# The  Book of Daily Prayer

# THE LIVING BOOK
# OF DAILY PRAYER

## MORNING AND EVENING

**Kim Martin Sadler**

EDITOR

THE PILGRIM PRESS
CLEVELAND

The Pilgrim Press, 700 Prospect Avenue, Cleveland, Ohio 44115-1100
thepilgrimpress.com
© 2008 by The Pilgrim Press

Biblical quotations are primarily from the New Revised Standard Version
of the Bible, © 1989 by the Division of Christian Education of the National
Council of the Churches of Christ in the U.S.A., and are used by permission.
Adapted for inclusivity.

♻ Printed in the United States of America on
acid-free paper that contains post-consumer fiber.

13    12    11    10    09    08        5    4    3    2    1

Library of Congress Cataloging-in-Publication Data

The living book of daily prayer : morning and evening / Kim Martin Sadler, editor.
p. cm.
ISBN 978-0-8298-1785-0 (alk. paper)
1. Devotional calendars.    2. Prayers.    I. Sadler, Kim Martin.
BV4810.L56    2008
242'.8—dc22                        2008028351

# CONTENTS

# INTRODUCTION

From 1997 to 2004, The Pilgrim Press published the annual devotional resource, *The Book of Daily Prayer, Morning and Evening*. By the time the series ended in 2004, *The Book of Daily Prayer* had amassed a large and devoted readership. Over the years since then, I have received numerous emails requesting that we reconsider our decision to end the series. I was moved to learn how *The Book of Daily Prayer* had been a blessing to loved ones serving in Iraq, loved ones who were ill, loved ones who were incarcerated, as well as for those who just wanted to grow in faith.

I, along with The Pilgrim Press staff, am pleased to release *The Living Book of Daily Prayer*. This devotional resource is a compilation of previously printed prayers from *The Book of Daily Prayer* that many of you grew to love. It is my prayer that you will be refreshed anew as you devote yourselves to Christ in prayer. And finally, "Do not worry about anything, but in everything by prayer and supplication with thanksgiving let your requests be made known to God. And the peace of God, which surpasses all understanding, will guard your hearts and your minds in Christ Jesus."

Blessings,
*Kim Martin Sadler*

*The Living Book of Daily Prayer* is to be used for daily devotion in the morning and evening. To use the book as a personal devotional guide, begin by reading the scripture passage for the day, followed by the opening (morning or evening) prayer. Read the meditative prayer next. This prayer is written in the style of writing known as "praying the Scripture." This allows your meditative prayer to be more than an interpretation of the day's reading.

    The intercessory (morning or evening) prayer follows. Here, you should offer prayers for those in need of God's blessings and other personal concerns. You might find it helpful to maintain a prayer list that can be used during intercessory prayer. It may be followed by the Prayer of Our Savior or another suggestion by the author. Both morning and evening devotional times end with a closing prayer.

    Those who use *The Living Book of Daily Prayer* in a group setting can follow the same pattern described for personal use. One person can read the scripture verses aloud, and another can lead the prayers. The meditative prayer may be said in unison or read silently. You may decide that each group member will share her or his prayer concerns during intercessory prayer. The Prayer of Our Savior and the closing prayer may be recited by the entire group in unison.

    No matter how you choose to use this wonderful resource, you are encouraged to develop your own method(s). It is our prayer that you will grow in faith and develop a closer walk with our Savior, Jesus Christ.

# January 1

## New Year's Day

*(Read Luke 3:15–17)*

**MORNING**

Mighty Redeemer, cleanse my eyes so they may see
your presence in this new time.

**EVENING**

Mighty Redeemer, what will I resolve to see in others? The faults
that we all bear? Or the opportunity to love despite human frailty?

O Living Waters, the future seems veiled, but let me be a bearer of good news—that the God of hosts lives and is a cleanser of souls! Let me resolve to cleanse my life of the sins that prevent me from loving fully. Let me resolve to cleanse my heart of despair, knowing that you alone, God, are a bearer of light where there is darkness. Let me show others in this new time through words and deeds that I am a follower of Jesus Christ.

**MORNING**

Provider of life, put a new song in my heart.
Give me direction where I need guidance. Let me be a beacon
of light to someone who has become lost along the way.
*(Prayers of Intercession)*

**EVENING**

Provider of life, how glorious is your name above all others.
Thank you for life.
*(Prayers of Intercession)*

**PREPARE ME, GOD, FOR THE BEGINNING OF A NEW SEASON.**
*(Pray the Prayer of Our Savior.)*

**MORNING**

O faithful and gracious God,
provide tender mercies this day, and
renew my spirit that I may be
instrumental in renewing the spirits
of others. In accordance to your will,
Jesus. In the name of Jesus. Amen.

**EVENING**

God, I thank you and praise
your holy name, for your everlasting
love flows freely. In the name
of Jesus. Amen.

# January 2

*(Read Luke 3:21–22)*

**MORNING**

Sweet Lily of the Valley, let me pause throughout this day
and pray for someone in need.

**EVENING**

Sweet Lily of the Valley, did I remember to give thanks
to you today for answered prayers?

O God, too often my prayers begin with a plea for help. Let me always remember before praying to give thanks to you for the many prayers you have already answered in my life. Let me remember to pray for the needs of others less fortunate than myself. Let me remember the importance and power of intercession. And even when I feel too anxious or weary to pray, guide me to pray.

**MORNING**

O Sovereign God, allow me to take time today to pray earnestly
for someone who is unwilling or unable to ask.
*(Prayers of Intercession)*

**EVENING**

Thank you, Jesus, for your prayer life. Help me to grow stronger
in my prayer life. Help me to pray as you do.
*(Prayers of Intercession)*

**PRAYER CHANGES THINGS.**
*(Pray the Prayer of Our Savior.)*

**MORNING**

I praise the wonderful and
marvelous name of our Savior.
How good it is to know your
goodness is everlasting. Thank you for
listening to my silent prayers when I
cannot speak. In the name of Jesus.
Amen.

**EVENING**

Thank you, God, for my blessings.
Thank you, God, for answering the
prayers of others in need.
In the name of Jesus.
Amen.

# January 3

*(Read Isaiah 43:1–7)*

**MORNING**
Blessed Savior, as I go forward this day,
may I take comfort in knowing you are walking right beside me.

**EVENING**
Blessed Savior, thank you for never leaving me and never forsaking
me. Protect me from fearful thoughts as I sleep.

As I go through this life, I have so often been trapped by fear—the fear of failure, the fear of disapproval, the fear of reproach, even the fear of blessings. Let me remember that in your name, blessed Jesus, I find courage. You, Creator, will place a shield of protection around me. You, Holy One, will uphold and console me.

**MORNING**
God, you continue to strengthen me, to comfort me,
to love me. For this, I will forever bless your name. In you,
I find the spirit of love, not fear.
*(Prayers of Intercession)*

**EVENING**
Through another day, you have shown me that despite
my resistance to surrender all to you, I can still find a safe haven
in your love.
*(Prayers of Intercession)*

**IF GOD IS WITH ME, WHO SHALL BE AGAINST ME?**
*(Sing "Blessed Assurance" or another familiar song.)*

**MORNING**
Help me, God, to brush aside fear,
and to boldly proclaim the way of
salvation to someone today.
In accordance with your will, Jesus.
In the name of Jesus. Amen.

**EVENING**
Thank you, Jesus, for surrounding
me with a hedge of safety. You are
my Rock. You are my High Tower.
I lift up your name above all others.
I glorify your name. In the name
of Jesus. Amen.

# January 4

*(Read Psalm 29:1–3)*

**MORNING**

Sovereign God, thank you for awakening me to live among your creation. You alone are worthy of all praise. I will gladly worship your name for the life you breathe into me daily.

**EVENING**

Sovereign God, all plans did not go as smoothly as anticipated. I thank you, however, for teaching me patience and for allowing me to wait on you. I am grateful.

O Wonderful Counselor, I ask so much of you. I expect everything when I am owed nothing and am unworthy even to speak your name. Show me, God, how I can give of myself freely to you. Help me to give of my time to work in your vineyard. Grant me the ability to give of my finances to uphold your Word. Let me praise you when I am tired and full of despair. Open a place in my life so that I can experience you anew.

**MORNING**

Precious Savior, let me find new reasons to stop and give praise.
Help me show others how to worship you continually.
*(Prayers of Intercession)*

**EVENING**

Royal High Priest, for how you bless me, for when you bless me,
for being an ever-present help when I need you, for salvation, I thank you.
*(Prayers of Intercession)*

---

**YOU ALONE, GOD, ARE WORTHY TO BE PRAISED.**
*(Sing "Bless God, O My Soul" or another familiar hymn.)*

---

**MORNING**

You allow me to see a new morning, God. All good things I achieve today are a testament to your grace and power. In the name of Jesus. Amen.

**EVENING**

Thank you for the blessings of this day. I worship you. I adore you. I give my life to you. I love you. In the name of Jesus. Amen.

# January 5

*(Read Psalm 29:4–9)*

**MORNING**

Savior, help me to listen to you today amid the noise.

**EVENING**

Savior, as I sleep, speak to me in your small, sweet voice.

Gracious God, you often speak to me, but I don't always hear. Allow me to remain still and listen to your voice. Let me hear your will and not my own. The path that you set for me is holy and good and righteous. Enable me, with strength, to boldly live the Word of God.

**MORNING**

Sweet Jesus, thank you for allowing me another opportunity to serve. Glory to your name.
*(Prayers of Intercession)*

**EVENING**

Great Majesty, thank you for still caring for me despite my selfish thoughts and actions.
*(Prayers of Intercession)*

**PLEASE LET ME BE A DOER OF THE WORD AND NOT JUST A HEARER.**
*(Pray the Prayer of Our Savior.)*

**MORNING**

I begin this morning desiring to hear your Word through others around me. May I remember that you place people in my life to teach me your way. Let me open my ears to hear the lessons of today.
In accordance with your will, Jesus.
In the name of Jesus.
Amen.

**EVENING**

Thank you, God, for this time to rest. May my mind and body be renewed as I sleep. May I wake with a bountiful spirit. In accordance with your will, Jesus. In the name of Jesus.
Amen.

# January 6

### Epiphany

*(Read Psalm 29:10–11)*

**MORNING**

Giver of peace, when trials emerge, you are my refuge.
Let me look to you for encouragement.

**EVENING**

Giver of peace, thank you for your faithfulness today.
You are the God of all comfort.

When tribulations abound and help seems at a distance, may I not look to myself for all of the answers. I am simply not strong or wise enough. Let me remember to whom I belong, and let me call on the name of Jesus in times of trouble. For you, God, are the peace giver, and when I am at my weakest, you provide unyielding strength. You, who called peace into stormy waters, are able to calm my fears. Glory to your wonderful name.

**MORNING**

May I be grateful for the obstacles you bring my way.
I know that I have been made stronger by depending on you.
*(Prayers of Intercession)*

**EVENING**

As long as I continue to trust you, God, I can weather any storm.
*(Prayers of Intercession)*

**IN CHRIST, ALL THINGS ARE POSSIBLE.**
*(Sing "Leaning on the Everlasting Arms" or another favorite hymn.)*

**MORNING**

Help me, God, to see that I can find peace in any situation. Help me remember that I am never alone today. In accordance with your will, Jesus. In the name of Jesus. Amen.

**EVENING**

Thank you, Jesus, for salvation and for being my battle shield. I win with you. In the name of Jesus. Amen.

# January 7

*(Read Acts 8:14–17)*

**MORNING**
Gracious God, do I allow myself to be guided
by the Holy Spirit, or am I leading the way?

**EVENING**
Gracious God, I humble myself before you. Holy Spirit,
work within me. Help me to let go and follow your lead.

God, you have provided me with a voice, a vision, a compass, and a conscience. It is the Holy Spirit—a beacon that gives light and guidance in the night. Help me to become reacquainted with the Holy Spirit. Let it rise up in my soul and renew my life.

**MORNING**
God, may I be guided by the Holy Spirit within me.
Let me pray for healing for someone in need today.
*(Prayers of Intercession)*

**EVENING**
You, God, are awesome. You provide for my every need.
Thank you for those you guided to pray for me throughout my life.
*(Prayers of Intercession)*

**PRAY CONTINUALLY AND BELIEVE FAITHFULLY.**
*(Pray the Prayer of Our Savior.)*

**MORNING**
Help me, God, to pray more
consistently; live firmly in your Word;
listen to you more carefully; love you
more deeply; trust you fearlessly;
praise and worship your name faithfully; and forgive and love myself
steadfastly. In the name
of Jesus. Amen.

**EVENING**
Faithful God, I will forever
thank you and worship you. You
saved my life. Show me your plan for
my life, and help me fulfill your
design for it. In the name
of Jesus. Amen.

# January 8

*(Read Isaiah 60:1–6)*

### MORNING
Illuminating One and Light of the World, as a moth is attracted
to a flame, so I desire to make conscious contact with you,
the light of life, at the beginning of this day.

### EVENING
Illuminating One and Light of the World, God of the day and of
the night, as the shades of evening fall around me and I assess the day
that is coming to a close, I once again turn to you in the spirit of prayer.

Your prophet of old reminds me that you are the creator of all nations
and all people; so I know that you are my God. You desire to dispel
the gloom that sometimes creeps into the world with the radiance of
your love. You desire to enrich life with the gifts of your Spirit—love,
joy, peace, patience, kindness, generosity, faithfulness, gentleness, self-
control. You also call me to brighten the lives of others with your love.

### MORNING
May what I say and do in the hours to come emulate the example
I have experienced in Jesus, who taught his followers to pray.
*(Prayers of Intercession)*

### EVENING
Forgive me, Enlightening One, if throughout this day, in any way,
I have hurt rather than helped, clouded rather than brightened,
made poorer rather than richer, any life that intersected with mine.
*(Prayers of Intercession)*

ILLUMINATING ONE, YOU ARE THE LIGHT OF THE WORLD. MAY I LEARN FROM MY MISTAKES
SO THAT TOMORROW MY LIFE WILL MORE FULLY REFLECT YOUR WILL AND WAYS.

### MORNING
God, be now my light throughout
the light of this day! In the name
of the Light of Life. Amen.

### EVENING
God, grant me rest, I pray,
in the knowledge that I am in the
loving care of you who neither slum-
bers nor sleeps. In the name of
the Light of Life. Amen.

# January 9

*(Read Psalm 72:1–7, 10–14)*

### MORNING
Just and righteous God, as the psalmist prayed that the leaders
of his day might rule in a fashion acceptable to you, I offer my
prayers for the leaders of the earth's nations.

### EVENING
Just and righteous God, my prayers tonight are for all who are oppressed
for any reason. May they feel your presence and know your love and care,
and may their oppression cease.

May your Spirit lead all who are in positions of authority to be sensitive to and address the needs of the poor, the homeless, the hungry, and any who are oppressed because of their race, creed, or sexual orientation. May they strive for peace on earth and good will to all. May they find an example for their sovereignty in the justice, righteousness, and deliverance that characterize your rule of the worlds you have created.

### MORNING
Great Ruler of the universe, may I somehow today, through personal
example and perhaps through contact with an elected official, do something
to help bring to fruition at least one of these ideals.
*(Prayers of Intercession)*

### EVENING
Thank you, gracious God, for the opportunity I had today to minister
to someone who was in need or oppressed. (Reflect on your day.)
Grant me sleep that will refresh and strengthen me to continue
to act in your behalf in the days to come.
*(Prayers of Intercession)*

### YOU ARE A JUST AND RIGHTEOUS GOD.

| MORNING | EVENING |
|---|---|
| Now may I go forth in the spirit of your prophet Micah to do justice and to love kindness as I walk humbly with you. In the name of the Light of Life. Amen. | Tomorrow may my eyes continue to see someone, my ears hear someone, and my heart lead me to respond to someone in need. In the name of the Light of Life. Amen. |

# January 10

*(Read Ephesians 3:1–12)*

**MORNING**

Infinite God of grace, although my finite mind cannot
completely comprehend you, you have created in me a
God-shaped vacuum that I now invite you to fill.

**EVENING**

Infinite God of grace, as the shadows deepen and I anticipate a
night of rest, I pause to ponder your Word once again.

Like Paul, I want to be a prisoner of the Christ so that I can commit
myself to being as Christ-like as I can. In this role, may I share with
others the good news and the boundless riches of your child—not in
arrogance or judgment—but as a beggar telling them where I have
found bread. Thank you for the church that binds me to those who
have made similar commitments. Although we, the many members of
the body of Christ, differ in our skills and gifts, you desire that we celebrate our uniqueness and be your servants in a variety of ways.

**MORNING**

You are the creator of all. Today enable me to catch
a glimpse of your Spirit in everyone I meet.
*(Prayers of Intercession)*

**EVENING**

Gracious God, as the shadows deepen and I anticipate a night of rest, I pause to
share my thoughts and feelings. I must confess, "For I do not do the good I want,
but the evil I do not want is what I do." Forgive me, Pardoning Parent.
*(Prayers of Intercession)*

---

MAKE ME ATTENTIVE TO THE GOOD IN OTHERS, NOT TO THEIR FAULTS;
AND TO WHAT I HAVE IN COMMON WITH THEM, NOT TO OUR DIFFERENCES.

---

**MORNING**

Guide me, great Jehovah,
as I seek to serve, not for my glory,
but for yours. In the name of
the Light of Life. Amen.

**EVENING**

Give us all a refreshing sleep so
that we may awaken strengthened
for tomorrow. In the name of
the Light of Life. Amen.

# January 11

*(Read Matthew 2:1–12)*

### MORNING
God of my Savior, today may I be like the Magi; wise enough
to seek to find and know Jesus, the Christ; wise enough to pay him homage
by letting the Babe of Bethlehem become the man of Nazareth and my Savior;
wise enough to dedicate to God's service my gifts of time, treasure, and talent.

### EVENING
God of my Savior, thank you, for offering me throughout this day, as
you offered the Magi, direction, purpose, and a goal for which to strive.

God of Jesus and my God, I commit myself to "finding" the Christ.
Thus, I will do my best to emulate your Child: to love as Jesus loved,
to serve as Jesus served, and to be one of your expressions in the world
in what I say and do. Just as Jesus grew in faith and knowledge of you,
I will strive to do the same by turning daily to your Word, which is "a
lamp to my feet and a light to my path."

### MORNING
Thank you, O God, for those people of old who have helped me
find the Christ in the stories they wrote about him and
through his teachings that they preserved.
*(Prayers of Intercession)*

### EVENING
Forgive me, parent of Christ Jesus and my parent, for the times
today when I failed to "follow the star" and instead followed Herod,
who sought to betray Jesus—the one who became the light of the world.
*(Prayers of Intercession)*

### I SEEK THE CHRIST.

### MORNING
Eternal Guide, I greet this day with
the prayer that my life will cast light
and not shadows on all whom I meet!
In the name of the Light of Life. Amen.

### EVENING
Guiding Light, grant me a good night's
rest in the assurance that I can be wiser
tomorrow. And I will try to be! In the
name of the Light of Life. Amen.

# January 12

*(Read Genesis 1:1–5 and Psalm 29)*

### MORNING

Creator and creating God, thank you for ancient, timeless stories reminding
me of who you are and whose I am. As I open my eyes to the light of this
new day, my heart sings with the one who wrote "How Great Thou Art."
You are great, O God, for you called the worlds into being.

### EVENING

Creator and creating God, thank you for ancient, timeless stories reminding
me of who you are and whose I am. Thank you for the signs of your presence.

I live amid countless evidences of your creating power: sun, moon,
stars, mountains, rivers, trees, shrubs, flowers, animals, and birds. I hear
you in the thunder, see you in the lightning, and feel you in the wind.
But I sense that the greatest evidence of your creativity is in my own life
and in the lives of my family, friends, and neighbors. We all have been
created in your image. I have been created to be like you—with the ca-
pacities to love, care, reason, relate, create, and choose. Thank you,
Great One, for the breath of life and for the resources of the world in
which I live. Grant me the strength to care for and use them wisely.

### MORNING

May I begin this day mindful of all of your natural
and personal expressions that will surround me.
*(Prayers of Intercession)*

### EVENING

Ever-present God, whose Spirit has surrounded and embraced me
throughout this day, grant me a night of peaceful rest.
*(Prayers of Intercession)*

THANK YOU FOR THE GIFT OF THIS DAY AS WELL AS FOR THE GIFT OF THIS NEW YEAR.

| MORNING | EVENING |
|---|---|
| I commit myself to being a faithful steward of your many gifts that fill my life. In the name if the Light of Life. Amen. | May I greet tomorrow's dawn with new resolve to be the person you created me to be. Amen. |

# January 13

*(Read Acts 19:1–7 and sing the first verse of the hymn
"Holy Spirit, Truth Divine" or another familiar hymn)*

### MORNING

Holy Spirit of God, may I, throughout this day, be aware of and
receptive to your presence within and around me.

### EVENING

Holy Spirit of God, you have been with me this day.
Therefore I was able to face whatever came my way.

I praise you, O God, for all that I have learned about you this week
from your holy Word. I was reminded that the various facets of the
world in which I live speak to me of your creative power. You are the
one who called the worlds into being and created me in your image.
The scriptures also proclaim that I see you revealed in the life of Jesus,
whose birth I celebrated not long ago—the one who taught and showed
me how to live. Now the apostle Paul has focused my attention on your
Holy Spirit, which is present within and around me at all times.

### MORNING

Spirit of the living God, fall upon me. Thus, may your
Holy Spirit guide and sustain me throughout this day, resulting
in my living as you want me to live.
*(Prayers of Intercession)*

### EVENING

For the comfort and power of your Spirit that has been with me
this day, thank you, O God!
*(Prayers of Intercession)*

### HOLY SPIRIT, YOU ARE TRUTH DIVINE.

### MORNING

Thank you, Eternal Contemporary,
for the assurance that during this day
I will never walk alone! In the name
of the Light of Life. Amen.

### EVENING

May sleep now descend on me as
I relax my mind and body, knowing
that I am always in your love and
care. In the name of the Light
of Life. Amen.

# January 14

*(Read Mark 1:4–11)*

### MORNING
Forgiving and renewing God, into whose Spirit I have been
baptized, reading the story of Jesus' baptism challenges me to revisit my
own baptism. (*Either*) Although I was too young to remember, I have
heard of the vows taken by my loved ones on my behalf.
(*Or*) I recall the day when I took my baptismal vows.

### EVENING
Forgiving and renewing God, into whose Spirit I have been
baptized, reading the story of Jesus' baptism challenges me to revisit
my own. I can rest tonight confident that I am yours.

Just as centuries ago Jesus was baptized by John and proclaimed to be
your Child, through my baptism, the uniqueness, value, and worth of
my life as your child were affirmed! My life was dedicated to you as I
have come to know you through the Christ. And it was promised that
I would grow in my faith as a part of the church, the body of Christ.
Where I have been faithful to these vows, may I continue to be. Where
I have failed to live up to them, forgive me.

### MORNING
Imperfect as I am, bathe me in your love, clothe me with your
presence, and feed me the bread of life that comes only from you.
*(Prayers of Intercession)*

### EVENING
May I turn away from that which is displeasing to you. And tomorrow may I be
more the person you want me to be—more like Jesus, your Child, and my Savior.
*(Prayers of Intercession)*

### HOLY SPIRIT OF GOD, DESCEND ON ME.

### MORNING
Descend on me, Holy Spirit, so that
my life today will give you reason to
say, "With you I am well pleased." In
the name of the Light of Life. Amen.

### EVENING
May sleep descend on me like a
descending dove. May I be refreshed,
so your Spirit will be evident tomorrow
in what I say and do In the name of
the Light of Life. Amen.

# January 15

### Martin Luther King Jr. Birthday

*(Read Psalm 19)*

#### MORNING
Glorious God, open my eyes to the full awareness
of your presence in this day.

#### EVENING
Glorious God, open my heart to full attentiveness
to your presence this night.

Surprising and all-encompassing God, you are everywhere. I ask for re-assurance, expecting words—and you reveal yourself in the sky! In the protective, persistent warmth of the sun! I ask for your guidance, expecting mandates—and you give me the gentle protection of your law. Every day of my life is your sweet message, joyously poured out to me; every one of my encounters with the scriptures, a reward.

#### MORNING
Revive me for this day, sweet God.
Enlighten me to the needs of others.
*(Prayers of Intercession)*

#### EVENING
Tonight, I remember and rejoice in the many
subtle revelations of your presence in this day.
*(Prayers of Intercession)*

#### CLEAR ME FROM MY HIDDEN FAULTS, O GOD.
*(Pray the Prayer of Our Savior.)*

#### MORNING
Let my words reflect you today,
O God, my rock and my redeemer.
In Jesus' name. Amen.

#### EVENING
May the meditations of my heart
be acceptable to you, O God, my rock
and my redeemer. In Jesus' name.
Amen.

# January 16

*(Read Nehemiah 8:1–3, 5–6)*

**MORNING**
Tender and gracious God, I lift my hands to you this day in praise.

**EVENING**
Tender and gracious God, I bow my head to you this night
with thanksgiving.

O God, how generous you have been to us—all people, women and men—through all generations. Now, when we stand in worshipful attentiveness, we know that you will speak to us as you once did through Moses and Ezra. We thank you that the loving words you gave them have been preserved for our benefit in scripture. Open our ears to your faithful leaders of this time, too. Show us how and when to say "Amen, Amen" to your living Word today.

**MORNING**
Let the words of my mouth and the meditation of my heart be
acceptable to you, O God, my rock and my redeemer.
*(Prayers of Intercession)*

**EVENING**
Let the words of my mouth and the meditation of my heart be
acceptable to you, O God, my rock and my redeemer.
*(Prayers of Intercession)*

---

**AMEN, AMEN.**
*(Pray the Prayer of Our Savior.)*

---

**MORNING**
Bless us this day, great God, so we might show in all our actions that we are your servants. In Jesus' name. Amen.

**EVENING**
We bow our heads this evening with thanks to you, great God, for all the blessings of this day. In Jesus' name. Amen.

# January 17

*(Read Nehemiah 8:8–10)*

**MORNING**

Savior God, I greet you on this holy day. As I read your Word
this morning, bless me with a deeper understanding.

**EVENING**

Savior God, I bless you for this holy day. As I read your Word
this evening, bless me with a deeper understanding.

Most loving God, sometimes I am so overwhelmed by my own inadequacies that all I can do is weep. Only your amazing, grace-filled love comforts me in those times. When I remember your love, I see that every day of my life is your holy gift to me. I am then strengthened by the joyful knowledge of your inestimable care for me. Then I am shaken from mournful immobility. Then I can go on.

**MORNING**

Lead me, God, to those who are unprepared for your
magnanimity. And give me the generosity of spirit to make
their preparations for them.
*(Prayers of Intercession)*

**EVENING**

Let me rest this night, O God, reassured that today
I have given sweet portions to others on your behalf.
*(Prayers of Intercession)*

**GOD'S JOY IS MY STRENGTH.**
*(Pray the Prayer of Our Savior.)*

| **MORNING** | **EVENING** |
|:---:|:---:|
| This day, grant me peace. | This evening, grant me rest. |
| In Jesus' name. | In Jesus' name. |
| Amen. | Amen. |

# January 18

*(Read Luke 4:14–21)*

**MORNING**

My God, I greet you this morning as my parent,
my love, and my dearest friend.

**EVENING**

My God, I honor you this evening as my protector,
redeemer, and guide.

Saving God, when I am poor you provide for me. When I am trapped by the world's one-sided views and oppressed by its greedy demands, you set me free. When I am blind to love, you open my eyes. What great good news you have sent to me in your savior son, Jesus! Fix my eyes on him that I might know the power of your fulfilling Spirit.

**MORNING**

Fill me with your spirit this day, O God that I, too, might bring
good news to the poor and open the eyes of the blind.
*(Prayers of Intercession)*

**EVENING**

Let your spirit rest in me this night, O God, releasing me
and others who worry from all oppressive thought.
*(Prayers of Intercession)*

---

**GOD'S JOY IS MY STRENGTH.**

*(Pray the Prayer of Our Savior.)*

---

**MORNING**

May I walk today in the spirit of
Christ, proclaiming God's great favor.
In Jesus' name. Amen.

**EVENING**

May the blessings of the triune
God be upon us all this night.
In Jesus' name. Amen.

# January 19

(Read 1 Corinthians 12:12–13)

**MORNING**
Creator God, I remember and honor my baptism
as I begin this day.

**EVENING**
Creator God, I thank you for my place in your communion.

God, I marvel at the flourishing complexity of your creation. It is beyond my comprehension. I am stunned by stars, by history, by the many wise leaders you have raised up for us throughout the generations. I am stunned, even, by myself—by my unique body and my distinct personality, which also display your infinite abundance. I am further awestruck that you have made all of this amazing variety one in Jesus Christ. In you, Creator God, wonders never cease.

**MORNING**
God, you know no boundaries. Open my eyes to the many,
mysterious ways in which your Spirit moves through all
whom I meet this day.
*(Prayers of Intercession)*

**EVENING**
God, I have judged others among your children harshly today.
Forgive me.
*(Prayers of Intercession)*

THE BLESSINGS OF THE TRIUNE GOD BE ON US ALL.
*(Pray the Prayer of Our Savior.)*

**MORNING**
Assured in Christ that I am filled
with the power of the Spirit, I go into
this day. In Jesus' name. Amen.

**EVENING**
Blessed by God through Christ,
I rest assured this night.
In Jesus' name. Amen.

# January 20

*(Read 1 Corinthians 12:14–26)*

**MORNING**

Tender Jesus, I have need of your presence this day.

**EVENING**

Tender Jesus, I rejoice in your presence this evening.

Teach me your compassion, Christ. All around me, I see others in the body of Christ whom I simply cannot understand. They seem too intolerant or too permissive, too narrow-minded or too loose, too prejudiced or too accommodating. And yet, it is not you, but I who judge them. You reassure me that you have need of all the members of your body, that, mysteriously, many single members will be needed if your realm is to be made. Let me honor all as you do—with care and love.

**MORNING**

Compassionate Christ, comfort those who are suffering today.
*(Prayers of Intercession)*

**EVENING**

Compassionate Christ, comfort those who are suffering this night.
*(Prayers of Intercession)*

**TENDER JESUS, I THANK YOU FOR MY PLACE IN YOUR COMMUNION.**
*(Pray the Prayer of Our Savior.)*

| **MORNING** | **EVENING** |
|---|---|
| May I meet the world with your compassion throughout this day. In Jesus' name. Amen. | Bless me tonight, sweet Christ, with the dissolution of all this day's dissension. In Jesus' name. Amen. |

# January 21

*(Read 1 Corinthians 12:27–31)*

**MORNING**
God of all good gifts, I open my heart to you this morning.

**EVENING**
God of all good gifts, I thank you for the blessings of this day.

God, you reassure me that I have particular gifts for your realm. But sometimes I wonder just what they are. I see so many other gifted individuals in the world: teachers, preachers, healers, compassionate movers-and-shakers. What am I compared to them? I feel so inadequate. Show me what you would have me do. And remind me that, through Christ, I have the strength to do it.

**MORNING**
God, I offer prayers this morning for all the workers in your realm
but most especially for those who seem confused and disheartened.
*(Prayers of Intercession)*

**EVENING**
God, bless all the workers in your realm and relieve them
of this day's burdens.
*(Prayers of Intercession)*

LET US ALL, TOGETHER, STRIVE FOR GREATER GIFTS.
*(Pray the Prayer of Our Savior.)*

**MORNING**
Bless me, God, that I might use
my particular gifts this day for you.
In Jesus' name. Amen.

**EVENING**
Thank you, God, for the gift of this
day and for my part in making it
yours. In Jesus' name. Amen.

# January 22

*(Read 1 Samuel 3:1–10, [11–20])*

**MORNING**

Gracious God, another day is here. Help me to be faithful
to the tasks you are calling me to do.

**EVENING**

Gracious God, as I reflect upon the day, help me to count my blessings.
Help me tomorrow to be a blessing to someone in need.

Revealing Word of Life, I praise you for calling me by name. Thank you for insisting on my attention. God, you called Samuel in the days of his youth when your Word had not yet been revealed to him. You were always there as he went about his temple duties. It is scary and comforting to know you are calling me: scary because I do not know what you will ask of me, yet comforting because I know you will provide my needs and make a way. God, keep calling my name until you have my undivided attention. Reveal to me that special task you have reserved just for me. Grant me the courage to respond as Samuel did: "Here I am, for you called me."

**MORNING**

God, I pray for myself and others who need your protection today.
Do not leave us alone as we go, but keep us in your care.
*(Prayers of Intercession)*

**EVENING**

Today I encountered some who are disconnected from your love and grace.
Grant unto them your peace and the courage to acknowledge your presence.
*(Prayers of Intercession)*

**HERE I AM, FOR YOU CALLED ME.**

**MORNING**

Caring God, let me not be distracted
by petty things, but rather help me to
focus on your goodness. In the name
of Jesus. Amen.

**EVENING**

Caring God, the day now ends.
Brood and hover over me in the night.
Then, with the dawn, bring forth
courage and wisdom. In the name
of Jesus. Amen.

# January 23

(Read 1 Samuel 3:1–10 [11–20])

### MORNING
Eternal God of power and mercy, in the quietness of this hour,
prepare me to face the uncertainty of this day with fortitude and grace.

### EVENING
Eternal God of power and mercy, this day was a good one because
I felt your presence. I pray for those who have no peace.

God of mystery and patience, I praise you for being a God who hears and listens. Too often, dear God, my days are busy. I fill each day with too many things to do and I disrupt the quiet with noise. I refuse to slow down. The quiet and stillness are terrifying. Yet, O God, you challenge me to be still and know that you are God. In the stillness of the night, before the dawning of the day, you called Samuel. Breathe upon my anxiety and fear; transform them into confidence and courage. Open my ears to hear your still, small voice beckoning me closer to you.

### MORNING
God, I am tempted to fill this time with noise and activity.
Help me to center and focus on you.
*(Prayers of Intercession)*

### EVENING
Thank you, God, for this personal and private retreat from the
hustle and bustle of life. As I prepare for sleep, I rest in
the comfort of your care.
*(Prayers of Intercession)*

**OPEN MY EARS TO HEAR YOUR STILL, SMALL VOICE.**

### MORNING
God of calmness, thank you for these moments of peacefulness. When the day becomes busy, help me to remember how it feels to be quiet and still in your presence. In Jesus' name. Amen.

### EVENING
God of rest, as I sleep tonight, let me retire in the assurance of your love. May I awake on the morrow with only this prayer: "Sovereign, speak! For your servant hears." In Jesus' name. Amen.

# January 24

**MORNING**

Gentle God of strength, thank you for awakening me so gently
with your touch of love and mercy. I am ready to face the day.

**EVENING**

Gentle God of strength, I rejoice and pray for those who struggle
both during the day and during the night. Be for them what you
have been for me: a steady presence of strength.

All-knowing God, I praise you because you love me in spite of my
thoughts and deeds. Merciful God, I confess that I am not worthy of
your love. I am impatient with those who struggle. I am blind to the
pain of the oppressed. I am tempted to be selfish and greedy. I am cynical when I should be caring; apathetic when I should be involved; pas-
sive when I should be bold. These and other frailties I lay before you.
God of grace, I come before you seeking your transforming grace and
never-ending mercy. Refashion me in your image and likeness.

**MORNING**

Eternal and loving God, create in me a clean heart and contrite spirit.
Leave me not to my own devices and whims, but fill me with your grace.
*(Prayers of Intercession)*

**EVENING**

God, take my failures, shortcomings, and weaknesses
and transform them into opportunities to glorify you.
*(Prayers of Intercession)*

"EVEN THERE YOUR HAND SHALL LEAD ME, AND YOUR RIGHT HAND SHALL HOLD ME FAST."

**MORNING**

Creator God, I know not what this
day holds for me—joy or tragedy,
prosperity or poverty. I stand in the
light of your love, knowing that whatever happens, you are still with me.
In Jesus' name. Amen.

**EVENING**

Thank you for the grace and
mercy that sustained me today. Life is
difficult, yet you brought me through
again. I am grateful. In Jesus' name.
Amen.

# January 25

*(Read 1 Corinthians 6:12–20)*

### MORNING
Creator of all that is good and true,
I arise and give thanks for this day.

### EVENING
Creator of all that is good and true, take my life, all that is in it
and in me, and make it a thing of joy and beauty.

Maker of all there is, I praise your wisdom in making real for us the beauty and majesty of creation. In the days of the apostle Paul, some thought the physical body was not worthy of consideration. For them, the only important thing was the soul and spirit. Yet, O Wise One, you created us from the dust and breathed into our bodies the breath of life. Your Word became flesh, dwelt among us, died, and was raised up for us. Through your mighty Word and deeds, you elevate human beings to a place of dignity and worth. Your Spirit lives in us, and we are yours. Help us to live as your temples on earth.

### MORNING
Loving God, help me distinguish between that which is good to me
and that which is good for me. Grant me the courage to choose wisely.
*(Prayers of Intercession)*

### EVENING
O God, my rock and refuge, strengthen me with your Holy Spirit. Grant me
the wisdom to love and care for all of creation, which you pronounced good.
*(Prayers of Intercession)*

---

"FOR YOU WERE BOUGHT WITH A PRICE; THEREFORE GLORIFY GOD IN YOUR BODY."

---

| MORNING | EVENING |
|---|---|
| It is easy to judge my neighbor. I thank you for Christ Jesus, who looked beyond the superficial and bade us to love one another. In the name of Jesus I pray. Amen. | As sleep brings rest and renewal, O God, may I awake with new zeal and fresh energy for the journey. In the name of Jesus Christ I pray. Amen. |

# January 26

*(Read John 1:43–51)*

### MORNING

All-knowing and ever-present God, who knows what this day will bring? Help me to live this day as if it were my last. Be with me, and let my will be your will.

### EVENING

All-knowing and ever-present God, there is a restlessness within me that I cannot explain or understand. Use this energy for your glory. In Jesus' name.

Rock of Ages, you are made known to us in Jesus of Nazareth. Empower me to share the good news. Word of Life, I am not always comfortable sharing my faith. I feel awkward and unsure when I try to tell others what Christ has done for me. Give me the confidence to tell others what I have experienced. Give me the boldness to echo the words of Philip: "I have found him about whom Moses in the law and also the prophets wrote, Jesus son of Joseph from Nazareth." As this day unfolds, loosen my tongue and let me speak of what I know. If I am questioned about my faith, let me not cringe in shame or fear, but rather let me invite others to "come and see."

### MORNING

I envy the ease with which the disciples responded to Jesus' invitation to join him. Remind me of where I have been and where I am now.

*(Prayers of Intercession)*

### EVENING

God of creation, I pray for those who do not know Christ Jesus. I pray for their salvation even as I rest in the blessed assurance of my own.

*(Prayers of Intercession)*

---

**"DO YOU BELIEVE BECAUSE I TOLD YOU THAT I SAW YOU UNDER THE FIG TREE?"**

---

### MORNING

O God, through the ages, you have revealed yourself. Today, I can tell others what you have done for me through Christ Jesus. I pray for boldness in telling my story. In Jesus' name. Amen.

### EVENING

Eternal and loving God, as night blankets this day, forgive me and grant me the courage to stand up for Jesus in the days ahead. In Jesus' name. Amen.

# January 27

*(Read John 1:43–51)*

**MORNING**

Most loving God, thank you for the rest of last night and for the gift of a new day.

**EVENING**

Most loving God, may I rest in the knowledge that in a changing
and chaotic world, you are steadfast and immovable.

God of peace, I praise you for being a God who calls and commissions. Make me an instrument of your peace in the world. Jesus saw Nathaniel sitting under the fig tree before Philip interrupted his meditation. The fig tree, a symbol of peace, is shady and leafy. Many have sat under its branches to rest and meditate. God, grant me the shade of a fig tree wherever I am, and show me how I can bring peace to the part of the world I inhabit. Help me to smile when I would rather curse; to whisper when I would rather scream; to comfort when I would rather strike out; to love when I would rather hate. In a broken, hurting, warring, and hungering world, use me as your instrument of healing, love, hope, and peace.

**MORNING**

You promised to give power to the faint and strength to the powerless. I pray for myself and others who wait for you to renew our strength. Hear my prayer, O God.
*(Prayers of Intercession)*

**EVENING**

O God, as I lay my weary head down this night, grant me a
peaceful sleep, safe within the circle of your love and mercy.
*(Prayers of Intercession)*

**"YOU WILL SEE GREATER THINGS THAN THESE."**

**MORNING**

Fill me with the power of your
Holy Spirit so that I may boldly live
this day. In the name of the Bringer
of Peace, I pray. Amen.

**EVENING**

Somewhere tonight, mothers and
fathers fear for their lives and the lives
of their children. Be with them.
In the name of the Bringer of Peace,
I pray. Amen.

# January 28

*(Read John 1:43–51 and Joel 2:28–29)*

**MORNING**

Good Provider, be present in my life today. Give me the will to think and do what is right. Guide my steps and order my ways according to your good pleasure.

**EVENING**

Good Provider, thank you for a day filled with miracles of love, life, companionship, and nourishment. Envelop me tonight in your grace and mercy.

Giver of every good and perfect gift, I praise you for making all things new. You declared, O Ancient of Days, that in the fullness of time, you would pour out your Spirit upon all flesh. According to your Word, men and women, young and old, slave and free, would dream dreams, see visions, and prophesy. You sent Jesus to show us a more excellent way—a way of peace, justice, harmony, and love. God of creation, do a new thing and begin with me. Kindle within me your vision for creation. Ignite in me a fire to do your will. Stir up within me the desire to serve your people. Put me where you can use me.

**MORNING**

Sovereign, here I am! Send me into your creation to bring healing, health, and wholeness wherever I can.

*(Prayers of Intercession)*

**EVENING**

God of serenity, allow me a night of rest and peacefulness, knowing that tomorrow is another opportunity to serve and glorify you.

*(Prayers of Intercession)*

**I PRAISE YOU FOR ALL THINGS NEW.**

**MORNING**

O God, this is the beginning of a new day and a new week. The possibilities are endless. Make me worthy of the challenges that lie ahead.
In Jesus' name. Amen.

**EVENING**

Eternal God, I confess that I was not perfect today. Thank you for being a God who does not ask perfection of us. In Jesus' name. Amen.

# January 29

*(Read Deuteronomy 18:15–20)*

**MORNING**

Holy and awesome God, at the beginning of a new day, let wonder
stir me and awaken me. I would be alert to your life-giving presence.

**EVENING**

Holy and awesome God, this day, your gift to me, is nearly done.
I thank you that your Word is a living Word.

Revealing God, I praise you that you have not left me alone. You have
provided and appointed me with messengers, prophets, teachers, and
apostles of your surprising new creation. Holy One, as your people,
Israel, came into the new and the promised land, you provided
prophets who would be alert, attentive, and faithful to your Word. I
know, O God, that I really cannot live by bread alone; that the bread of
this world, even in ample supply, leaves me famished for your Word
and presence, upon which I truly depend. Grant me the courage to listen for your Word, to watch for your presence.

**MORNING**

As I look to this new day, I hold before you those who are in
special need of your encouraging Word.
*(Prayers of Intercession)*

**EVENING**

I praise you for this day, and, as I ponder its experiences, I seek what you
would have me learn. I pray for sisters and brothers in need of your Word.
*(Prayers of Intercession)*

---

**WITH A HEART OPEN TO YOUR WAY, I PRAY THE PRAYER JESUS TAUGHT.**
*(Pray the Prayer of Our Savior.)*

---

**MORNING**

Send me into this new day, listening
for your living, giving Word and open
to your presence. In the matchless
name of Jesus. Amen.

**EVENING**

I give myself to you, confident that I
rest in the shelter of your wings. In
the matchless name of Jesus. Amen.

# January 30

*(Read Deuteronomy 18:15–20)*

### MORNING

Calling God, even as the dawn calls forth a new day, you have
called and claimed me, loving and holy God.

### EVENING

Calling God, I offer this day, with its incomplete words and deeds,
to you in whom completion is found.

I praise you, O Holy One, for the persons and events, the stories and the
experiences, by which you have called me to know and to serve you.
Gracious God, sometimes your Word is like fire in my bones. You have
called me to speak your Word, to bear witness to your truth. I confess
that it is not easy to be a messenger, a prophet, a witness, an apostle of
your way. Often I am unsure of your Word and your will. I would rather
leave this task to another. I lose heart. I fail to speak the Word you have
entrusted to me. I am afraid of what it might cost me. Forgive the ways
I have shut your Word up within me. Help me to tell your truth in love
and to trust your power to use me for the healing of your world.

### MORNING

For your prophets and martyrs today, for all who fearlessly speak
your Word, and for the church throughout the world, I pray.
*(Prayers of Intercession)*

### EVENING

You who have called the worlds into being, you who know the tiniest sparrow,
hear my prayers for the needs of others and for my own needs.
*(Prayers of Intercession)*

---

**WITH A HEART OPEN TO YOUR WAY, I PRAY THE PRAYER THAT JESUS TAUGHT.**
*(Pray the Prayer of Our Savior.)*

---

### MORNING

Called to love and serve you, I go to
this new day confident of your presence.
In the matchless name of Jesus. Amen.

### EVENING

Now, hearing your promise,
"Do not be afraid," grant me rest and
peace. In the matchless name of Jesus.
Amen.

# January 31

*(Read 1 Corinthians 8:1–13)*

### MORNING

Patient and Gracious God, I am grateful for the relationships in which you
have placed me and ask for your guidance to strengthen them.

### EVENING

Patient and Gracious God, I praise you, Holy One, for you exist
in relationship: Creator, Redeemer, and Sustainer.

O God, whose new creation summons and creates a new community, help me to hear in the story of your people in Corinth possibilities of grace and growth for every congregation. O God, you are at work in the lives of congregations and communities. Sometimes in our congregations we too imagine that we are "in the know," that we are brighter, freer, more knowledgeable, or more spiritual than others. O God, whose ways are not our ways, I see that my knowledge counts for little unless it is guided and directed by love. Help me to place my knowledge and gifts in the service of a love that builds up others, that builds up the community as a witness to your gracious way and patient truth.

### MORNING

You have placed me in a fabric of human community.
I pray for the needs of others and for my own needs in this day.
*(Prayers of Intercession)*

### EVENING

Grant me patience with others, even as you have been patient with me. I pray
for those who have been patient with me and for those who need my patience.
*(Prayers of Intercession)*

---

**WITH A HEART OPEN TO YOUR WAY, I PRAY THE PRAYER THAT JESUS TAUGHT.**
*(Pray the Prayer of Our Savior.)*

---

| MORNING | EVENING |
|---|---|
| Open my eyes to the opportunities of this day to build up others and to strengthen the weak. In the matchless name of Jesus. Amen. | Assured of your constant care for all your creation, I ask that you would grant me restful sleep. In the matchless name of Jesus. Amen. |

# February 1

*(Read 1 Corinthians 8:1–13)*

### MORNING

O God in whom all things exist, the light of your love opens
my eyes to the connection of all that is, and I thank you.

### EVENING

O God in whom all things exist, I open myself in prayer
to your restoring compassion for me and for all.

Compassionate God, I praise you for your vision of a new community, and I seek that possibility as I listen to the story of your people and church at Corinth. Perhaps, O God, our individualism is but an illusion, a chimera, and confusion. Perhaps you have not called us one by one, but community by community. Perhaps at the judgment we shall not stand before you alone or one by one, but community by community, congregation by congregation, people by people, that you may see what kind of community we have been together, that you may see who we have left out. Compassionate God, grant me grace to see the connections, to reweave the fabric where it has been frayed, and to discover that, in thinking of others, it is myself I have thought of as well.

### MORNING

In prayer for the needs of others, as well as my own,
I would restore and strengthen our connections.
*(Prayers of Intercession)*

### EVENING

As I remember in prayer before you my sisters and brothers,
heal, I pray, your broken body.
*(Prayers of Intercession)*

---

**WITH A HEART OPEN TO YOUR WAY, I PRAY THE PRAYER JESUS TAUGHT.**
*(Pray the Prayer of Our Savior.)*

---

### MORNING

As I go to love and serve you, I am not
alone. I am surrounded by all the faithful.
In the matchless name of Jesus. Amen.

### EVENING

You know me, O God. In this is my
rest and my safety. In the matchless
name of Jesus. Amen.

# February 2

*(Read Mark 1:21–27)*

**MORNING**
Liberating God, break me open, and make me new this day.

**EVENING**
Liberating God, by your gracious powers, I am sustained
and granted healing and wholeness.

I marvel at you for your astonishing power as I listen to the story of Jesus encountering demonic powers in the sanctuary. Holy One, you come to engage the powers of evil. You come to challenge everything that distorts, diminishes, and disfigures your intention for humankind. Evil knows you. It senses your presence, your power, your threat. You find it in its sacred sanctuaries. Forgive me that I have made peace where you engage in struggle. Forgive me that too often I have dismissed the astonishing, the miraculous, and the transforming possibility. Let the report of your disturbing power to change, challenge, and heal spread in our lives, congregations, and world.

**MORNING**
Your power to make all things new is nearer than I imagine.
Bring newness and hope to those engaged in the struggle with evil.
*(Prayers of Intercession)*

**EVENING**
I pray now for those whose lives are distorted by pain,
evil, or oppression.
*(Prayers of Intercession)*

---

**WITH A HEART OPEN TO YOUR WAY, I PRAY THE PRAYER JESUS TAUGHT.**
*(Pray the Prayer of Our Savior.)*

---

| **MORNING** | **EVENING** |
|---|---|
| Today, grant me the grace to trust your promises and to live into them. In the matchless name of Jesus. Amen. | Your power is beyond my grasp, yet within reach of my trust. In trust would I rest now. In the matchless name of Jesus. Amen. |

# February 3

*(Read Mark 1:21-27)*

**MORNING**

Passionate God, Astonishing One, speak with authority,
that I may know that this day counts.

**EVENING**

Passionate God, let me now ponder with wonder
and awe your presence in the day that is ending.

Jesus the teacher, teach me. Teach me of your life-giving power and your claim as author of my life. We learn little—strangely—from Mark's story of what Jesus actually taught. We do learn that his teaching had power—life changing, demon-disturbing, awe-inspiring, people-healing power. Amazing! Help me to know anew the power of the gospel, of the Word, of the church. Deliver me from all discounting, domesticating, and dismissing of this amazing power that has, in some measure, been entrusted to me. Free me from fear. Set me free to share, to trust, to teach, and to live with the power of God's good news.

**MORNING**

I look to this new day with its possibilities for healing
for others and for myself.
*(Prayers of Intercession)*

**EVENING**

Tonight I hold in prayer those who have given up hope
and those who hide from hope.
*(Prayers of Intercession)*

**WITH A HEART OPEN TO YOUR WAY, I PRAY THE PRAYER JESUS TAUGHT.**
*(Pray the Prayer of Our Savior.)*

**MORNING**

I surrender myself to you, O God,
to love and serve you as fully as I am
able this day. In the matchless name
of Jesus. Amen.

**EVENING**

Quiet my anxieties that even as
I sleep I may be receptive to your love
and truth. In the matchless name
of Jesus. Amen.

# February 4

*(Read Psalm 111)*

### MORNING
Holy and Awesome God, with this new day I remember
your mercies throughout this week, and your abiding care.

### EVENING
Holy and Awesome God, a day of recalling your constant care now
ends. Let me rest in the knowledge that you do care for me.

Faithful God, guided by the psalmist, today I tell of your goodness,
your faithfulness, your trustworthiness. Some days and seasons, holy
one, you seem hidden and far off; and it takes courage to say so. Not
today. Today, my whole being sings. Today I praise you because of your
great works. Praise is also an act of courage. Today, Gracious One, I
praise you in the midst of the congregation, offering my own testimony
to all who would hear of your enduring love. May I so lose myself in
your love that I may be found more authentically in your service.

### MORNING
In the confidence of your care, I pray for the needs
of the world and of the church.
*(Prayers of Intercession)*

### EVENING
I thank you for the people of the congregation,
and I ask your care for them.
*(Prayers of Intercession)*

---

**WITH A HEART OPEN TO YOUR WAY, I PRAY THE PRAYER JESUS TAUGHT.**
*(Pray the Prayer of Our Savior.)*

---

### MORNING
I want to know joy today.
Help me to seek the one needed
thing, your presence. In the matchless
name of Jesus. Amen.

### EVENING
Your praise, O God, endures forever;
sung by night stars, by the breath of
wild creatures, and by me. In the
matchless name of Jesus. Amen.

# February 5

*(Read Deuteronomy 18:15–20)*

### MORNING

Loving God, my ears awake to the sounds of this day.
May I listen as the sun sings the melody of the morning.

### EVENING

Loving God, my ears have been filled with the many sounds
of this day. May I put them to rest with your singing of the stars.

It is often hard to hear you. The voices of the world stuff my ears as if
with the cotton called confusion. Other times it is only my own voice
to which I listen. Then I wonder why your voice remains silent to my
ears. But you promise not to leave me without guidance. You promise
to send me those who speak for you. Help me practice the art of discernment. Give to me the gift of recognizing your voice.

### MORNING

From a still place that comes from walking in your promises,
strengthen me to be your voice to others.
*(Prayers of Intercession)*

### EVENING

From a still place that comes from resting in your love,
let me remember all those who couldn't hear you today.
*(Prayers of Intercession)*

---

"GOD, SPEAK TO ME THAT I MAY SPEAK IN LIVING ECHOES OF YOUR TONE."
*(Frances Ridley Havergal)*

---

| MORNING | EVENING |
|---|---|
| God of morning and melody, meet me in the many voices I hear today and let me know through whom you speak. Thanks be to Christ. Amen. | God of stars and song, speak to me even as I sleep that even in my dreams I may discern your will. Thanks be to Christ. Amen. |

# February 6

*(Read Deuteronomy 18:15–20)*

### MORNING
God of History, let me know as I awake this morning that today
belongs to you as surely as yesterday and tomorrow.

### EVENING
God of History, as I go to sleep tonight, remind me that my history is yours to hold.

You are a God who acts in history. It is easier for me to believe you sent
prophets to people only in the past. I resist recognizing that I am one
who would rather seek comfort rather than do justice and love kindness.
It is also easier for me to believe that you called people only in the past
to be prophets. I resist discovering what it means to be one who speaks
for you. Remind me that your prophets always speak by your authority.

### MORNING
God of action and authority, I acknowledge that you
are in control. May I not seek to control this day or any
whom I may encounter.
*(Prayers of Intercession)*

### EVENING
God of word and deed, forgive me if I left words unspoken,
or actions undone, that could have been of encouragement to others.
*(Prayers of Intercession)*

---

"GOD'S SPIRIT FREELY FLOWS, HIGH SINGING WHERE IT WILL;
GOD SPOKE OF OLD IN PROPHET'S WORD; THAT WORD SPEAKS STILL."
*(Moses Maimonides)*

---

### MORNING
With humility, I accept the gift
of this day with all its possibilities
knowing it belongs to you. Thanks be
to Christ. Amen.

### EVENING
With humility, I give back to you
the gift of this day knowing that all I
accomplished today was by your grace.
Thanks be to Christ. Amen.

# February 7

*(Read 1 Corinthians 8:1–13)*

### MORNING

Compassionate God, while my head is on the pillow, remind me
that this I know for sure, I am known and loved by you.

### EVENING

Compassionate God, before I return to my bed, remind me that
this I know for sure, I am loved and known by you.

I like to think I am in the know. I want to see in black and white and
act surprised when everyone else is not in step with me. Life, though,
is most often lived in shades of gray. What is right is discovered less by
how much I know than by how much I love. I want the freedom that
comes from living in you and yet am not eager for the responsibility
that comes with it. Let me use the gift of conscience to discern where
on the path I should walk today.

### MORNING

Open me to what I may come to know from
those I will walk with this day.
*(Prayers of Intercession)*

### EVENING

Help me to embrace what I have come to know from
those I walked with this day.
*(Prayers of Intercession)*

---

**"O GRANT US LIGHT THAT WE MY KNOW WISDOM THAT YOU ALONE CAN GIVE."**
*(Lawrence Tuttiett)*

---

### MORNING

Let me measure my steps this day,
not from my own understanding
but by your love. Thanks be to Christ.
Amen.

### EVENING

May I rest at the close of this day,
in the knowledge of having walked
in your love. Thanks be to Christ.
Amen.

# February 8

*(Read 1 Corinthians 8:1–13)*

### MORNING
Companion God, I rise from my bed
drawn by a dawning awareness of your presence.

### EVENING
Companion God, I will return to my bed,
wrapped in the warmth of your love.

You have given me the awesome joy and responsibility of freedom in Jesus Christ. But you have not done so for me to go off on my own without regard for my sisters and brothers. For I am a creature of community. You have created me to be in relationship with all of humanity, to be interconnected with all of creation. I live with the knowing that all that I do and say has impact. It is with tenderness and loving kindness that I go out to greet the world.

### MORNING
Lead me to those for whom an encounter
of respect and caring would be empowering.
*(Prayers of Intercession)*

### EVENING
If I had encounters today in which I did not respond
with respect and caring, let there be healing.
*(Prayers of Intercession)*

---

"BLESSED BE THE TIE THAT BINDS OUR HEARTS IN CHRISTIAN LOVE;
THE SHARING OF A COMMON LIFE IS LIKE TO THAT ABOVE."
*(John Fawcett)*

---

### MORNING
Called to care, I do so in the
knowledge that I am not alone.
Your presence sustains me. Thanks be
to Christ. Amen.

### EVENING
I end this day in the care that only
your presence can bring. I rest in the
knowledge that I am not alone.
Thanks be to Christ. Amen.

# February 9

*(Read Mark 1:21–28)*

### MORNING
Author of my days, just the fact that I can breathe deeply
and fill my lungs with the beginning of the day is a miracle.

### EVENING
Author of my days, just the fact that I can exhale
and release all that might keep me from sleep is a miracle.

In the dimness of this world, all Jesus has to do is walk among the people to be seen as light, to teach a word that is recognized as having such authority that even evil spirits obey him. Open my eyes to your light so that even the corners of my life are lit with your love. Open my ears to your word that even the evil that seeks to hide in my life may find no cover. Let me recognize the authority by which I may do ministry in your name.

### MORNING
Lead me to the corners within my interactions
with others that need the light of your love.
*(Prayers of Intercession)*

### EVENING
Let me recognize the places in my interactions
with others that may become places for evil to hide.
*(Prayers of Intercession)*

---

"REMEMBER, GOD, YOUR WORKS OF OLD, THE WONDERS THAT OUR PEOPLE TOLD.
NONE EVER CALLED ON YOU IN VAIN. GIVE PEACE, O GOD, GIVE PEACE AGAIN."
*(Henry W. Baker)*

---

### MORNING
God of light, it is in you that I rise
to greet the day. Thanks be to Christ.
Amen.

### EVENING
God of truth, it is in you that
I find my rest. Thanks be to Christ.
Amen.

# February 10

*(Read Psalm 11:1–6)*

**MORNING**

Gracious and merciful God, your works that greet my eyes
this day fill me with awe.

**EVENING**

Gracious and Merciful God, it is with reverence
that I give thanks for the gifts of this day.

When I look at the glory of your creation and your works among your people, my response must be to give praise to you. You create mountains but are trustworthy to not ignore the low places. You are a God of majesty, but you are merciful to those who call on you. Embody my words of thanks into the deeds of my living. Consecrate my daily actions, so that every part of my walk with you gives you honor.

**MORNING**

Keep me mindful that I am not a reflection of your mercy
by myself but in company with others.
*(Prayers of Intercession)*

**EVENING**

Remind me when I look in the mirror that it is not
my own reflection I seek, but the reflection of how I have been
your mercy to others.
*(Prayers of Intercession)*

"YOUR MERCIES HOW TENDER, HOW FIRM TO THE END,
OUR MAKER, DEFENDER, REDEEMER, AND FRIEND."
*(Robert Grant)*

**MORNING**

You provide for those who hunger.
Feed me now so that I can do your work.
Thanks be to Christ. Amen.

**EVENING**

You provide for those who hunger.
Feed me now so that I may rest in you.
Thanks be to Christ. Amen.

# February 11

*(Read Psalm 111:7–10)*

### MORNING

Faithful One, I awake this morning knowing that I am a work in progress. I trust that you are guiding me to become who I am.

### EVENING

Faithful One, I come to the close of this day trusting that you know me by name and that by your grace I am becoming who I am.

Your Word is a source of comfort and guidance for me. Discerning your truth is often difficult, since even my own best intentions can get in the way. Plant me firmly in what I know for sure. I know I may gain understanding when I value your wisdom above the "wisdom" of the world. I know that I am called to be in relationship not only with you, but with your people. Grant me wisdom and understanding when by the work of my hands I seek to do justice.

### MORNING

Illuminate the moments and interactions in my day
with which I need to practice what I know to be wise and true.
*(Prayers of Intercession)*

### EVENING

Remind me of the moments and interactions in my day
from which I might discern your wisdom.
*(Prayers of Intercession)*

---

**"You are my best thought by day or by night,**
**waking or sleeping, your presence my light."**
*(Mary E. Byrne)*

---

### MORNING

May I take your promises
with me as I seek to live out a faithful
response to your love. Thanks be
to Christ. Amen.

### EVENING

As I seek understanding,
may I rest in your promises and praise
you with every breath. Thanks be
to Christ. Amen.

# February 12

*(Read Psalm 147:1–6)*

**MORNING**

O mighty God, my spirit, soul, and body praise you!

**EVENING**

O mighty God, during the course of this day I have seen your
hand at work in my life and in all creation. I truly praise you.

Mighty, Creator God. Sometimes in the business of life, I fail to see
your hand at work in my life and in the lives of those around me. Like
a faithful physician, you have always tended to my wounds, and your
gentle Spirit always has given me comfort. Today, as I begin a new work
week, may I serve as your agent of healing within my family, my
church, and my community. Use me, O God, to lift and uphold the
brokenhearted and the downtrodden.

**MORNING**

Thank you for your healing power and presence.
Make your power known today.
*(Prayers of Intercession)*

**EVENING**

Today I saw you in the midst of my life. Thank you, loving God!
*(Prayers of Intercession)*

MAY WE REST IN THE KNOWLEDGE THAT A HEALING, CREATING, AND GRACIOUS
GOD IS ACTIVELY INVOLVED IN OUR LIVES, OUR FAMILIES, AND OUR COMMUNITIES.
*(Pray the Prayer of Our Savior.)*

**MORNING**

Help me trust you to meet
my hopes and needs so that I may be
free to serve as your agent of healing
and peace. In Jesus' name I pray.
Amen.

**EVENING**

Give me rest, that tomorrow I may
continue to see your hand at work.
In Jesus' name I pray.
Amen.

# February 13

*(Read Psalm 147:7–11)*

**MORNING**

Almighty and loving God, this is the day that you have made.
I sing praises for your creation.

**EVENING**

Almighty and loving God, my song to you has not ended
for the evening. It is as beautiful as the morning.

I sing to you, gracious God, because you do not tire of working. I sing to you because you constantly create complex and simple things, large and small things, dangerous and harmless things, beautiful and repulsive things—all providing the perfect balance for life. I sing to you because I rejoice that your constant presence gives me comfort and peace. I pray that your presence will help me to be present to others who need comfort and peace. May I be your vessel, imparting your love, your healing, your peace, and your justice.

**MORNING**

I sing to you, rejoicing in your gift of life, O God.
*(Prayers of Intercession)*

**EVENING**

Maker of wonders, I rejoice in the wonderful things
that you have done today.
*(Prayers of Intercession)*

---

**GOD CREATED THIS DAY, WITH ITS HIGH AND ITS LOW POINTS.**
**LET US REJOICE IN THE PRESENCE OF GOD IN THE WORLD AND IN OUR LIVES.**
*(Pray the Prayer of Our Savior.)*

---

**MORNING**

Do not allow me to forget
that you are at work in my life today
and always. In Jesus' name I pray.
Amen.

**EVENING**

Give me rest, that tomorrow I may
bear your good news to a world in
need of healing. In Jesus' name I pray.
Amen.

# February 14

Valentine's Day

*(Read 1 Corinthians 9:16–23)*

**MORNING**

Loving Jesus, strengthen me to be a bearer
of the good news in my family and community.

**EVENING**

Loving Jesus, I praise you because I was not silent
and had the courage to share your good news today.

Mighty Savior, help me not to be ashamed of the gospel. Help me to understand the good news as your power for salvation for everyone who has faith. May I be your instrument of liberation, healing, peace, justice, and reconciliation in my family and in my community. Help me, O God, never to be silent. Help me to share the good news freely with everyone around me: the cashier in the supermarket, the members of the PTA, and all those you call my neighbors.

**MORNING**

Savior of creation, may your strength and power allow me
to serve you today.
*(Prayers of Intercession)*

**EVENING**

Loving Savior, today I have experienced the exhilarating power
of the gospel in my life, and I saw your light shine in those around me.
*(Prayers of Intercession)*

---

LET US DRESS OURSELVES IN THE POWER OF THE GOSPEL. WE MUST NOT BE SILENT!
LET US SHARE THE GOOD NEWS OF SALVATION WITH EVERYONE.
*(Pray the Prayer of Our Savior.)*

---

| **MORNING** | **EVENING** |
| --- | --- |
| Help me not to be silent today. | Give me rest, that tomorrow I may |
| In Jesus' name I pray. Amen. | share fearlessly with others the healing |
| | and transforming power of Jesus. |
| | In Jesus' name I pray. Amen. |

# February 15

*(Read Mark 1:29–34)*

**MORNING**

Healer of creation, bring healing, wholeness,
and liberation to my life.

**EVENING**

Healer of creation, thank you.
Your power has been a real presence in my life today.

Gracious Savior, I rejoice in knowing that your healing power has been at work from the beginning of time and that you continue to heal and restore your creation. I have experienced the power of the gospel in the healing that your presence brings to my life, my family, and my community. Allow me to discern your healing hand at work in the midst of the people around me, that I may glorify your name. Heal our souls, our spirits, and our bodies, liberating us from the fear and the feeling of hopelessness that come from illness and disease.

**MORNING**

Almighty God, bring wholeness to my life
and the people around me.
*(Prayers of Intercession)*

**EVENING**

Healing Christ, continue to heal and restore your creation.
*(Prayers of Intercession)*

REJOICE! THE HEALING POWER OF JESUS IS REAL,

AND IT BRINGS WHOLENESS AND LIBERATION TO OUR LIVES.

*(Pray the Prayer of Our Savior.)*

| **MORNING** | **EVENING** |
|---|---|
| Drive away my fear of your healing power and restore my wholeness. In Jesus' name I pray. Amen. | Give me rest, that tomorrow I may be your agent of healing. In Jesus' name I pray. Amen. |

# February 16

*(Read Mark 1:35–39)*

**MORNING**
Living God, renew my soul, that today I may serve
with new diligence.

**EVENING**
Living God, you have filled this day with exciting
and powerful experiences.

I awake, O God, receptive to new possibilities for service and ministry. Fill me with your power, Holy One, in a new and exciting way. Fill me to overflowing with your healing power that it may flow through me to others. Fill me with your renewing and restoring power, that I may be able to make a difference in my community. I pray that today I may be an instrument of your love, power, and grace.

**MORNING**
In the dawn of this new day, O God,
fill my life with your presence.
*(Prayers of Intercession)*

**EVENING**
In the twilight of this day, O God, I rejoice in your mighty works.
*(Prayers of Intercession)*

---

THE GOD OF NEW BEGINNINGS HAS CLEANSED US WITH THE RIVERS
OF RIGHTEOUSNESS. BRIMMING WITH THE SPIRIT OF CONVICTION, OUR LIVES NOW
EMBRACE AND SHARE THE HEALING POWER OF CHRIST.
*(Pray the Prayer of Our Savior.)*

---

**MORNING**
I am your agent of healing;
empower me for this ministry today.
In Jesus' name I pray. Amen.

**EVENING**
I place the weariness of my daily
toil in your arms; in them may I find
comfort. Give me rest that I may awake
regenerated and ready to begin again.
In Jesus' name I pray. Amen.

# February 17

*(Read Isaiah 40:21–26)*

**MORNING**

Mighty God, I see you in the newness of this day.

**EVENING**

Mighty God, I have seen your work today, and I am thankful.

I lift up my eyes, and I see your glory, O Holy One. Your mighty works surround me, and I am amazed at the intricacy and openness of your creation. I am truly in awe of you, God. I am in awe that your mercy, love, and power can be seen in all of creation. Make your righteousness known in my life and in my community, that all may be transformed by your marvelous grace. Today, I worship your holy name.

**MORNING**

I rejoice today in your righteousness and your mighty works.
*(Prayers of Intercession)*

**EVENING**

I rejoice because today you have been at work
transforming the world.
*(Prayers of Intercession)*

---

OUR GOD IS MIGHTY AND POWERFUL. LET US PUT ALL OUR TRUST IN GOD,
AND WE WILL SEE GOD'S GLORY.
*(Pray the Prayer of Our Savior.)*

---

| **MORNING** | **EVENING** |
| --- | --- |
| Almighty God, lead me to quiet streams where I may encounter the new revelation that comes through your constant presence in my life. In Jesus' name I pray. Amen. | Give me rest, that tomorrow I may experience your power and revelation afresh. In Jesus' name I pray. Amen. |

# February 18

*(Read Isaiah 40:27–31)*

**MORNING**

Creator of heaven and earth, renew my strength today.

**EVENING**

Creator of heaven and earth, your strength has not failed me.

Almighty God, you know my ups and downs; you know my fears and joys; you know my wants and needs. But sometimes I fail to trust you fully. I pray that in your love, grace, and power you will transform and renew my life. Loving God, empower me to live as you desire and strengthen me for the journey of life.

**MORNING**

I rejoice in your steadfast love, power, and glory.

*(Prayers of Intercession)*

**EVENING**

You give me everything I need for wholeness and peace.

*(Prayers of Intercession)*

O GOD, YOUR POWER WILL RENEW OUR STRENGTH.

EMPOWER US AND TRANSFORM OUR LIVES.

*(Pray the Prayer of Our Savior.)*

**MORNING**

Give me strength for a new day.
I need your power today.
In Jesus' name I pray.
Amen.

**EVENING**

Give me rest, that tomorrow
I may continue on my journey
as you walk with me.
In Jesus' name I pray.
Amen.

# February 19

*(Read Hosea 2:14–20)*

**MORNING**

Divine Love, wake me today with your renewing love.

**EVENING**

Divine Love, as I prepare for rest, may I reflect on today
and become aware of times I was faithful to your covenant.

God of Reconciliation and Hope, as you did with ancient Israel, woo us back into a loving relationship with you. As I live this day, call me to acts of righteousness and mercy. Let me reach out to others who live in brokenness. Together may we put the pieces back into a whole, allowing hope to be restored.

**MORNING**

Righteous and Merciful God, you desire all your creation to be
in harmony. Grant your peace and hope to those for whom I pray.
*(Prayers of Intercession)*

**EVENING**

Grant me, Loving One, a restful night. Hold and rock me in
your arms, lulling me to sleep. Watch over those for whom I pray.
*(Prayers of Intercession)*

LET ME BE AN INSTRUMENT OF YOUR HOPE, PEACE, AND RECONCILIATION.

**MORNING**

As I go out into the world today,
Hope of the World, awaken my senses
to cries of justice. In Christ's name.
Amen.

**EVENING**

As I close my eyes, I am comforted
knowing your Light shines in the
darkness. In Christ's name. Amen.

# February 20

*(Read Psalm 103:1–5)*

### MORNING
Giver-of-All-Good-Gifts, I rise singing your praises.
My very being—body, mind and soul—blesses your holy name.

### EVENING
Giver-of-All-Good-Gifts, I lie down singing your praises.
Thank you for the blessings of this day.

Bless the Lord, O my soul. I praise you, my God and Redeemer. You know our needs and satisfy our longings with good gifts. You forgive us our sins and do not remember our wrongdoings. You heal our bodies, minds, and souls of the ills that plague them. Your love is everlasting. Great is your mercy to your children. Nothing in this world can separate us from the love in Jesus Christ our Sovereign.

### MORNING
Wondrous God, I give you thanks for your blessings.
Bestow your blessings upon those for whom I pray.
*(Prayers of Intercession)*

### EVENING
Merciful God, thank you for the blessings given me today.
Watch over and keep safe those for whom I pray.
*(Prayers of Intercession)*

---

**BLESS THE LORD, O MY SOUL, AND ALL THAT IS WITHIN ME BLESS GOD'S HOLY NAME.**

---

### MORNING
I rejoice in your love, my God.
It strengthens me for the challenges
that await me today.
In Christ's name. Amen.

### EVENING
I rejoice in your love, my God.
It gives me peace as I close my eyes
and rest for the night.
In Christ's name. Amen.

# February 21

*(Read Psalm 103:6–13, 22)*

**MORNING**

Compassionate One, Loving Parent, you coax me awake
with the whispers of the morning light.

**EVENING**

Compassionate One, Loving Parent, you lull me to sleep
with the lullabies of the evening wind.

As all children wander from their parents, so we, your children, have strayed from your path. Out of prejudice, fear, and hatred we have turned on each other and broken your commandments. We have not lived in peace. God, you are slow to anger and you abound in steadfast love. You are the Sovereign of all the earth. Remove from us our transgressions, and use us as your instruments of compassion.

**MORNING**

Lift us above our failings. Set us on your straight path.
Show compassion for those for whom I pray.
*(Prayers of Intercession)*

**EVENING**

As night falls on those for whom I pray, may they feel
your presence with them, your loving arms around them.
*(Prayers of Intercession)*

**GOD IS SLOW TO ANGER AND ABOUNDS IN STEADFAST LOVE.**

| **MORNING** | **EVENING** |
|---|---|
| I give you thanks, God, for I go out in joy knowing I am forgiven and loved. Guide me this day. In Christ's name. Amen. | I give you thanks, God, for your love is as high as the heavens. Grant me rest this night and renew my soul. In Christ's name. Amen. |

# February 22

*(Read 2 Corinthians 3:1–6)*

**MORNING**

God of all life, I begin this new day in anticipation of all
that you have planned for me.

**EVENING**

God of all life, I end this day grateful for the many ways
you have been revealed to me.

We read the headlines, watch the news, and become discouraged and
sometimes depressed. Often we become caught up in the events of the
world and do not notice the reflections of your glory happening around
us. Your surprises break out in unexpected ways and places. Help us to
learn how to pay attention and recognize them.

**MORNING**

Awaken me to your surprising glory.
Encourage and strengthen those for whom I pray.
*(Prayers of Intercession)*

**EVENING**

I give you thanks for the ways you made yourself known
to me today. Protect those for whom I pray.
*(Prayers of Intercession)*

**WATCH. WAIT. ANTICIPATE GOD AT WORK IN THE WORLD.**

| **MORNING** | **EVENING** |
|---|---|
| Let me be mindful | Grant me peace and rest, |
| of your glory. Surprise me! | refreshed for a new day. |
| In Christ's name. | In Christ's name. |
| Amen. | Amen. |

# February 23

*(Read 2 Corinthians 3:1–6)*

**MORNING**

Creator God, I greet this day with joy. I am your baptized child.

**EVENING**

Creator God, I am contented. I know you are always with me.

We live in a society defined by fast and throwaway. Nothing is made to last, but to be replaced. We are captivated by the latest fashion and newest model. Today Paul reminds us that what is truly dependable and trustworthy is you, O God. In Christ we are free. Freedom is a gift that liberates us to be the people you created us to be.

**MORNING**

I give you thanks for your saving grace.
Extend your grace to those for whom I pray.
*(Prayers of Intercession)*

**EVENING**

What peace I feel knowing in Christ I am free.
Grant your peace to those for whom I pray.
*(Prayers of Intercession)*

**THE TRUTH SHALL SET US FREE.**

**MORNING**

I woke this morning feeling rested
and renewed in the knowledge that the
Truth shall set me free.
In Christ's name.
Amen.

**EVENING**

God of quietness and rest,
calm my heart, mind, and soul.
Grant me a peaceful night.
In Christ's name.
Amen.

# February 24

*(Read Mark 2:13–17)*

**MORNING**

God who is above all naming, you call my name
and bid me to arise and shine.

**EVENING**

God who is above all naming, you soothe my soul
and bid me to rest and be renewed.

Jesus saw past the barriers society built around people. Jesus saw through the masks worn by those who wanted to hide their true selves. He saw the true being and called them to follow. He deemed them worthy to be part of his ministry. Often we think we are not worthy of your love and forgiveness, Friend-of-the-friendless, Help-for-the-helpless. Some are plagued by addiction, lies, deceit, anger, and low self-esteem. Yet Jesus calls them. He calls us all to put aside what weighs us down and to find new life in him. Reconcile us to you, O Love Divine, and each other.

**MORNING**

Call me to serve you this day, my Savior.
May those for whom I pray feel your acceptance and love.
*(Prayers of Intercession)*

**EVENING**

Lay your hands upon me this night.
Bless me and those for whom I pray.
*(Prayers of Intercession)*

---

**THE MERCY OF GOD IS FROM EVERLASTING TO EVERLASTING.**

---

**MORNING**

Energize me this day to serve you.
Let me hear your voice above all other
sounds. Let me hear and listen.
In Christ's name. Amen.

**EVENING**

You whisper my name and gently
command me not to be anxious but
to place my very being in your loving
care. I am safe in your arms. In
Christ's name. Amen.

# February 25

*(Read Mark 2:13–22)*

**MORNING**
God of Expectation, this is your day.
In celebration I worship you.

**EVENING**
God of Expectation, I thank you for this day.
I continue to worship you.

Jesus, you shared many meals with your followers. You looked beyond social prejudice against people. You called outcasts to be your followers and break bread. Today, you continue to prepare the table before us; inviting us to eat and drink. As we break bread together in your name, let us make this meal an opportunity to be reconciled with one another. Let it be an occasion for healing. As we lift the cup in your name, let us break down barriers that exclude others. Help us to reach out to the oppressed, the outcast, and those held in contempt. May we all sit in unity.

**MORNING**
Giver of the Sabbath, I come before you with thanksgiving.
Bless those for whom I pray.
*(Prayers of Intercession)*

**EVENING**
Giver of the Sabbath, I go through my bedtime ritual
and ponder all the wonders of you that I encountered this day.
Bless those for whom I pray.
*(Prayers of Intercession)*

---

**WE HAVE FULLNESS OF LIFE IN CHRIST.**

---

**MORNING**
I hold in my heart the gift of life you give me today. May I worship you in all that I do. In Christ's name. Amen.

**EVENING**
I hold in my heart the blessing given me today. I rest secure in your love. In Christ's name. Amen.

# February 26

*(Read Psalm 99:6–9)*

### MORNING
Welcoming God, I awaken to continue my journey
into your presence.

### EVENING
Welcoming God, I rejoice in the wonderful ways
you greet me and accept me.

God, you are a friend and a guide to your people throughout the ages, and we praise you with thanks and joy. To countless people who have cried out to you, you have shown your mercy, you have revealed your love, and you have spoken your word. You offer to all who faithfully seek you the assurance of your steadfast love and presence. Greet us in this time as we bring our lives and hopes to you. Reach out to us and draw us near so we can gain strength and courage from your power.

### MORNING
I greet this new day knowing that you hear my prayers, O God.
*(Prayers of Intercession)*

### EVENING
Even as I rest, O God, you hear those who call your name,
and you greet them in love and mercy.
*(Prayers of Intercession)*

AS WE DRAW NEAR TO YOU, WONDERFUL GOD, YOU DRAW NEAR TO US.
THANK YOU FOR YOUR STEADFAST COMPANIONSHIP.

### MORNING
I sense your nearness, holy God;
my spirit stretches for your Spirit, and
I listen for your guiding voice.
Praise be to Christ. Amen.

### EVENING
In the peace of your protecting
embrace, God, I rest and gain
new energy for tomorrow.
Praise be to Christ. Amen.

# February 27

*(Read Luke 9:28–36)*

**MORNING**

Loving God, from the valleys I travel. I come now to your holy
mountain in search of your transforming word.

**EVENING**

Loving God, when I have stumbled on the journey to you, you
have given me strength and courage.

God, Jesus knew the value of taking special time to be with you. He frequently separated himself from the tasks and business of daily living to
be renewed in your presence. And you greeted Jesus each time he
sought your holy touch and wisdom. He knew you as a loving, intimate
Parent, ready to receive and embrace him. Let us hear again Jesus' invitation to draw close to you with him; claim us together with Jesus as
your chosen cherished ones.

**MORNING**

God, you seek to make yourself known to every person
in unique ways.
*(Prayers of Intercession)*

**EVENING**

How have you greeted people today, God?
What blessings have you poured into someone's life?
*(Prayers of Intercession)*

I WILL SPEND SOME SPECIAL TIME TODAY TO BE WITH YOU, GOD,
KNOWING YOU ACCEPT ME AS YOUR OWN PRECIOUS CREATION.

**MORNING**

God, today I seek to be in your
presence. Let me not miss your voice
when you speak. Praise be to Christ.
Amen.

**EVENING**

Tonight I will rest comfortably,
God, because I know you will greet
me again in the new day. Praise be
to Christ. Amen.

# February 28

*(Read Exodus 34:29–35)*

**MORNING**
Brilliant God, this new day embraces me just
as your radiant love encircles me.

**EVENING**
Brilliant God, my heart is aglow with your power,
and my soul is aflame with your Spirit.

O God, we confess we often fail to share our faith and show your love because we are uncomfortable talking about spirituality at home, in the workplace, and in the neighborhood. We come to you, but we do not go for you. We cover faith as Moses covered his face, and we place our relationship with you in separate compartment of our lives. Forgive us for failing to be courageous when you need us most. Embolden us today. Send us out to live and work for you and for your realm.

**MORNING**
Use me to change lives today, God; call me into your service.
*(Prayers of Intercession)*

**EVENING**
Thank you for sending me on a mission for you today, O God.
*(Prayers of Intercession)*

---

**GOD, I AM A VESSEL THROUGH WHICH YOU POUR LOVE ON THE WORLD.**

---

**MORNING**
Light of the world, today help me
introduce even one person to you.
Praise be to Christ. Amen.

**EVENING**
Light of the world, your radiance
pierces the night and brings a new
dawn each morning. Praise be
to Christ. Amen.

# March 1

*(Read Luke 9:37–43)*

**MORNING**

Empowering God, you are the source of healing and restoring.

**EVENING**

Empowering God, you make new the lives of your people
whom you cherish.

God, Jesus' life demonstrates that you greet us and make yourself
known to each of us for a special purpose. Jesus returned from his
mountaintop experience in your presence and immediately healed a
child and transformed a family's life. Our relationship with you kindles
within us a commitment to loving action in your name. We gain power
from your presence and commit to use that power to make a positive
difference for others. Guide us to people for whom we can be a special
blessing in Christ's name.

**MORNING**

Strengthen and encourage me in my work for you, O God.
*(Prayers of Intercession)*

**EVENING**

Thank you for the resources and inspiration
you have given me for devoted service, O God.
*(Prayers of Intercession)*

---

I AM GOD'S AGENT OF HEALING AND RESTORATION IN THIS WORLD.
*(Sing "Spirit of the Living God" or another familiar hymn.)*

---

| **EVENING** | **MORNING** |
| --- | --- |
| Thank you, God, for the honor of representing you. Praise be to Christ. Amen. | God, today let me be the instrument of your compassion. Praise be to Christ. Amen. |

# March 2

*(Read 2 Corinthians 3:12–18)*

**MORNING**
Open my heart today, God, that I may radiate praise and joy.

**EVENING**
Open my heart tonight, God.
You have cleared my vision to see you.

God, you know we create barriers that prevent us from fully experiencing and enjoying our relationship with you. These barriers are veils that leave us unable to gaze at your glorious workings in our lives. We fear trusting you fully. We fear treading into the changed future that you prepare for us. We hesitate to accept your vision of who we can be tomorrow because we have grown comfortable today. Forgive us, we pray. Unlock our vision and creativity. Free us to tap into your creating and renewing force to enjoy all kinds of sight, including foresight, hindsight, and insight—each pointing beyond outer realities to a deeper reality within us.

**MORNING**
God, increase our sensitivity to the needs of your people.
*(Prayers of Intercession)*

**EVENING**
Tonight, God, I pray for those who, like me,
are struggling to shed veils and tear down barriers.
*(Prayers of Intercession)*

---

**GOD'S GLORY IS REVEALED TO ME EVERY DAY IN JESUS CHRIST,
AND MY SOUL IS OPEN TO RECEIVE YOU, GOD.**

---

| **MORNING** | **EVENING** |
|---|---|
| Inspiring God, help me to stay open to new ideas and to feast on what is fascinating, memorable, and beautiful. Praise be to Christ. Amen. | Inspiring God, reveal to us your hopes for tomorrow. Praise be to Christ. Amen. |

# March 3

*(Read 2 Corinthians 4:1–2)*

**M O R N I N G**

Dearest God, I freely offer you all of my hopes and dreams for this new day.

**E V E N I N G**

Dearest God, I place all of my successes and failures of this day in your hands.

O God, your loving compassion and forgiveness make it easy to be open and vulnerable in my relationship with you. I fully trust my heart in your tender care, knowing you will never ridicule me, condemn me, or turn away from me. But it is hard to be as honest and truthful in relationships with other people. We often hide our emotional and spiritual core by protecting ourselves from exposure and imagined harm. Reassure us, God; loosen this tight grip that clenches our hearts. Let your love inspire us to develop relationships based on unconditional trust and openness. Empower us with courage to draw from your energy and build love, generosity, and mutual concern into our relationships, just as Jesus did with people in his life.

**M O R N I N G**

Help me to risk loving so that I may truly live for you, O God.
*(Prayers of Intercession)*

**E V E N I N G**

Thank you for encouraging me and uplifting me today as I sought
to nurture meaningful connections with people.
*(Prayers of Intercession)*

**I AM AN EXPRESSION OF GOD'S LIFE AND LOVE IN THE LIVES OF PEOPLE I MEET.**

| **M O R N I N G** | **E V E N I N G** |
|---|---|
| I am excited to go with you into this day, loving God, and meet the people you'll draw to me. Praise be to Christ. Amen. | Thank you for your companionship today, loving God, and I ask that tomorrow I may be a companion to another. Praise be to Christ. Amen. |

# March 4

*(Read Psalm 99:1–5)*

**MORNING**
Almighty God, hear my joyful praise today.
With a glad and grateful spirit, I worship you.

**EVENING**
Almighty God, the universe is full of divine presence.

God, today I recall and celebrate your mighty acts across the centuries, caring for people and drawing them close to you through faithful love, reaching out to embrace and uplift. You sent Jesus to establish your realm of justice and truth in people's hearts so we may establish it for you in this world. You are always present to offer new beginnings and new opportunities. You bring joy and hope where there were lifelessness and despair. Today, use us to further your purposes; make your intentions for us known, and fulfill your promises in us.

**MORNING**
I offer you my life, O God, to use for your goals.
*(Prayers of Intercession)*

**EVENING**
Thank you for this day and all the blessings
you have revealed, God.
*(Prayers of Intercession)*

---

**I LOVE GOD WITH ALL MY MIND, HEART, AND SPIRIT. PRAISE GOD!**
*(Sing "Joyful, Joyful, We Adore You" or another familiar hymn.)*

---

**MORNING**
This is your holy day, God;
I will rejoice and be glad in it.
Praise be Christ. Amen.

**EVENING**
Thank you, God, for receiving my
praise. I now look forward to another
week of partnership with you.
Praise be to Christ. Amen.

# March 5

*(Read John 4:5–42)*

**MORNING**

God, as I arise to this new day that you have made,
I rejoice and trust my life to you.

**EVENING**

God, allow my heart and soul to reflect
your everlasting love for me.

Good and caring God, allow us to quench our thirst and our hunger for justice and peace through your Word. Intervene with your power in the places that deny dignity and wholeness to your children. Fill us with your life-giving water, so we can spread your ministry of peace and justice every day of our lives.

**MORNING**

When I thirst for justice, help me to recognize
your living waters in others.
*(Prayers of Intercession)*

**EVENING**

It is well with my soul because you, my Creator God,
have delivered me from my enemies. I am overflowing
with the presence of your love.
*(Prayers of Intercession)*

"GOD IS SPIRIT, AND THOSE WHO WORSHIP GOD
MUST WORSHIP IN SPIRIT AND TRUTH."

**MORNING**

Praising God, make my
days joyful. Shower us with your
power, so that your people can
worship your greatness in deed and
in spirit. In Jesus' name. Amen.

**EVENING**

In others we find the way to our
own wellness. Thank you, God, for the
challenge of this day and the joy of life.
In Jesus' name. Amen.

# March 6

*(Read John 4:5–42)*

**MORNING**

O God, thank you for your child, Jesus, and for the privilege
of living a new day. May the harvest of this day be pleasing to you.

**EVENING**

God, I have planted seeds of your love in many places today.
Many "crops are ready to be harvested" by the power of your Holy Spirit.
Let it be done.

Creator God and supreme Authority over all creation, hear our prayers.
Women and children find themselves in fields of anger, hatred, racism,
and death. God, lift them out of this misery and plant in their lives love
and mercy, so they can reap a harvest of justice and peace. Hear our
prayers, loving God. Use us as your workers in the field by empowering
us with your Holy Spirit.

**MORNING**

Jesus the Christ is the Savior of the world. This I believe and trust.
*(Prayers of Intercession)*

**EVENING**

We plant fields for justice in your name, though our eyes
may never see the harvest. May all praise be given to you,
for your everlasting love.
*(Prayers of Intercession)*

---

**"ONE PERSON PLANTS, ANOTHER PERSON REAPS."**

---

| **MORNING** | **EVENING** |
|---|---|
| Allow your will to be done in our lives in the world. Be with us all of our days. In Jesus' name. Amen. | In peace I rest and trust that your blessings will awaken me to new experiences and perhaps some harvest. In Jesus' name. Amen. |

# March 7

*(Read Exodus 17:1–7)*

### MORNING

God Almighty, Creator of heaven and earth, Giver of all that is good
and wonderful, guide my footsteps and the words I use to address others.
As your humble servant, open my eyes to know your will.

### EVENING

God Almighty, Creator of heaven and earth, teach me how to
please you in every place. May all that is good and pleasing in your
sight be raised to you in worship and praise.

God, at times we find ourselves in a desert, feeling hot and thirsty, because of wrongs done to us or because of our own guilt and sin against you and others. Forgive us if we have sinned against you, and forgive those who have sinned against us. At times we put you to the test. Forgive us if we have become cynical and forgetful of the times when you have endured our shortcomings and led us to victory! Praise be to you, God Almighty! *Gloria a Dios!*

### MORNING

There is no mountaintop or desert, no waters, nor any place in creation over
which you, our God, have no dominion. God, you will be with me always.
*(Prayers of Intercession)*

### EVENING

Human we are, and we must rest to regain energy and enjoy silence. Meanwhile,
O God, prepare us to continue our journey and speak to us in our dreams.
*(Prayers of Intercession)*

### "IS GOD WITH US OR NOT?"

| MORNING | EVENING |
|---|---|
| Loving and wise God, you have provided for my needs, and for this I am grateful. Help me to continue to trust in your goodness and love. In Jesus' name. Amen. | Teach me to trust in you more each day and to believe in your miraculous powers. In Jesus' name. Amen. |

# March 8

*(Read Psalm 95)*

**MORNING**
Creator God, receive our worship today by allowing it
to manifest into loving and caring behavior toward all whom
we may encounter in our world.

**EVENING**
Creator God, we kneel before you in thanksgiving for all the
good you have provided us. We pray that our worship is pleasing
in your sight and is your will.

From the depths of our thoughts and hearts, we can hear your tender voice tell us that all is well. You have made your Word flesh in Jesus Christ, which clarifies all other words. We pray that in our faith journey you will continue to speak to us and clarify your Word to us. Precious is our dialogue with you, for you are our Creator and Savior.

**MORNING**
God, you make my days joyful.
*(Prayers of Intercession)*

**EVENING**
God, thank you for today's challenges.
*(Prayers of Intercession)*

---

**"HUMBLE OURSELVES AND LISTEN TODAY TO WHAT GOD SAYS."**

---

**MORNING**
O God, who scatters the proud, who fills the hungry and sends the rich away empty, receive this morning joyful songs of praise. In Jesus' name. Amen.

**EVENING**
There is no God greater than you! You have watched over us when our good intentions have gone astray, when our ears have not heard and our tongues have not spoken. We plead for your forgiveness and for a depth of faith that will make a difference in us and in the world. In Jesus' name. Amen.

# March 9

*(Read Romans 5:1–11)*

### MORNING

God, how great is your love for us! You sacrificed your child,
Jesus Christ, to die for us, knowing that we were still sinners. Thank you
for giving us your peace and a relationship that has no end.

### EVENING

God, your love is with us always. May our dreams be of you
and our rest be for your service.

O God, we know that there is nothing in this world that can separate us from your love. You have baptized us with your Holy Spirit, and you shield us with your love and peace. Teach us, loving and caring God, to do what is just and righteous, to show constant love, and to live in humble relationship with you.

### MORNING

God, use my body as a vessel for your Holy Spirit.
*(Prayers of Intercession)*

### EVENING

Thank you for giving us your peace.
*(Prayers of Intercession)*

### "CHRIST DIED FOR US."

### MORNING

Use my body as a vessel for your
Holy Spirit to spread the good news
of Jesus the Christ. In Jesus' name.
Amen.

### EVENING

The greatest gift was given to
us through your child, Jesus Christ,
while we were still sinners.
God is good all the time! And all the
time, God is good! *Gloria a Dios!*
In Jesus' name. Amen.

# March 10

*(Read Romans 5:1–11)*

### MORNING

O hallelujah, wisdom is for us! Ours is a union
now won in Jesus. Ours is a union now won in Jesus.
O Redeemer Power, hallelujah, God.

### EVENING

O hallelujah, wisdom is for us! Your victory over death
is my hope and salvation every day of my life.

May your reign on earth be seen in our church. Kindle your Word in us to make your children wiser. Grant us your victory through good and bad times. Glory be to you, our God, our discerning power. Wisdom from on high is ever with us. O hallelujah, our faith in you has made us free!

### MORNING

I will walk with my Jesus in victory all day long.
*(Prayers of Intercession)*

### EVENING

What a friend I have in Jesus, who cares for me
all day and night. Guide my dreams, strengthen my body,
and awaken me to your tender care.
*(Prayers of Intercession)*

---

**"IN KNOWING JESUS AS YOUR SAVIOR, YOU ARE UNITED TO GOD YOUR CREATOR."**

---

### MORNING

Holy Spirit of God, abide in me.
Teach me your ways. Glory and honor
are yours alone. In Jesus' name.
Amen.

### EVENING

Speak to my heart, O Holy One.
You are my great Parent, and I am
your child. Reside in my dwelling,
and I become one in the Spirit
with you. In Jesus' name.
Amen.

# March 11

*(Read Psalm 95)*

**MORNING**

Protector God, walk with us.
Provide us with words of courage and clothe us with your love.
Let a new song stir my heart.

**EVENING**

Protector God, praise and glory to you for your saving actions.

Praise be to you, O God! When I think of the wondrous gifts of love you have given freely and unconditionally, I humbly kneel before you, my Creator. I lift up my hands to give you glory and praise! Rule over our lives; you are our Maker. Let the world sing a new song unto you.

**MORNING**

God is ruler of all heaven and earth.
*(Prayers of Intercession)*

**EVENING**

You have provided for my every need; for this I thank you.
You, my God, care and give joy to my heart.
*(Prayers of Intercession)*

**"GOD IS MIGHTY, SING JOYFUL SONGS OF PRAISE."**

**MORNING**

Holy Spirit of God,
glory and honor are yours.
In Jesus' name. Amen.

**EVENING**

Speak to my heart
and reside in me.
In Jesus' name. Amen.

# March 12

*(Read Exodus 24:12–18)*

### MORNING
God, thank you for inviting me into your presence one more time.

### EVENING
God, thank you for keeping me close to you this day.

God of love, you have set before us the way. You have given us light for our journey. You have provided us with food, drink, shelter, garments, and love. You have cared for our every need. And you have given us a place to wait on your love. Caring God, you have given us a place in your heart. Hear us this day as we live our lives as monuments to you.

### MORNING
God, as I face the challenges of this day,
be with me and let me know that you are there.
*(Prayers of Intercession)*

### EVENING
God, I ask for forgiveness if, in my haste,
I missed your intent for my life today.
*(Prayers of Intercession)*

### IN A STATE OF GRACE I PRAY.
*(Pray the Prayer of Our Savior.)*

### MORNING
I pray for the power of patience
to heed your call—when you call,
and not when I want to hear.
In Jesus' name. Amen.

### EVENING
You were more patient with me
than I was with you. Forgive me, and
help me to do better tomorrow.
In Jesus' name. Amen.

# March 13

*(Read Psalm 2)*

**MORNING**

Loving God, I awake into a sinful and hateful world.
Please help me to show your love to someone new today.

**EVENING**

Loving God, thank you for guiding me past
the hidden dangers that lay in wait for me today.

God, I just want to say thank you to you, who in your expressions of
might can hold all life in the palm of your hand, yet in your expression
of love smiled on me this day. You rule with authority, yet you are not
brutish like us, your children. I declare to you, you who inhabit the heavens,
that my heart is open to rest in you. Visit me in your Holy Spirit and
dwell within me, so my soul will always shout and sing praises to you.

**MORNING**

Saving God, help me to withstand the evil
that I will confront this day.
*(Prayers of Intercession)*

**EVENING**

Thank you, God, for not letting me be overcome
by the enemy today.
*(Prayers of Intercession)*

**IN A STATE OF THANKFULNESS I PRAY.**

*(Pray the Prayer of Our Savior.)*

**MORNING**

God do not laugh at me today.
Fill me with your Holy Spirit, so all
that I do is pleasing in your sight.
Without you, what reason do I have
to be? In Jesus' name. Amen.

**EVENING**

You found me lacking in faith
this day, yet you still watched over
me. You found me unable to witness
with my whole life, yet you still
allowed me to take refuge in you.
I have no words other than "thank
you." In Jesus' name. Amen.

# March 14

*(Read Psalm 99)*

### MORNING

Sovereign God, guide me this day. Show me the way that
I should go. Entrust me to your charge, and do not let me stray.

### EVENING

Sovereign God, thank you for guiding me this day. You kept me
safe, and I will praise you for having mercy on a sinner like me.

God, you are mighty, and you are all powerful. Sometimes in my arrogance, I think that you need me. Thank you for showing me that it is you who are to be exalted, and not me. Loving God, I am but a speck in the universe, yet you know me by my name. It is not because of me, but because of your love for me, that I am able to achieve success in life. God, I praise your name. I exalt your name, and I will worship you—not just with my mouth, but with my life. Praise be to your blessed and holy name.

### MORNING

God, I look for your pillars this day—not of smoke, but of those
you have placed in my life who are God-filled and Spirit-led.
*(Prayers of Intercession)*

### EVENING

My day was cluttered with the voices of deceitful people,
but through all the clamor, I heard you call me by name. Thank you.
*(Prayers of Intercession)*

### IN A STATE OF AWE I PRAY.
*(Pray the Prayer of Our Savior.)*

### MORNING

God, allow me the privilege
to pray at your feet today.
In Jesus' name. Amen.

### EVENING

God, you heard my cries this day
and lovingly responded.
In Jesus' name. Amen.

# March 15

*(Read 2 Peter 1:16–21)*

**MORNING**

Jesus, this day let me live in the knowledge of your being.

**EVENING**

Jesus, I saw your power in action as you helped me
through this day.

Loving God, once more I was blessed by your grace. When I was feeling sad, I saw you in the smile of a stranger. When I was feeling hurt, I was comforted in the arms of your angel. When I was angry, you sent a ray of sunshine through my window. God, I was an eyewitness to your mercy today. Gracious God, thank you for being my God. Thank you for being real in my life.

**MORNING**

As you love Jesus, please love me as well.
*(Prayers of Intercession)*

**EVENING**

I did my best today to be found pleasing in your sight.
Help me again tomorrow to serve you with my all.
*(Prayers of Intercession)*

---

**IN A STATE OF LOVE I PRAY.**
*(Pray the Prayer of Our Savior.)*

---

**MORNING**

Jesus, be with me this day so I may
hear your voice calling to me. In your
name. Amen.

**EVENING**

I found solace today by standing
on the mountain of your love. I need
you, and I thank you for caring
for me. In Jesus' name.
Amen.

# March 16

*(Read 2 Peter 1:16–21)*

**MORNING**

God, as I awaken to the sounds of life,
may I hear your Word in all that I see.

**EVENING**

God, when I thought I knew more than you today,
your light shone through to correct me.

Patient God, today as I was going astray in my thoughts, your Holy
Spirit entered and guided me back on the right track. How foolish I
am, sometimes replacing your will with mine! How selfish of me to
think that I am the only one who understands you. I have but a piece
of the truth. Savior, keep me in your arms, so I can share the truth I
know with the truth you have shared with others.

**MORNING**

God, let me read your Word anew today.
*(Prayers of Intercession)*

**EVENING**

I was upheld by your Word today.
It has never failed to help me in times of difficulty.
*(Prayers of Intercession)*

**IN A STATE OF BELIEVING I PRAY.**
*(Pray the Prayer of Our Savior.)*

**MORNING**

Savior, I offer you my life today.
May it be worthy of your use.
In Jesus' name. Amen.

**EVENING**

God, without you, I would have
failed to show love to a stranger today
who needed my help. Thank you for
not letting me pass by unnoticing.
In Jesus' name. Amen.

# March 17

*(Read Matthew 17:1–9)*

**MORNING**

God of light, shine. God of light, shine.
God of light, shine through me.

**EVENING**

God of light, I pray that I was used today to show the light
of Christ to someone who was lost.

God of wonder, I pray for your healing touch today. My body is racked with the pain of a world that does not know you. Heal me, so I can go and proclaim your Word by the witness of my life. Transform me from my selfish state to a state of Christ-centeredness. This day, Savior Christ, control every aspect of my life according to your holy will.

**MORNING**

It is good to be found in the land of the living.
May I live today in new ways that show your love in my life.
*(Prayers of Intercession)*

**EVENING**

This was a great day. All day long, I knew that you were with me.
*(Prayers of Intercession)*

---

IN A STATE OF EXPECTATION I PRAY.
*(Pray the Prayer of Our Savior.)*

---

**MORNING**

Savior, today cover me with your Spirit, so all that I do is a reflection of my life in Christ. In Jesus' name. Amen.

**EVENING**

Caring God, thank you for speaking through me today when I did not have the words to comfort my neighbor who was in need. In Jesus' name. Amen.

# March 18

*(Read Matthew 17:1–9)*

### MORNING

God, no one has a greater love than you.
You loved me enough to give and redeem my life.

### EVENING

God, you showed me how much you loved me today
when you picked me up from my fall.

God, give me voice today to proclaim to the world that Christ has taken control of my life. Lead me away from sinful desires. Guide me in a way that will cause others to follow you into all truth. Let the power of your resurrection fill my body. Renew me in the power that can come only from you. Let me show my love for you through the ways I show my love to others.

### MORNING

Precious God, this day let me comfort someone
who has lost a loved one by pointing them toward you.
*(Prayers of Intercession)*

### EVENING

Blessings unto you, loving God. May I praise your name forever.
*(Prayers of Intercession)*

---

**IN A STATE OF RENEWED HOPE I PRAY.**
*(Pray the Prayer of Our Savior.)*

---

| MORNING | EVENING |
|---|---|
| Help me, God, to build a lasting monument to your steadfast love. Mold me in your image, so all can see what you can do—even with someone like me. In Jesus' name. Amen. | Thank you, Jesus, for rising from the grave. When the gravity of sin is pulling me down, I know that I believe in a God who believes in getting back up. In your name I pray. Amen. |

# March 19

*(Read Genesis 15:1–12, 17, 18)*

**MORNING**
Extravagant and Loving God,
I am in awe as I think of your gifts to me.

**EVENING**
Extravagant and Loving God,
I see the countless stars tonight and remember your gifts.

God, when I think of our ancestors in the faith, I marvel that they spoke to you so freely. Abram's faith challenges me. But it is your power that astounds me. The one who created the stars knows we can never count them all. Holy God, you are light in the darkness, a shield against danger. When I feel your presence, I am not afraid. Give me courage to follow wherever you may lead.

**MORNING**
I do not know what challenges this day may bring.
Thank you, God, for being with me.
*(Prayers of Intercession)*

**EVENING**
Dear God, thank you for all this day has brought me.
*(Prayers of Intercession)*

**I PRAY FOR . . .**
*(Pray the Prayer of Our Savior.)*

**MORNING**
Today, help me keep my promises
to you and to the people in my life.
Thanks be to God. Amen.

**EVENING**
As I prepare for sleep I will close my
eyes and quietly count the blessings of
this day. Thanks be to God. Amen.

# March 20

(*Read Psalm 27:1–5*)

**MORNING**

Dear God, I woke up this morning and saw the sun rise.
As I see a new day's light, I remember your light and guidance.

**EVENING**

Dear God, now even as the sunlight begins to fade,
I know that you still give light to my life.

I am fearful. I read and listen to the news. I learn of crimes in my own city, of terror in the nation, of wars and starvation around the world. I am overwhelmed with the evil that seems to thrive. The world is full of angry, violent people. I want to run and hide. I ask, how can I protect myself? Then I remember your presence always with me, God, and I feel your protection. I become calm as I reflect that you are with me in all times and places.

**MORNING**

I am confident that whatever difficulties I face today, you will be
with me, God. I thank you for your comforting presence.
*(Prayers of Intercession)*

**EVENING**

Thank you, God, for being with me today. You still my anxiety
and calm my fears. May everyone find your peace.
*(Prayers of Intercession)*

**I PRAY FOR . . .**
*(Pray the Prayer of Our Savior.)*

**MORNING**

As I go about my day,
may I remember that everyone I meet
is your child and that you love us all.
Thanks be to God. Amen.

**EVENING**

Dear God, today the news
was frightening, but I remember that
the world is in your hands.
Thanks be to God. Amen.

# March 21

*(Read Psalm 27:6–14)*

### MORNING
God, can you hear me? I need to know that you are near
and that you will be with me throughout all of this day.

### EVENING
God, through this day, I felt your presence many times.
Be with me now as the day ends.

God, how can I praise you as I go about my day? Could I sing as I drive
to work? Can I pray before I eat my lunch? Trusting God, as I meet all
the different people who will cross my path this day, may a confident
smile be the sign of my trust in you. I pray that my path will be smooth
today, that the people I have to deal with will be trustworthy, that my
friends and family will be on my side. But I know that whatever happens, God, you will be with me. I will be aware of your goodness from
morning until night.

### MORNING
Help me, God, to use the experience of this day to learn more
about your goodness and love. Make me aware of your presence
every moment.
*(Prayers of Intercession)*

### EVENING
Dear God, I take these few moments to reflect on my day and to remember
the times when I felt your presence. Thank you for being with me.
*(Prayers of Intercession)*

### I PRAY FOR . . .
*(Pray the Prayer of Our Savior.)*

### MORNING
As my day begins, dear God,
I will look for signs of your holy presence and I will praise you. Thanks be
to God. Amen.

### EVENING
The day has been long and I am
ready for sleep. Help me to slow down
and let go of all that has happened.
Thanks be to God. Amen.

# March 22

*(Read Philippians 3:17–4:1)*

### MORNING

Loving God, I think of the faithful people recorded in your Holy Scriptures.
I pray that you will help me to imitate them and to become like them.

### EVENING

Loving God, I come to you now with the experiences of my day.
I know that many times I fell short. I ask for your forgiveness.

Creator God, who supplies all of my needs, I am often torn between the two worlds that claim me. Paul calls on Christians to be citizens of heaven, to have spiritual matters as our main concern. The world calls in a louder voice. Compete! Be successful! Buy this. It will make you beautiful. Wear that; you will be in style. In the race to succeed at what I do, it is so easy to neglect time for reading, for reflection, and for prayer. In wanting to be admired, I spend time and money on unnecessary things. The search for new and interesting things to do sets a hectic pace. But, Loving God, when I keep my focus on my faith in Jesus Christ, when I remember with thanks his dying on the cross, then my priorities seem to easily sort themselves out. I am then at peace with myself and the world.

### MORNING

I thank you, God, for your gift of new life in Jesus Christ.
By his death and resurrection I have been made a citizen of heaven.
*(Prayers of Intercession)*

### EVENING

Thank you, God, for the times when I felt at peace. I pray that those
with whom I had contact felt that I treated them with fairness and respect.
*(Prayers of Intercession)*

### I PRAY FOR . . .
*(Pray the Prayer of Our Savior.)*

| MORNING | EVENING |
|---|---|
| Just for today, God, may I stop my busyness and tend to my spirit. Just for today. Thanks be to God. Amen. | As I prepare for sleep, let me set aside all my earthly worries and concerns. May I always rest in you. Thanks be to God. Amen. |

# March 23

*(Read Luke 13:31–33)*

### MORNING
Good morning, God. As I think about the day ahead of me,
I need to feel the courage and strength that comes from you.

### EVENING
Good evening, God. My day is nearly over and I am weary and carrying
many burdens. Please come to me, God, so that I may lay them down.

God, Jesus' courage in this passage astounds me. He called the king a fox—a sly, vicious killer. This is not "gentle Jesus meek and mild"; this is not a cooing baby in a manger. This is an angry prophet who speaks the truth clearly and without fear. Jesus is so firm in his calling and purpose. I long for that same certainty. I long for the courage to name and to speak against all that is hindering your realm. It is so easy to confuse being Christian with being nice. It is so easy to confuse working for your peaceable realm with simply "going along to get along." Oh, I long for courage.

### MORNING
God, I know that you will be with me this day and that your
presence will guide me and give me strength. Thank you.
*(Prayers of Intercession)*

### EVENING
God, I thank you for the times during the day when you gave me
the right words to speak and the courage to speak them.
*(Prayers of Intercession)*

### I PRAY FOR . . .
*(Pray the Prayer of Our Savior.)*

### MORNING
Today, may I speak truth with courage
and with love. And may my words
also be received with courage and
love. Thanks be to God. Amen.

### EVENING
God, as my day closes, I think about
tomorrow and I place it in your care.
Thanks be to God. Amen.

# March 24

*(Read Luke 13:34–35)*

**MORNING**
Loving God, I know I can come to you as a protective mother
and loving father. I put my whole trust in you.

**EVENING**
Loving God, I feel safe and secure when I rest
in the shadow of your wings.

I watch ducks in a pond near my home. They follow their mother so closely, looking only at her. They trust that she will lead them to food and away from danger. As evening comes they return to the spot she has chosen and they gather close to her for warmth and shelter. Parent God, how often I have wished for a guide to lead me through my days, for someone to watch for danger and make sure I find what I need. I know that I have such a guide—if I trust and follow, looking only to you.

**MORNING**
I thank you, God, knowing that as I begin this day
I may look to you for everything I need.
*(Prayers of Intercession)*

**EVENING**
I thank you, God, that I am one of your children and
have felt your shelter and protection all through this day.
*(Prayers of Intercession)*

**I PRAY FOR . . .**
*(Pray the Prayer of Our Savior.)*

**MORNING**
As I am carrying out many
responsibilities today, remind me that I
am your child and I am in your care.
Thanks be to God. Amen.

**EVENING**
Dear God, night has come and I am
weary. I nestle in the comfort of your
love and care. Thanks be to God.
Amen.

# March 25

*(Read Luke 9:28–36)*

**MORNING**

Great God, as my day begins, keep me awake and watchful
for signs of your presence and glory.

**EVENING**

Great God, I know that I often go through my day noticing only
the humdrum and missing your miracles. Please forgive me.

Imagine almost sleeping through the Transfiguration! Luke says, "Peter and his companions were weighed down with sleep." They came too close to missing this wonderful revelation of who their leader really was. Omnipotent God, Jesus stands clearly in the tradition of your chosen, Moses and Elijah. What do we miss when we "sleepwalk" through our days?

**MORNING**

God, I thank you for the ways you reveal your glory each day.
Today, may I be alert to the signs of your presence.
*(Prayers of Intercession)*

**EVENING**

I thank you, God, that I was able to "see" you today—in the kind
smile of a stranger, in a hug from my child, in a brilliant sunset.
*(Prayers of Intercession)*

**I PRAY FOR . . .**
*(Pray the Prayer of Our Savior.)*

**MORNING**

As this day unfolds before me,
let me find time for rest, for worship,
and for basking in the dazzling light
of Jesus. Thanks be to God.
Amen.

**EVENING**

I feel at peace as this day ends.
Guard me through the night; my trust
is in you. Thanks be to God.
Amen.

# March 26

*(Read John 9:1–23)*

**MORNING**

O God, in the warm brilliance of the sunshine,
your name is to be praised!

**EVENING**

O God, in the cool shadows of twilight,
your name is to be praised!

Eternal God, I confess to you my meager vision, my limited discernment and awareness, my lack of expectation and hope. I turn away from the light that would give growth and meaning to my life. Open my mind and my art to the surprises of your healing grace and mercy that I may rejoice in your works, which are revealed day by day. In your mercy, transform my despondency into joy and affirmation.

**MORNING**

Today, O God, help me to be aware of those about me
who do your work and who reveal your divine purposes.
*(Prayers of Intercession)*

**EVENING**

Thank you for the evidence I have witnessed today of your grace,
which overcomes hopelessness and despair.
*(Prayers of Intercession)*

---

**"O SEND OUT YOUR LIGHT AND YOUR TRUTH; LET THEM LEAD ME."**
*(Pray the Prayer of Our Savior.)*

---

**MORNING**

In this new day, open me to
perceive and to receive your leading
and your will. In Jesus' name.
Amen.

**EVENING**

Grant me rest, O God,
this night, in the confidence of your
encompassing love. In Jesus' name.
Amen.

# March 27

*(Read John 9:24–41 and Mark 2:13–17)*

**MORNING**

Creator God, you have made this day; I will rejoice in it.

**EVENING**

Creator God, your name is to be praised as the sun goes down.

Dear God, how well you must know my illusions. I imagine that I am competent, that I have everything under control and all figured out, that my intelligence and achievements will assure me favor in your sight. Help me, O God, to cast away my illusions, that I may see myself more clearly as I really am. Grant me the courage and honesty to admit my faults and to open my eyes to see my daily need for your redeeming mercies.

**MORNING**

This morning help me to remember with gratitude
all those who, although perhaps despised and at risk,
faithfully witness to the realm of God.
*(Prayers of Intercession)*

**EVENING**

Help me at the close of the day to see myself,
as with all of your children in all places of your creation,
within the bonds of your love.
*(Prayers of Intercession)*

---

"JUST AS I AM, WITHOUT ONE PLEA BUT THAT YOUR BLOOD WAS SHED FOR ME."
*(Pray the Prayer of Our Savior.)*

---

| **MORNING** | **EVENING** |
|:---:|:---:|
| In this new day, God, have mercy. | At bedtime, God, have mercy. |
| Christ, have mercy. God, have mercy. | Christ, have mercy. God, have mercy. |
| In the name of our Savior, I pray. | In the name of our Savior, I pray. |
| Amen. | Amen. |

## March 28

*(Read 1 Samuel 16:1–7)*

**MORNING**
O God, all creation rejoices in you this morning!

**EVENING**
O God, all creation rests in you this night!

Eternal One, you know how much we rely on outward appearances, how much we judge one another by culture, skin color, and social class, and how dazzled we are by success and celebrity. Help me to understand more clearly what is really important and to repent of my reliance on the superficial. Grant to me the mind of Christ that I may see beneath the surface and find in all your children the enduring worth that is valuable in your sight.

**MORNING**
Grant me this day, O God, deeper insight into
what is really important in life.
*(Prayers of Intercession)*

**EVENING**
Cleanse the thoughts of my heart,
that I may see your way and follow in faith.
*(Prayers of Intercession)*

GOD, YOU KNOW THE INNERMOST THOUGHTS AND SECRETS OF MY HEART,
AND YET YOU DO NOT TURN AWAY FROM ME. HOW WONDERFUL! AMAZING GRACE!
*(Pray the Prayer of Our Savior.)*

**MORNING**
Help to me go forth confident
of your love, O God. In the name
of Christ, I pray. Amen.

**EVENING**
Grant rest and peace this night
to me and to all those whom I hold
dear. In the name of Christ,
I pray. Amen.

# March 29

*(Read 1 Samuel 16:8–13)*

**MORNING**

"Morning has broken, like the first morning."
(Eleanor Farjeon)

**EVENING**

"Day is dying in the west; Heaven is touching earth with rest."
(Mary A. Lathbury)

Great and wonderful God, you are not silent but speak, calling forth those who are to do your works of love, justice, and reconciliation in the world. Help me to hear your voice and to know my calling according to your will. Anoint me with your Holy Spirit, that I may faithfully be Christ to my neighbors and fulfill the high calling you have for all your people as partners with you in the work of healing and redemption.

**MORNING**

Open my ears this day, O God, to hear your call. Give me a grateful heart for all those who, in all walks of life, are committed to your service.
*(Prayers of Intercession)*

**EVENING**

Grant to me, at the close of the day, a deeper sense of your purpose for my life, O God.
*(Prayers of Intercession)*

---

"JESUS CALLS US, O'ER THE TUMULT OF OUR LIFE'S WILD, RESTLESS SEA, . . .
'CHRISTIAN, FOLLOW ME.'" (Cecil F. Alexander)
*(Pray the Prayer of Our Savior.)*

---

| **MORNING** | **EVENING** |
|---|---|
| Grant me the presence of the Holy Spirit throughout this day. In the name of Christ, I pray. Amen. | Grant me a restful night, that in the new day I may awaken to your service. In the name of Christ, I pray. Amen. |

# March 30

*(Read Psalm 23 and Isaiah 40)*

**MORNING**

"Comfort, O comfort my people, says your God."

**EVENING**

"God gives power to the faint, and strengthens the powerless."

How astonishing, O Holy One, that you would be our gentle shepherd—to cause us to rest in verdant pastures, to lead us beside still waters, and to restore our souls! This faith is a great comfort to me, O God, in the midst of the anxieties of my life. I often feel pulled in many different ways; help me to cleave to the center. As you comfort me, help me to comfort others that the peace of Christ may more and more be abroad in the world.

**MORNING**

I remember before you, O God, all those who are anxious and troubled, who live in the midst of turmoil, strife, and violence.
*(Prayers of Intercession)*

**EVENING**

Forgive me, dear God, for my thoughtlessness and lack of consideration toward others, which may have only added to their troubles during this day.
*(Prayers of Intercession)*

---

**"THOSE WHO WAIT FOR GOD SHALL RENEW THEIR STRENGTH, THEY SHALL MOUNT UP WITH WINGS LIKE EAGLES, THEY SHALL RUN AND NOT BE WEARY."**
*(Pray the Prayer of Our Savior.)*

---

| MORNING | EVENING |
|---|---|
| In the bustle of this day, help me to find a quiet place of repose in my soul. In the name of Christ, I pray. Amen. | Into your hands, O Shepherd, I entrust myself for tranquil sleep. In the name of Christ, I pray. Amen. |

# March 31

*(Read Psalm 23 and Romans 8:35, 37–39)*

### MORNING

O God, "I will sing aloud of your steadfast love in the morning."

### EVENING

O God, "The night is as bright as the day,
for darkness is as light to you."

Eternal and Holy God, you lead us even in the most shadowy times of our lives, or perhaps especially then. I want to believe your Word, that nothing can separate us from your love, revealed to us in Christ Jesus— not hardship or distress, not persecution or famine, not even death or anything in all creation. Help my unbelief; strengthen me in this faith. Deliver me from the fear of evil.

### MORNING

O God, be present with me this day so that I may radiate
more clearly the love you have for us, in Christ.
*(Prayers of Intercession)*

### EVENING

Give me a restful night, dear God, confident that your goodness
and mercy shall follow me all the days of my life.
*(Prayers of Intercession)*

### "IF GOD IS FOR US, WHO IS AGAINST US?"
*(Pray the Prayer of Our Savior.)*

### MORNING

New every morning are
your mercies, O God! Thus may it be
forever. In the name of Christ,
I pray. Amen.

### EVENING

Whether awake or asleep,
help me to live in the confidence that
I shall dwell in your house my whole
life long. In the name of Christ,
I pray. Amen.

# April 1

*(Read Ephesians 5:8–14)*

### MORNING

Dear God, as every Sunday recalls Resurrection day, help me this
day to witness to the triumph of life and to awaken to renewal.

### EVENING

Dear God, prepare me now through refreshing and restful sleep to greet
the coming new day as a day of service to you, with joy and thanksgiving.

On this day, O God, help me to reflect upon all that is good and right
and true, and to repent of my unfruitful works that are not pleasing in
your sight. Through the power of the Holy Spirit, awaken me from my
moral slumber that the light of Christ may shine upon me and through
me to all whom I know.

### MORNING

At worship this day, O God, help me to hear your redeeming and renewing Word,
that more and more I may live my life in ways that are pleasing in your sight.
*(Prayers of Intercession)*

### EVENING

I am mindful this night, dear God, of how far we are from your realm, of how
wrong, falsehood, and injustice seem to rule in many places. I pray for all who
suffer under the yoke of injustice, that they may know your compassion; and I
pray for those who harm others, that they may repent and turn from their ways.
*(Prayers of Intercession)*

"THIS LITTLE LIGHT OF MINE, I'M GONNA LET IT SHINE, LET IT SHINE,

LET IT SHINE, LET IT SHINE." (traditional spiritual)
*(Pray the Prayer of Our Savior.)*

| MORNING | EVENING |
|---|---|
| As I awaken to the day you have made, O God, awaken me to turn toward the light of Christ. In the name of Christ, I pray. Amen. | "All praise be yours, my God, this night, for all the blessing of the light. Keep me, kind Maker of all things, beneath the shelter of your wings." (Thomas Ken) In the name of Christ, I pray. Amen. |

# April 2

*(Read Isaiah 55:1–5)*

**MORNING**
Abundant God, I arise this morning in a spirit of gratitude.
I face the day knowing you are my Provider.

**EVENING**
Abundant God, I come to the end of this day in a spirit
of gratitude. I face the night knowing I can find my rest in you.

Too often I forfeit joy, yearning, and searching for the "one thing" that I believe will make me truly happy. I am stressed because my vocation or employment does not provide the comfort for which I strive. I destroy my spirit of gratitude because I just don't seem to have enough. O God, too often I live out of a perception of lack rather than a perception of abundance. The prophet calls us to look to a higher Source, and in these words I receive the promise of abundant life. *¡Aleluya!* Inclining my ears to these words, I want for nothing. Thank you, God, for my wholeness is in you.

**MORNING**
I go forth this day with my mind, soul, and heart open to your
Word. Israel's Holy One, I come to you remembering . . .
*(Prayers of Intercession)*

**EVENING**
O God, for the moments I doubted, complained, or caused pain
to another, forgive me.
*(Prayers of Intercession)*

---

TAKE HEED—THE ENEMY DESPISES GRATITUDE BECAUSE GRATITUDE LEADS
TO A PROFOUND SENSE OF SACREDNESS. IN ALL THINGS BE GRATEFUL.

---

**MORNING**
Lead me so that I might share
of your abundance with all those
I meet this day. In the Savior's name.
Amen.

**EVENING**
For your guidance, protection, and
love, thank you! In the Savior's name.
Amen.

# April 3

*(Read Isaiah 55:6–9)*

**MORNING**

Merciful God, I arise this morning in a spirit of blessed assurance.
I face the day knowing you are always near.

**EVENING**

Merciful God, I come to the end of this day in a spirit of blessed
assurance. I face the night knowing I am never alone.

Too often I seek success and miss my true calling. My competitive edge
does not allow me to appreciate the simple. The workplace receives all
of my time. My loved ones get what is left over or squeezed in. Busyness
is the attitude of the day. I have to do and be all. I spend little time on
reflection and renewal. Whose work have I been called to do anyway?
The prophet calls us to look to a wiser Source, and in these words I receive the promise of merciful guidance. *¡Aleluya!* Inclining my ears to
these words, I find meaning. Thank you, God, for my purpose is in you.

**MORNING**

Israel's God of mercy, I come to you remembering . . .
*(Prayers of Intercession)*

**EVENING**

Lead me, guide me, and use me for your will.
*(Prayers of Intercession)*

---

TAKE HEED—THE ENEMY DESPISES MEDITATION BECAUSE IT TAPS INTO THE POWER
OF GOD WITHIN. AT ALL TIMES BE AWARE OF THE GREAT I AM.

---

**MORNING**

I go forth this day with my mind,
soul, and heart open to your Word.
In the Savior's name. Amen.

**EVENING**

O God, for the moments I acted
out of self-interest and labored in
vain, forgive me. Thank you for your
guidance, protection, and love.
Thank you! In the Savior's name.
Amen.

# April 4

*(Read Psalm 63:1-4)*

**MORNING**

Eternal God, I arise this morning in a spirit of praise.
I face the day knowing you are my God.

**EVENING**

Eternal God, I come to the end of this day in a spirit of praise.
I face the night knowing you are watching over me.

The psalmist reveals what is in my soul, O God. I seek to know you, to follow your ways, to love as you love. I know my flesh is weak, yet I am created in your divine image. I know my heart is faint, yet Jesus gives me the power to love away sin and sadness. *¡Gloria a Dios!* My soul rejoices in you, O God. In an ever-changing world, you are a constant. Thank you, God! My whole being exalts in you.

**MORNING**

God of both King David and the woman at the well,
I come to you remembering . . .
*(Prayers of Intercession)*

**EVENING**

My whole being shall reveal the joy that is found in you.
*(Prayers of Intercession)*

---

TAKE HEED—THE ENEMY DESPISES PRAISE BECAUSE PRAISE CREATES AN OPPORTUNITY TO BE A LIVING WITNESS FOR OTHERS. PRAISE GOD IN ALL THINGS AND AT ALL TIMES.

---

**MORNING**

I go forth this day with my mind,
soul, and heart open to your Word.
In the Savior's name. Amen.

**EVENING**

O God, for the moments I reacted
out of anger and fear, forgive me.
Thank you for your guidance,
protection, and love. Thank you!
In the Savior's name. Amen.

# April 5

*(Read Psalm 63:5–8)*

**MORNING**
Almighty God, I arise this morning in a spirit of humbleness.
I face the day knowing you are my strength.

**EVENING**
Almighty God, I come to the end of this day in a spirit
of humbleness. I face the night knowing my help comes from you.

The psalmist describes an ageless truth: you are a present God. My peace comes in recognizing you are with me in the midst of my pain and you are at the center of my joy. I find strength in knowing that, although I sometimes stray from you, your love for me is unfailing. Bless your name, O steadfast One! Your love endures forever. O God, even in my finitude, your glory is revealed. Thank you, God. I will forever sing your praises!

**MORNING**
God of both Job and Mary, the mother of Jesus, I come to you remembering . . .
*(Prayers of Intercession)*

**EVENING**
Almighty God, my life is in your hands.
*(Prayers of Intercession)*

---

**TAKE HEED—THE ENEMY DESPISES HUMBLENESS BECAUSE IN YOUR HUMBLENESS IS FOUND THE STRENGTH OF GOD. REMAIN ALWAYS HUMBLE BEFORE GOD.**

---

**MORNING**
I go forth this day with my mind, soul, and heart open to your Word. In the Savior's name. Amen.

**EVENING**
O God, for the moments I boasted, scorned another, or chose the spotlight over hard work, forgive me. Thank you for your guidance, protection, and love. Thank you! In the Savior's name. Amen.

# April 6

*(Read Luke 13:1–9)*

### MORNING
Creator God, I arise this morning in a spirit of agape.
I face the day knowing you are a just God.

### EVENING
Creator God, I come to the end of this day in a spirit of agape.
I face the night knowing your love is unconditional.

Hearing Jesus' words, I realize we are all equal in your sight, O God. As I witness the pain and suffering around me, I claim, "I am blessed." But does this mean those who endure violence, poverty, and oppression are less blessed? No! All are blessed by having been created by your hand. I believe when even one of your creations perishes, you mourn. Creator God, allow me an understanding of the vastness of your unconditional love. Thank you for revealing this love in Jesus.

### MORNING
God of the rich and of the poor, I come to you remembering . . .
*(Prayers of Intercession)*

### EVENING
I will see the world with the lenses of your love.
*(Prayers of Intercession)*

---

**TAKE HEED—THE ENEMY DESPISES UNCONDITIONAL LOVE BECAUSE THIS FORM OF LOVE HAS THE FREEDOM TO REACH ALL OF GOD'S CREATION. LOVE FREELY AND ALLOW YOURSELF TO BE LOVED IN RETURN.**

---

### MORNING
I go forth this day with my mind, soul, and heart open to your Word. In the Savior's name. Amen.

### EVENING
O God, for the moments I deemed myself or another unworthy of your love and blessings, forgive me. Thank you for your guidance, protection, and love. Thank you! In the Savior's name. Amen.

# April 7

*(Read 1 Corinthians 10:1–5)*

### MORNING

God of my ancestors, I arise this morning in a spirit
of faithfulness, and I face the day knowing you are a God
of the second chance.

### EVENING

God of my ancestors, I come to the end of this day in a spirit
of faithfulness, and I face the night knowing you are the same
yesterday, today, and tomorrow.

Paul asks us to remember our ancestors and to pay attention to and learn from their experiences. Whose responsibility is it that I know my history and the history of my people? Mine! I need to know where I came from in order to discern who I am and where I am called to be. You, O God, have been present in my life since before I was born. *¡Gracias mi Dios!* Through the growing pains and the joys, you have been the Source of grace and strength for all generations. *¡Aleluya!*

### MORNING

God of Moses and *de mi abuela*, I come to you remembering . . .
*(Prayers of Intercession)*

### EVENING

God of Moses and *de mi abuela*, I come to you remembering . . .
*(Prayers of Intercession)*

---

TAKE HEED—THE ENEMY DESPISES FAITHFULNESS BECAUSE AT THE CORE
OF OUR FAITHFULNESS IS A GOD WHO REMAINS FAITHFUL TO US.
REMAIN FAITHFUL THROUGH ALL SEASONS.

---

### MORNING

I go forth this day with my mind,
soul, and heart open to your Word.
I will remember from whom I have
come. In the Savior's name. Amen.

### EVENING

O God, for the moments I denied my
history and lost faith in my present,
forgive me. For your guidance,
protection, and love, thank you!
In the Savior's name. Amen.

# April 8

*(Read 1 Corinthians 10:6–13)*

**MORNING**

God of grace, I arise this morning in a spirit of righteousness,
and I face the day knowing you are the Rock on which I stand.

**EVENING**

God of grace, I come to the end of this day in a spirit of righteousness,
and I face the night knowing my life is in your hands.

Paul teaches us that we are to break the cycles that destroy us as people of God. God, this is not always easy. I want to be better, different, whole; but at times all I know is what I have endured. The cycles of violence, addiction, and oppression are alive and well. It is only by your grace that I have come this far. Thank you, God, for being my Refuge and my Strength. Thank you for the good news revealed in Jesus—I can become a new creation. I can break the cycle. *¡Gracias a Dios!*

**MORNING**

God of new beginnings, I come to you remembering . . .
*(Prayers of Intercession)*

**EVENING**

God of new beginnings, I come to you remembering . . .
*(Prayers of Intercession)*

---

**TAKE HEED—THE ENEMY DESPISES RIGHTEOUSNESS BECAUSE RIGHTEOUSNESS LEAVES LITTLE ROOM FOR SIN. FIND YOUR RIGHTEOUSNESS IN GOD.**

---

**MORNING**

I go forth this day with my mind,
soul, and heart open to your Word.
Give me strength to stop all injustice
and hurt I may witness today.
In the Savior's name.
Amen.

**EVENING**

O God, for the moments I turned
away in fear or allowed myself to be
engaged in wrongful acts, forgive me.
For your guidance, protection,
and love, thank you! In the
Savior's name. Amen.

# April 9

*(Read Acts 17:22–28)*

**MORNING**

Creator God, in whom we live and move and have our being,
immerse us this day in the splendor of your presence.

**EVENING**

Creator God, who made the world and everything in it,
and rested when you finished your work, allow us to rest from
this day's work and lie down in peace.

God, we search for you, only to discover that you have found us. We
grope to find you, only to find that you have taken us by the hand. You,
the "unknown god" for whom souls have searched since the beginning of
time, have been incarnated. We discover you in the face of Jesus Christ.

**MORNING**

You are not far from us, O God. Come close today to all who need
you and yearn to experience your renewing touch.
*(Prayers of Intercession)*

**EVENING**

We pray this evening for all who are searching for you, O God.
Let them know you are not far from them.
*(Prayers of Intercession)*

---

**IN GOD WE LIVE AND MOVE AND HAVE OUR BEING.**
*(Pray the Prayer of Our Savior.)*

---

**MORNING**

Sovereign of heaven and earth,
let us stand in awe of your presence as
we begin this new day. Take us in our
work to those places where we may
encounter you and be transformed
into your instruments of justice and
witness. In Jesus' name. Amen.

**EVENING**

May, O God, whatever we sought
to think, do, and say this day be an
offering that has been pleasing
in your sight. In Jesus' name.
Amen.

# April 10

*(Read Acts 17:29–31)*

**MORNING**

O God, you have made us your own and have called us kindred
with your people of every nation and generation. We praise you for
adopting us into such a diverse household!

**EVENING**

O God, you have called us into community with a world of differences that sometimes frightens us and causes us to isolate ourselves from people unlike us. Forgive us
when we fail to honor those who are near to us yet whom we have kept at a distance.

God, you are not the product of human imagination and fashioning.
You are not the creation of human experience and reasoning. Awe-inspiring God, you alone are God. You call us from the worship of whatever in the world would own us, to you, the one who molds us in the
image of yourself.

**MORNING**

We pray for those who this day will turn to the gods of human making.
Hold them, O Holy One, in your parental care.
*(Prayers of Intercession)*

**EVENING**

We pray for those who have been victimized. Assure them,
O Holy One, that nothing in all creation can separate them from your love.
*(Prayers of Intercession)*

---

**GOD IS NOT AN IMAGE FORMED BY THE ART AND IMAGINATION OF MORTALS.**
*(Pray the Prayer of Our Savior.)*

---

| **MORNING** | **EVENING** |
|---|---|
| In righteousness you have judged the world, O God. And through the resurrection of Jesus Christ you have overcome its power. Lead us to Christ, who is the way, the truth, and the life. In Jesus' name. Amen. | We repent, O God, and ask your forgiveness when we miss the mark you intend us to reach. Grant that we may rest in the assurance of Christ's reconciling love. In Jesus' name. Amen. |

# April 11

*(Read Psalm 66:8–15)*

**MORNING**

Bless you, O God, for keeping us through the night.
Keep us this day in the shelter of your protective care lest the
things we need to do overcome us.

**EVENING**

Bless you, O God, for bringing us through today's troubles.
We now bring to you the offerings of our praise and thanksgiving.

Sovereign One, praise is what keeps your people from slipping into the morass of self-centeredness. Praise on human lips and in human hearts keeps us looking beyond ourselves and the troubles that threaten to undo us. You, O Source of Life, you are the God who promises not to take away tough times but to lead us through tough times to your grace.

**MORNING**

Hear, O God, our prayers for those with burdens on their backs
too heavy to bear. Strengthen them and keep them from falling.
*(Prayers of Intercession)*

**EVENING**

Hear, O God, our prayers for those who lives are being tested.
Deliver them from the evil that lures them and keep their feet from stumbling.
*(Prayers of Intercession)*

**"BLESS OUR GOD, O PEOPLES, LET THE SOUND OF GOD'S PRAISE BE HEARD!'**
*(Pray the Prayer of Our Savior.)*

| MORNING | EVENING |
|---|---|
| Blessed be you, O God. When we will be in trouble today, take us to the other side of our troubles, where we may discover the spacious freedom of your mercy and find wisdom and courage for the living of this day. In Jesus' name. Amen. | Blessed be you, O God, for bringing us safely to the end of this day. We give you the gift of our lives to fulfill the promises we made when we were in trouble and thank you for deliverance from today's distress. Now let us rest in peace. In Jesus' name. Amen. |

# April 12

*(Read Psalm 66:16–20)*

**MORNING**

O God, how awesome is your presence! How wonderful are all the
things you have done for me! Blessed be your name.

**EVENING**

O God, if in my heart I had cherished anything that was contrary
to your will, you would not have listened to me. Yet, when I have
prayed to you, you truly have given heed to my prayers.

Patient God, you promise neither to reject us nor to reject our prayers.
You promise never to forget us and to listen to our prayers. Loving God,
you listen to us, affirm us, and love us. All who have reverence for you
should tell the good news of what you have done!

**MORNING**

You have promised to listen to my prayers, O God.
Hear me as I pray for others and for myself, and keep me
in prayer throughout this day.
*(Prayers of Intercession)*

**EVENING**

You have heard my praying, O God. Listen now as I pray for those
close and far away, known and unknown, for others and for myself.
*(Prayers of Intercession)*

**"TRULY GOD HAS LISTENED AND HAS GIVEN HEED TO THE WORDS OF MY PRAYER."**
*(Pray the Prayer of Our Savior.)*

| MORNING | EVENING |
|---|---|
| O God, may not only what I say to you but also what I say to others be words to which you will listen today. May not only what I do for you but also what I do for others be prayers to which you will give heed. In Jesus' name. Amen. | Truly, O God, you have listened to me today. You have heard my prayers and protests, even when my thinking and speaking and doing have not been well pleasing to you. Forgive me, and let me abide the night in a prayerful silence. In Jesus' name. Amen. |

# April 13

*(Read John 14:15–17)*

### MORNING

O Holy Spirit, this day open me to your comforting presence,
that I may know you are with me in all I am and do and say.

### EVENING

O Holy Spirit, I know you have been with me throughout this day. Now let
me rest in the assurance that you will be with me this night and forever.

O Holy Creator, the good news for this day is that Jesus promised that
the presence of the Holy Spirit will be with us as our Advocate,
Comforter, and Intercessor. There isn't a moment when we are outside
of the Spirit's embrace. The Spirit abides with us; stays with us; and accompanies us as our constant companion. The best news of all is that
the promise has no expiration date! The Spirit stays with us forever!

### MORNING

O Holy Spirit, enter into the hearts of all who need you this day,
and begin your gracious work of redeeming love.
*(Prayers of Intercession)*

### EVENING

As you have interceded for me today, sometimes in sighs too deep
for words, O Holy Spirit, my Advocate, I now come to you to intercede for all who need your presence.
*(Prayers of Intercession)*

---

**"IF YOU LOVE ME, YOU WILL KEEP MY COMMANDMENTS. . . ."**
*(Pray the Prayer of Our Savior.)*

---

### MORNING

O Spirit of the Living God,
send me into this new day and abide
in me throughout whatever this day
may bring so that others may see in
me some sign of a truth greater than
the world can give. In Jesus' name.
Amen.

### EVENING

Stay with me, Abiding Spirit,
as this day ends. Assure me that you
will be with me as I sleep and that
you will awaken me to a new day
tomorrow in Christ Jesus.
In Jesus' name. Amen.

# April 14

*(Read John 14:18–21)*

### MORNING

Jesus, you promise never to abandon us, even when we forget you
and even deny you. Come to us again this day and stay with us.

### EVENING

Jesus, you have been in our being and doing and thinking this day.
Thank you for holding us in a love that will not let us go.

Wondrous beyond all imagining, Wondrous God, is the good news that
because Jesus lives we shall live also. There is nothing in all creation that
can separate us from Jesus' resurrection presence. Those in the world,
so unable to see past the idols of culture and commerce, no longer can
own us. Jesus reigns! We can live in peace.

### MORNING

Jesus, you have claimed us as your own. Hear now the prayers we
offer for those whom the world has orphaned and abandoned, that
they may never feel alone.
*(Prayers of Intercession)*

### EVENING

Jesus, you love us more than we love you. Hear our intercessions
for those whom the world cannot and will not love, that they may
be touched by a love that defies human expectations.
*(Prayers of Intercession)*

---

### "I WILL NOT LEAVE YOU ORPHANED; I AM COMING TO YOU."
*(Pray the Prayer of Our Savior.)*

---

### MORNING

Jesus, our divine companion,
go with us into this new day and
assure us that no moment will be
outside the circle of your loving care.
In Jesus' name. Amen.

### EVENING

Jesus, our morning joy and our rest,
let us now leave behind whatever has
burdened us this day, and let us go to
sleep in you. In Jesus' name.
Amen.

# April 15

*(Read 1 Peter 3:13–22)*

### MORNING

O Savior, when morning gilds the skies, our hearts, awakening,
cry: "May Jesus Christ be praised!" Let us profess our hope in you
boldly today, yet always with gentleness and reverence.

### EVENING

O Savior, abide with us: fast falls the eventide; the shadows deepen,
with us abide. Hold your cross before our closing eyes this night and let us
rest assured that no one will harm us if you are by our side.

Our only comfort in body and soul, in life and in death, is that we belong not to ourselves but to our faithful Savior, Jesus Christ.

### MORNING

Savior Christ, as you have interceded for us, so now we bring to you all
who need you, especially those who this day will suffer for your sake.
*(Prayers of Intercession)*

### EVENING

Savior Christ, as you have suffered for our sins, so now we intercede for
the victims of violence and injustice, that they may be assured that you are
with them and they are not alone.
*(Prayers of Intercession)*

### IN YOUR HEARTS SANCTIFY CHRIST AS LORD."
*(Pray the Prayer of Our Savior.)*

### MORNING

Put to shame, O Christ, all those who
will seek to abuse any of your own
this day. Defend all those, who in the
strength of their conscience, will claim
you as their only Savior amid cultures
that want them to claim multiple allegiances and optional loyalties. In
Jesus' name. Amen.

### EVENING

As the sun sets on yet another
continent, O Christ, your reign has no
end. In many nations and many
tongues your praise has been sung this
day. Continue to strengthen your
church, that we may be your faithful
witnesses and continue to tell the amazing story of your love for the entire
world. In Jesus' name. Amen.

# April 16

*(Read Acts 10:44–48)*

### MORNING
God of all people, I greet this new day with thanksgiving; as I share
the gospel, enable me to think of others in an inclusive manner.

### EVENING
God of all people, help me to understand that your word is for
everyone and that human differences should not be allowed to
stand in the path of sharing the gospel.

Can you imagine not being baptized in the faith because of your
human differences? God, you open the door for all persons to receive
the message of your gospel and your Holy Spirit.

### MORNING
O God, as I face brokenness and nonacceptance in the world,
help me move through the day and not allow human differences to
hinder my sharing your goodness with others.
*(Prayers of Intercession)*

### EVENING
As the day closes, let me not close my eyes to the needs of others
to hear the gospel and receive the Holy Spirit.
*(Prayers of Intercession)*

---

GOD IS NO RESPECTER OF PERSONS.
THE HOLY SPIRIT COMES NOT ACCORDING TO HUMAN EXPECTATIONS.

---

### MORNING
O God of all people: Help me to
show love toward others without fo-
cusing on differences. Help me to love
unconditionally and let God's love
provide a message in deed by sharing
with others. Through Christ, our
Liberator. Amen.

### EVENING
Thank you, God, for the privilege
of being a messenger for you today.
Enable me to continue to witness to
others in a loving mode and
remember that you are God of all
people. Through Christ,
our Liberator. Amen.

# April 17

*(Read 1 John 5:1–6)*

**MORNING**

O God of Love, I greet the morning acknowledging that your love
for me is like that of a parent for a child.

**EVENING**

O God of Love, thank you for loving me this day and
for the many visible manifestations of that love.

God, to love you is to obey your commandments. It is a response to
your goodness and a self-yielding to your will.

**MORNING**

O God, this world has so many places where love does not
abound. Help me to show love as I go through the day and
remember that to love you is also to love others.
*(Prayers of Intercession)*

**EVENING**

God of love, thank you for loving me.
Thank you for giving me guidelines for living, opportunities
to show love, and challenges to obey the commandments.
*(Prayers of Intercession)*

---

A PERSON WHO LOVES GOD WILL ALSO ACT IN LOVING WAYS TOWARD OTHERS.
COUNTING THE WAYS GOD SHOWS LOVE TOWARD HUMANS IS IMPOSSIBLE.
GOD IS LOVE.

---

**MORNING**

O Loving God, thank you for a new day of experiences. Help me to reach out in loving ways and let the commandments serve as a pattern for my actions. Help me to be strengthened in faith. Through Christ, our Liberator. Amen.

**EVENING**

Can I say I love God? Can I say I have obeyed God's commandments today? Can I say I have shown love to others today? If not, God, please give me another chance to show love and practice obedience. Through Christ, our Liberator. Amen.

# April 18

*(Read John 15:9–11)*
*Sing "Just a Closer Walk with Thee" or another familiar hymn.*

### MORNING

O God, as I awake from restful sleep, I realize that you
live in me and provide for my needs even when I am unaware
of your presence and actions.

### EVENING

O God, today I felt your presence with and in me. It is the
very essence of a powerful love engulfing me and reminding me
that you are an example for me to learn how to love others.

God, to abide in your love is to have you incarnated in my heart.

### MORNING

God, I yearn for a closer walk with you and
for a relationship that reveals that closeness.
*(Prayers of Intercession)*

### EVENING

Sometimes, O God, it seems that you are so far away.
Sometimes circumstances tend to force the question, "Where is God?"
But the challenge is to remain faithful and steadfast.
You are present even if we are unable to discern it.
*(Prayers of Intercession)*

THERE IS UNSPEAKABLE JOY IN ABIDING IN CHRIST JESUS.

### MORNING

Today, O God, bring me closer
to you. Help me to know your will
and accept it. Help me to yield myself
and open my heart so that I may be
consumed in your love. Through
Christ, our Liberator. Amen.

### EVENING

As the day draws to a close,
O God, never withdraw your love and
presence from me. The joy that comes
from a close relationship is not
describable. May that love never end.
Through Christ, our Liberator. Amen.

# April 19

*(Read John 15:12–15)*
*Sing "More Love to Thee, O Christ" or another familiar hymn.*

### MORNING

O God, I thank you for revealing the real meaning
of love through sacrifice.

### EVENING

O God, looking back over the day, what have I done in the way
of showing love through sacrifice? Were my actions done out of love?
If not, God, please forgive!

Loving God, there is no greater love than the love expressed when one
gives up one's life for the sake of another.

### MORNING

O God, as I approach this new day, help make me ready
to love you and keep your commandments. Help me show love,
even if it requires sacrifice.
*(Prayers of Intercession)*

### EVENING

God, I often wonder how to give my all, and the answer comes in
a look at Jesus, the living example of sacrifice.
*(Prayers of Intercession)*

AS YOU LIVE YOUR LIFE, FOCUS ON THE MEANING OF LOVE THAT IS EMBODIED
IN SACRIFICE. THERE IS A DIFFERENCE BETWEEN SELFISH CONDITIONAL
LOVE AND UNSELFISH SACRIFICIAL LOVE.

### MORNING

The sun rises with a beauty that
reveals your love for all of creation.
Help me greet the day and be an
expression of love to all I encounter.
Through Christ, our Liberator.
Amen.

### EVENING

O God of Love, may you continue
to enable us to express our love in
obedience to your commandments.
Let us rest from the labors knowing
that your love surrounds us.
Through Christ, our Liberator.
Amen.

# April 20

*(Read Psalm 98:1–3)*
*Sing "God Is So Good" or another familiar hymn.*

### MORNING

O God as I greet the day, I burst forth with a song of praise,
giving thanks for the many blessings of a new day.

### EVENING

O God, today was filled with numerous blessings, some of which
I took for granted. Help me to remember your goodness and
faithfulness on this day.

God, you are constantly faithful at working to provide blessings for all
of earth's creatures and to conquer evil.

### MORNING

As I awake, I hear the sounds of the morning. Many of the sounds
remind me that it is God who keeps the world turning.
*(Prayers of Intercession)*

### EVENING

Today, Creator God, many persons have refused to acknowledge
your goodness and gave credit to other sources. Help me to remember the true source of power.
*(Prayers of Intercession)*

GOD'S CONTINUOUS ACTION IN THE WORLD PROVIDES A REASON TO OFFER PRAISE.
GOD IS VICTORIOUS IN THE END.

### MORNING

I greet the day with a song that will
last all day long. I greet the day with a
song, a message of love in song.
I greet the day with a prayer, that I
will do no wrong. Through Christ,
our Liberator. Amen.

### EVENING

O God, I sing praises to you,
my Creator, Sustainer, Redeemer, and
Friend. I say thanks for the blessings
of the day and those blessing
unknown to me. I sing praises of
thanksgiving! Through Christ,
our Liberator. Amen.

# April 21

*(Read Psalm 98:4–6)*

*Sing the Doxology.*

### MORNING
Praise-deserving God, a new day dawns with another opportunity
to sing praises unto you. With my voice I will make music and
acknowledge you as the anchor of my life.

### EVENING
Praise-deserving God, how can I praise you?
With my whole being, I will offer praise to you.

## Praise-deserving God, to glorify you is to offer praise joyously.

### MORNING
When morning breaks, it is often with such haste that I fail
to take time to praise God. I am undeserving of God's goodness,
but God is worthy of praise. Let me praise God.
*(Prayers of Intercession)*

### EVENING
Music lifts the heart and calms one's spirit. Therefore,
I will sing or listen to music until I feel God's presence. (Sing "O for a
Thousand Tongues to Sing" or "Joyful, Joyful, We Adore Thee.")
*(Prayers of Intercession)*

---

**INSTRUMENTS OF ALL TYPES ARE USED TO MAKE A JOYFUL NOISE OF PRAISE TO GOD.**

---

### MORNING
O God, there are times when praise
is easy and there are times when
everything tends to crowd the time for
praise. Let me this day find time to
offer sincere praise. Through Christ,
our Liberator. Amen.

### EVENING
The day ends but my praise to
God will never cease. I will sing to the
glory of God. I will lift my hands in
praise. I will join others in praise and
tell of God's goodness. Through
Christ, our Liberator Amen.

# April 22

*(Read Psalm 98:7–9)*
*Sing "For the Beauty of the Earth," "From All That Dwells below the Skies,"*
*or another familiar hymn.*

### MORNING

Creator God, all of your creation finds ways to offer praise.
I can do no less.

### EVENING

Creator God, Jesus is coming back looking for those who have
been faithful. Let me always remember your promises as reasons to
offer praise.

The second coming will be a time of praise and judgment. God, you
will be righteous and just toward all people in judgment. Yet, God, you
also love and forgive.

### MORNING

As I look out of the window, I see the beauty of nature. I am reminded of the
destructive human behavior that pollutes and destroys nature's balance. Help me
to be more conscious of my actions that may upset some small aspect of nature.
*(Prayers of Intercession)*

### EVENING

To praise God is an expression of my love for God.
*(Prayers of Intercession)*

---

**GOD WILL HOLD EVERYONE ACCOUNTABLE.**

---

### MORNING

On the seashore, the waves declare
an expression of praise. On the
mountain top, the eagle soars in
graceful praise. On the riverbed, the
fish swim in effortless praise. But here
I sit, with only a frail voice to offer
praise. Through Christ,
our Liberator. Amen.

### EVENING

O God, being judged and held
accountable is often dreaded. But you
have given commandments and instructions regarding your desires for
living among other humans and
showing devotion to God. Let us prepare for God's return in praise and
thanksgiving. Through Christ,
our Liberator. Amen.

# April 23

*(Read Acts 2:42–47)*

**MORNING**

Gracious God, from whom all blessings flow, I thank you for this
day. May I use it to glorify and magnify you and your holy name.

**EVENING**

Gracious God, I thank you for every task and activity that
I performed during this day.

I wait upon you, O God, to display your many signs and wonders. May
I live in one accord with other believers and strive to serve those in
need. May my possessions and material goods become less important
and my human relationships become more significant from this day
forward. Continue to lead me, guide me, and show me the way, both
now and forevermore.

**MORNING**

May I commit this day to serving others with the gifts,
skills, and attributes with which you have blessed me.

*(Prayers of Intercession)*

**EVENING**

Creator God, as I end this day with a spirit of peace and joy,
may I continue to acknowledge the many signs and wonders
that you reveal to me.

*(Prayers of Intercession)*

---

**AS YOU INCREASE THE NUMBERS OF THOSE WHO ARE SAVED,
MAY I ALWAYS HOLD SACRED THE PRAYER OF OUR SAVIOR.**

*(Pray the Prayer of Our Savior.)*

---

| **MORNING** | **EVENING** |
|---|---|
| With a sense of joy, | Jesus Christ, anoint me |
| I wait upon Jesus today. In your | with the things that you have taught |
| name I pray. Amen. | me today. In your |
| | name I pray. Amen. |

# April 24

*(Read Acts 2:42–47)*

**MORNING**
Blessed Creator, Maker of all things that are good,
I give you praise and honor today.

**EVENING**
Blessed Creator, this day and all that is in it are gifts from you.
As I end this day, I commit to you all that I have done.

Loving God, those who came before me gathered in the temple, and they remembered you with praise as they ate their daily meals with glad and generous hearts. As I partake of my meals today, may I give you all the honor, the glory, and the praise, remembering that each morsel I consume is a manifestation of your love for me. God, I pray for those who dwell among us who have no food to eat. May you give me a heart of compassion that encourages me to take some action to contribute to alleviating hunger and homelessness. My hands are your hands, my feet are your feet, and my voice is your voice. May I be a voice for the faceless, voiceless, nameless sufferers who exist in our midst every day.

**MORNING**
God, I commit this day to doing things
that contribute positively to humankind.
*(Prayers of Intercession)*

**EVENING**
Magnificent God, I acknowledge that you are my God
and that I am one of your people.
*(Prayers of Intercession)*

**I AM SAVED.**

*(Pray the Prayer of Our Savior.)*

**MORNING**
With a sense of joy, Jesus,
I wait upon you today. In your name
I pray. Amen.

**EVENING**
Jesus Christ, anoint me with the
things that you have taught me today.
In your name I pray. Amen.

# April 25

*(Read Psalm 23)*

**MORNING**
My God, may the people bow down to you,
my Shepherd and my Provider.

**EVENING**
My God, as this day comes to a close,
I thank you for the green pastures that I have walked through today.
Come, holy Comforter, come!

Dear God, you are my beloved Creator, my blessed Shepherd, and my watchful Protector. Reveal yourself to those who do not know you as they merely exist on the highest mountains and in the lowest valleys. On this day, O God, I thank you for allowing me to experience the greener pastures of life during the good times and the tranquillity of the still waters during the challenging times. You and you alone have the power to restore my soul so I may experience the fullness of life.

**MORNING**
This morning I pray for the restoration of (name the individuals
and families you know who are in need) . . .
*(Prayers of Intercession)*

**EVENING**
This evening, I continue to lift up in my prayer . . .
*(Prayers of Intercession)*

**WITH RENEWED HOPE I PRAY.**
*(Pray the Prayer of Our Savior.)*

**MORNING**
I begin this day seeking
the restorative power of the Creator.
In the name of Jesus. Amen.

**EVENING**
I end this day acknowledging the
restorative power of the Creator.
In the name of Jesus. Amen.

# April 26

*(Read Psalm 23)*

**MORNING**
Gracious God, I rejoice and look forward
to this day with excitement and joy!

**EVENING**
Gracious God, I end this day acknowledging the hopes and fears
of those who have come from all walks of life.

Dear God, I thank you for allowing me to experience life another day. Where there are those exhibiting signs of love in the world, please encourage them. Where there are those doing evil, prick their hearts so that they may realize there is a better way. Let me remember on this day that you are a God of love and peace, not evil and war. And wherever there is unrest, I pray for and patiently await a miracle. When goodness and mercy follow me, let me acknowledge that they are gifts from you, as I diligently strive not only to dwell but to thrive in your house my whole life long.

**MORNING**
On this day I will fear no evil, for you will be with me.
I will rely on your rod and your staff as sources of comfort.
*(Prayers of Intercession)*

**EVENING**
As I rest at the table that you have prepared, I acknowledge the goodness
and mercy that you have bestowed upon me all the days of my life.
*(Prayers of Intercession)*

**WITH RENEWED HOPE I PRAY.**
*(Pray the Prayer of Our Savior.)*

**MORNING**
Holy Spirit, bring comfort
and peace to the world today.
In the name of Jesus. Amen.

**EVENING**
Let the world continue to
experience your comfort and peace.
In the name of Jesus. Amen.

# April 27

*(Read 1 Peter 2:19–25)*

**MORNING**

Dear God, make me aware of your presence.

**EVENING**

Dear God, thank you for being with me today.

Gracious God, as I experience this day, let me feel your presence. Allow my body, mind, and spirit to endure all that this world has to offer. When my endurance appears low, remind me of Jesus, the One who endured the pain and suffering of the world, hanging on that old rugged cross. When I forget the suffering of Jesus, please order my steps, that I may again become an example of the One who came before, suffered, and triumphed more than two thousand years ago. Deliver me from complacency, so that I may seek righteousness and healing instead of sin and woundedness.

**MORNING**

I rejoice as I remain focused on the task of absorbing
your presence all the day long.
*(Prayers of Intercession)*

**EVENING**

I end this day in the presence of the
Shepherd and Guardian of my soul.
*(Prayers of Intercession)*

---

**I LIVE BY YOUR RIGHTEOUSNESS, SOVEREIGN JESUS.**

*(Pray the Prayer of Our Savior.)*

---

**MORNING**

I entrust this day into your hands,
O God. In the name of Jesus.
Amen.

**EVENING**

Free from sin, I strive for the
righteous life. In the name of Jesus.
Amen.

# April 28

*(Read John 10:1–10)*

**MORNING**

Loving God, may I usher in this day
through the gates of righteousness.

**EVENING**

Loving God, I end this day, calling upon you, our heavenly
Gatekeeper, to protect me through the night.

Magnificent God, Creator of heaven and earth, I thank you for this day. I trust in you to protect me from the evils of the world. May you keep your hedge of protection wrapped around me at all times, especially in those moments when you must move me beyond my comfort zone. Wherever you lead me, I will follow you as a sheep follows its shepherd. Wherever you tell me to go, I will press on with confidence, knowing that yours is voice of truth. My trust, my hope, and my life are in your capable hands. And I submit myself totally to you.

**MORNING**

Holy Spirit, empower me to hear and to yield to the voice of God.
*(Prayers of Intercession)*

**EVENING**

Dear God, I pause in silence. Let me hear your still, quiet voice.
Help me to be able to differentiate between your voice and the
voices of the false prophets who dwell among us.
*(Prayers of Intercession)*

---

**OUT OF THE DEPTHS OF SILENCE COMES A NEW REVELATION.**
*(Pray the Prayer of Our Savior.)*

---

| **MORNING** | **EVENING** |
|---|---|
| Be aware of the voice of the stranger. In the name of Jesus. Amen. | The voice of God shall always remain in the heart. In the name of Jesus. Amen. |

# April 29

*(Read John 10:1–10)*

### MORNING
Loving God, I thank you for Jesus, the Christ.
Because of Jesus I will receive the gift of abundant life.

### EVENING
Loving God, I retire this day humbly accepting
the experiences of an abundant life.

Dear God, I thank you, the Gatekeeper, for being eternally present at the gate that leads to abundant life. With your saving power, I look forward to the day when I will experience your bounty in the greener pastures of eternal life. But until that day, O God, I humbly seek your protection. Protect me from the violence that exists in the streets; shield me from lies and misinformation. When I have a doubting spirit, cleanse me. When I am anxious, calm me. When I am careless, guide me. When I am fearful, still my heart. For in you, O God, there is always a better way—the righteous way. And from this day forward, I extend my very being to you and to you alone, my Protector and Provider.

### MORNING
Help me to learn from my enemies today. Convert the anxieties
of my heart into experiences of love and joy.
*(Prayers of Intercession)*

### EVENING
I end this day with the blessed assurance that life
is a sacred gift, and I pray that I do not take it for granted.
*(Prayers of Intercession)*

---

### THE GATES OF HELL WILL NEVER PREVAIL!
*(Pray the Prayer of Our Savior.)*

---

### MORNING
Jesus said, "Very truly, I tell you, I am the gate for the sheep." As a sheep in the pasture, I assuredly wait at Jesus' feet. In Jesus' name. Amen.

### EVENING
"Whoever enters by me will be saved, and will come in and go out and find pasture." Thank you, God! In the name of Jesus. Amen.

# April 30

*(Read Psalm 23:1–3)*

### MORNING
Caring God, you are my compass and guide. I look to you for direction.

### EVENING
Caring God, I rest in the safety of your presence. Lead me into stillness.

Dear God, the psalmist reminds me that you, my Shepherd, are the one who knows what I need and leads me to it. In the hurry and heat of my days, I can be tempted to ignore or skip over my need for rest, nourishment, direction, or community. I can get caught up in accomplishing my goals and completing all on my agenda—forgetting that I am part of a wider community of your people. Overload can also come from the time and energy it takes to communicate and cooperate with others. God, you allow me to know when there is a time of "being" as well as "doing." Today and every day, lead me to timely pauses for re-creating, re-membering, and re-aligning myself with you and your people. Show me what is needed.

### MORNING
Compassionate God, refresh those in leadership
and the communities they serve.
*(Prayers of Intercession)*

### EVENING
Re-creating God, gather in your stressed ones
and lead them to a place of rest.
*(Prayers of Intercession)*

### GOD CALLS FOR "TIME-OUT."

| MORNING | EVENING |
|---|---|
| Dear God, in the living of today's possibilities, remind me of my relationship with you and others. In Jesus' name, I pray. Amen. | Refreshing God, I come to you for the rest I need to replenish my spirit this night. In Jesus' name, I pray. Amen. |

# May 1

*(Read Psalm 23:4–6)*

**MORNING**

Faithful One, I stand on the threshold of this day with you.
Strengthen me for what lies ahead.

**EVENING**

Faithful One, I come home with the joys and struggles
of this day to share them with you.

Shepherd God, you know how quickly darkness can transform the landscape of life into a dangerous place. In dark valleys, uneven ground, tree roots, and rocks become hazards, and landmarks are hard to see. Enemies can sneak up on me. I need direction and protection. It is such a gift to know that you are with me in dark times to provide not only light but also a table overflowing with grace—a table where I can meet my enemies face to face. O God, give me courage to meet my enemies in the power of your transforming love.

**MORNING**

Dear God, I bring my prayers for all who find themselves
in despair today.
*(Prayers of Intercession)*

**EVENING**

O God, I bring my enemies one by one into your loving embrace.
*(Prayers of Intercession)*

---

**GOD LEADS ME FORWARD THROUGH DIFFICULT TIMES.**

---

**MORNING**

Dear God, protect and encourage me as I face the challenges of this day. In Jesus' name, I pray. Amen.

**EVENING**

Generous God, my heart overflows with thanks for your unconditional love, which I experienced today. In Jesus' name, I pray. Amen.

# May 2

*(Read Acts 9:36–39)*

**MORNING**

Ever-present God, help me to be still enough to recognize your
calling for me this day.

**EVENING**

Ever-present God, I recall your messengers and my response.
Help me to hear your affirmation and/or forgiveness.

Peter responded to the message to come quickly. He drew near to death
and listened to the people, the situation, and you, Patient God. I too
have found myself in grief-filled scenes. The sense of loss can be overwhelming and tear-filled with the transition between the death of what
was and the birth of what is yet to be. Time is needed to listen with
compassion, to remember and cherish life, and to share in the longing
for new life. I, like others, am tempted to short-circuit, limit, discount,
stay away from, or put off this prayerful pause. God of all Seasons, help
me to be present to seasons of change, loss, and death. Teach me to listen carefully and to cherish stories for the sake of new life.

**MORNING**

O God, Comfort those who grieve losses
(loved one, relationship, job, health, aging).
*(Prayers of Intercession)*

**EVENING**

O God, I pray for families of those who
have lost someone or something dear today.
*(Prayers of Intercession)*

IN TIME AND BY THE GRACE OF GOD, DEATH AND GRIEF WILL OPEN INTO NEW LIFE.

| **MORNING** | **EVENING** |
| --- | --- |
| Dear God, help me to cherish and | O God, thank you for the gift |
| affirm the people in my life today. | of a community in times of life, |
| In Jesus' name, I pray. Amen. | death, and new life. In Jesus' name, |
| | I pray. Amen. |

# May 3

*(Read Acts 9:40–43)*

**MORNING**

Dear and Gracious God, I come to you humbly to connect
with your power to bring new life.

**EVENING**

Dear and Gracious God, bring to my awareness prayers
spoken and unspoken this day.

Peter cleared the room to be alone with you and a seemingly impossible situation. O God, help me to clear prayer space today so that I may come to you to offer my deepest concerns. Peter looked at the lifeless form of Tabitha and fell to his knees in heartfelt prayer. Believing in your resurrection power, he asked you for new life out of death. O God, encourage me to pray your hope, peace, joy, love, and new life into the impossibilities of my life and the lives of others. In this case, Peter saw the answer to his prayer, but it is not always given to me to see or to understand the unfolding of your response to my prayers. Gracious God, help me to be faithful in prayer even when I cannot see the outcome.

**MORNING**

Loving God, I ask your healing for those facing death and loss.
*(Prayers of Intercession)*

**EVENING**

Gracious God, encourage your people to ask for what they need
for new life.
*(Prayers of Intercession)*

JESUS' PRAYER-FULL MINISTRY CONTINUES IN ME.

**MORNING**

Dear God, I go forth into this day
to pray and live boldly. In Jesus'
name, I pray. Amen.

**EVENING**

Gracious God, thank you for
the loving way you answer prayer.
Keep me praying. In Jesus' name,
I pray. Amen.

# May 4

*(Read John 10:22–25)*

**MORNING**

Faithful and Loving God, I come in faith,
acknowledging my doubts and fears.

**EVENING**

Faithful and Loving God, thank you for your love offered, received,
and passed on today. Forgive me and help me to forgive others.

The religious gathering in the temple challenged Jesus, "If you are the Messiah, tell us plainly." O God, I see my own doubts and fears reflected here. There are times when I too want your identity and your leading written in big letters on a big sign so there is no mistaking that it is you. You know the times when I choose to back away and the times when I choose through loving service to declare the ongoing presence of Jesus the Christ. You know my frustration and discouragement with those who reject ministry in your name. Forgive my hesitation O God, and challenge me to deeper faith. Make me more aware of your presence every day. Give me courage to name and share in your ministry of love.

**MORNING**

Dear God, I pray for those in the church and world
struggling with unbelief.
*(Prayers of Intercession)*

**EVENING**

O God, I pray for those who struggle to teach
and for those who struggle to learn.
*(Prayers of Intercession)*

---

**MY LIFE IS LIVED IN JESUS' NAME.**

---

**MORNING**

Dear God, may my living today point to Christ's ongoing ministry and mission. In Jesus' name, I pray. Amen.

**EVENING**

Generous God, thank you for Christ's ministry of love, which I experienced today. In Jesus' name, I pray. Amen.

# May 5

*(Read John 10:26–30)*

**MORNING**

Shepherd God, I come as one known and loved by you,
to listen for your voice.

**EVENING**

Shepherd God, I come this night to meditate
on your loving care. Thank you.

Sheep recognize the loving concern of their shepherd's voice and they follow where he leads. There are many voices (friends, family, teachers, leaders, coworkers, children, and my own voice within) that I hear daily. I also hear the voices of strangers. Sometimes I hear the voice that short circuits my best intentions saying, "You can't do that!" or "You're hopeless!" At other times, I hear the voice that says, "You can do it!" Assuring God, help me to discern your loving voice in scripture, situations, people, and in the silence of my heart. I want to make sure it is you whom I am following.

**MORNING**

Dear God, I pray for the church to hear Jesus' voice
in their decision making.
*(Prayers of Intercession)*

**EVENING**

Loving God, I pray for lost and lonely ones
that they may know you are with them.
*(Prayers of Intercession)*

I LISTEN FOR CHRIST'S LEADING.

**MORNING**

Dear God, I enter this new day
committed to following your lead in
Jesus. In Jesus' name, I pray. Amen.

**EVENING**

Thank you, God, for the joy
and the pain of belonging with others
in your family of faith. In Jesus' name,
I pray. Amen.

# May 6

*(Read Revelation 7:9–17)*

**MORNING**

Almighty God, I join with disciples around the world today
to sing your praises.

**EVENING**

Almighty God, I reflect on your presence
in the challenges of this day.

Almighty God, in this reading from Revelation, I see a wonderful vision of a congregation of Christians gathered from all around the world. They are not present to debate or defend their holiness, their theology, or their differences. They are there as one body in their experience of journeying in faith through painful and difficult times with Christ and for Christ. They are gathered at the throne of grace to sing and praise you because they know what you have done for them. Loving God, where in my life have I experienced such moments of faithful celebration of your presence and provision? O God, bring me in touch with what enables and what hinders worship for me. Draw me into community and communion as I worship you with my faith family today.

**MORNING**

Dear God, give courage and hope in Christ to those facing crises.
*(Prayers of Intercession)*

**EVENING**

O God, I pray for the worldwide Christian church
that we may be faithful.
*(Prayers of Intercession)*

**I COME TO THIS PLACE TO WORSHIP GOD.**

| **MORNING** | **EVENING** |
|---|---|
| Dear God, lead me to a place of belonging and loving service. In Jesus' name, I pray. Amen. | Thank you for today's gathering, God. I continue to celebrate your saving grace. In Jesus' name, I pray. Amen. |

## May 7

(Read Acts 10:14–43)

**MORNING**
Source of my life, help me not to take this day for granted.

**EVENING**
Source of my life, day and night are alike to you.
Thank you for being present in all your creation.

Often in our hearts and in our secret thoughts, we harbor negative perceptions of and hostile feelings toward persons different from ourselves in race, culture, or religious faith. Impelled by the need to protect cherished self-images and comforting feelings of innate superiority to others, we allow attitudes and actions to go unchallenged. These views denigrate and demean individuals only because their culture, history, place of origin, or appearance are different from our own. It takes courage to challenge comfortable stereotypes that contribute to our privilege and ease. We need to hear afresh Peter's great declaration: "I perceive that God is no respecter of persons."

**MORNING**
Creator God, help me to affirm the personhood and dignity of
persons and to make my actions consistent with that affirmation.
*(Prayers of Intercession)*

**EVENING**
Increase the depth and breadth of my gratitude by enlarging my care and
appreciation for everyone and everything that you have created.
*(Prayers of Intercession)*

---

BE ASSURED THAT NO CIRCUMSTANCE CAN TAKE FROM US
THE LOVING AND CARING PRESENCE OF GOD.
*(Pray the Prayer of Our Savior.)*

---

**MORNING**
Make me bold to act consistently
with your will, according respect to
persons different from myself.
In Christ's name. Amen.

**EVENING**
May your benediction rest upon
all that I have done today.
In Christ's name. Amen.

# May 8

*(Read Isaiah 25:6–9)*

**MORNING**

Eternal God, allow me today to be an instrument fit for your use.

**EVENING**

Eternal God, I am grateful for your providential care today.

God, a paradox of being human is the awareness that though we are created in your image, we are not divine. You are eternal. Only you are good. We are mortal, finite, frail creatures who are destined to die and who possess only limited power to determine the course of our existence. The most treasured dimensions of our lives, our faith, our loves, our hopes, and our eternal destiny are gifts from your loving hand. These gifts are incarnate in the life, death, and resurrection of Jesus Christ. The ground of all of our hopes is rooted not in our goodness, but in the experience of your forgiveness and care. How can we fail to marvel at your compassion and mercy?

**MORNING**

Deliver me from presumptions of the sufficiency of my own
powers of body and mind in the journey of this day.
*(Prayers of Intercession)*

**EVENING**

Loving God, help me to relinquish into your keeping the care,
frustrations, and anxieties of this day.
*(Prayers of Intercession)*

---

**GOD'S GRACE IS SUFFICIENT FOR US.**

*(Pray the Prayer of Our Savior.)*

---

**MORNING**

O God, illumine my mind and embolden my heart so that I may enjoy the liberty that your divinity confers. In Christ's name. Amen.

**EVENING**

As I recall the involvements of this day, help me to hold in balance its pain and its peace, its tears and its laughter, its joys and its sorrows. In Christ's name. Amen.

# May 9

*(Read Psalm 118:1–2; 14–24)*

### MORNING

Our Creator, we stand in awe of your creation and marvel
that you have granted us the gift of life.

### EVENING

Our Creator, I pray that today we have been good stewards
of the life we have been given.

In trying to obey the admonition to praise you, caring God, sometimes we
evaluate worship by the level of the response of the participants. We must
not merely assume that spirited singing and fervent prayers of thanksgiving
fulfill the command to praise you at all times. We must remember the
prophets' counsel that the highest worship to you is embodied in service
rendered in your name to our neighbors and to the world. Redeemer God,
we praise you not because you need it, but because we cannot refrain from
expressing gratitude for your love, mercy, care, and forgiveness.

### MORNING

We express our gratitude to you for empowering us to participate with you
in the establishment of justice and freedom.
*(Prayers of Intercession)*

### EVENING

I pray that our lives today have been anthems of praise expressed
through the service we rendered to others.
*(Prayers of Intercession)*

---

**OUR SERVICE TO OUR NEIGHBORS IS OUR ENACTED PRAISE OF GOD.**
*(Pray the Prayer of Our Savior.)*

---

### MORNING

O God, grant to me a true sense
of proportion today; may I perceive
clearly what matters much and what
matters most in your sight.
In Christ's name. Amen.

### EVENING

O God, I pray that today I invested
my energies, my talents, and my
passion in that which conforms most
nearly to your will and purpose.
In Christ's name. Amen.

# May 10

*(Read 1 Corinthians 15:1–11)*

**MORNING**

Redeemer God, before the onslaught of the day,
free my mind to seek your presence.

**EVENING**

Redeemer God, I thank you for the victories won today
and for the forgiveness you tendered for my failures.

Paul reveals how difficult it is for him to resist the temptation to claim as personal achievements his success in ministry and his efforts to serve you. His experience mirrors our own struggles. It is humbling to acknowledge that salvation cannot be earned; it can only be accepted as a gift from you, loving God. While we understand the gospel message that you acted through Jesus of Nazareth to redeem us, it is a message that our hearts labor to understand. We comprehend the pathos of the petition "God, I believe; help my unbelief."

**MORNING**

Let me be open to the enabling power of your Holy Spirit
in my struggle to obey your Word.
*(Prayers of Intercession)*

**EVENING**

I am mindful of the high moments today when I felt
your presence and experienced your continuing care for me
and the world. Thank you.
*(Prayers of Intercession)*

---

**GOD'S GRACE IS SUFFICIENT FOR US!**
*(Pray the Prayer of Our Savior.)*

| **MORNING** | **EVENING** |
|---|---|
| Enable my life to reflect the breadth of the divine love revealed in Christ, as well as your continuing presence in the world. In Christ's name. Amen. | I commit my loved ones, the world you created, all the people who inhabit it, and me to your loving care. In Christ's name. Amen. |

# May 11

**MORNING**

O Holy One, deliver me from any thought or word that demeans your
divine presence and presumes to command you to do my bidding.

**EVENING**

O Holy One, we have peace as we remember that you do not
sleep, and that your providential care for us is not subject to day or
night, to sleeping or to waking, but is ever covering us.

We often cannot comprehend what our eyes have seen, because we live by
the axiom that "seeing is believing." Our experience proves its untruth.
Peter and John, who visited the tomb, saw its emptiness, but they did not
"see" its divine meaning. In subsequent encounters, they and others believed because they were in the physical presence of Jesus. Their experience
is at the heart of our faith. We have believed the testimony of the Spirit.
We have not seen you, God, but we have seen your divine love in our lives
and we have experienced the Spirit's transforming power in our hearts.
Only after we believed were our eyes opened to see your marvelous works.

**MORNING**

Illuminate my mind, so that I may see the world
around me through your loving eyes.
*(Prayers of Intercession)*

**EVENING**

As the day ends, we are reminded that everything is in your hands.
Grant us the peace that this certain knowledge bestows.
*(Prayers of Intercession)*

---

**BELIEVING IS SEEING.**

*(Pray the Prayer of Our Savior.)*

---

**MORNING**

O great Creator, give me faith to
discern your moving finger in the events
of this day. In Christ's name. Amen.

**EVENING**

We thank you for the glimpses we
have caught of your presence in the
world. In Christ's name. Amen.

# May 12

(*Read John 20:11–18*)

**MORNING**

Eternal God, we thank you for the capacity to inquire into the
mysteries of your creation and to think your thoughts after you.

**EVENING**

Eternal God, grant that after the unconsciousness of sleep,
we may awake with a heightened awareness of your presence.

Eternal God, human beings cannot ultimately frustrate your will. It prevails
even when, out of evil intent or ignorance, we deform creation or inflict
suffering upon one another. Despite Mary's myopia, she did recognize the
risen Christ, according to your intention. Unlike Mary, we become aware
of your presence through prayer and vigilant expectation. Thankfully, in
moments of illumination, we hear your call to us. We are reminded that
you have not abandoned the world or us, and we are liberated from the
hopelessness and despair to which the flow of human events gives rise.

**MORNING**

Open my eyes that I may see through the eyes of faith
and persevere, even in the face of apparent disaster.
(*Prayers of Intercession*)

**EVENING**

I pray that today your love was embodied in your servants
who walk among humankind.
(*Prayers of Intercession*)

GOD DOES NOT REQUIRE THAT WE BE SUCCESSFUL—ONLY THAT WE BE FAITHFUL.
(*Pray the Prayer of Our Savior.*)

**MORNING**

Enable us to be transparent to
your love in all of today's encounters.
In Christ's name. Amen.

**EVENING**

May our confidence in your
unswerving love and forgiveness usher
us into untroubled repose.
In Christ's name. Amen.

# May 13

*(Read Mark 16:1–8)*

**MORNING**

Eternal God, Creator and Sustainer of all that is, we thank you
for this day filled with opportunities to use our gifts of mind,
body, and spirit for the sake of your realm.

**EVENING**

Eternal God, quiet our minds and spirits and let your blessing rest upon us.

The compelling persuasiveness of the Scriptures is due, in no small measure, to the fact that we encounter ourselves in its pages. Mary the mother of James, Mary Magdalene, and Salome retreated into fearful silence after they saw the empty tomb and heard the testimony of the angel. Like these women, we are afraid in the presence of possible censure, ridicule, or derision. Unlike many martyrs and saints, and Jesus too, we are not exposed to risks of persecution and death for our witness. Nevertheless, in the presence of the forces of injustice and evil, we are silent, and Jesus is denied. If only we could hear anew the injunction of Jesus: "Inasmuch as you did it not to the least of these, you did it not unto me."

**MORNING**

Embolden us to break the shackles of fear when word and deed
would make visible the will and judgment of God.
*(Prayers of Intercession)*

**EVENING**

Expunge our guilt if, through our cowardice, we have failed to communicate
the good news of the gospel or manifested the love of God.
*(Prayers of Intercession)*

---

**TRUST IN GOD DELIVERS US FROM FEAR.**
*(Pray the Prayer of Our Savior.)*

---

**MORNING**

May I walk in the light of your grace
and be obedient to your will.
In Christ's name. Amen.

**EVENING**

I am grateful for having lived this
day and for the loving companionship
of the Holy Spirit along my journey.
In Christ's name. Amen.

# May 14

*(Read Philippians 2:5–8)*

**MORNING**

Loving God, thank you for Jesus, who came to earth to fully share
our humanity. Thank you, too, for his complete obedience to you.
May I this day be filled and live in his spirit.

**EVENING**

Loving God, thank you for this day and the knowledge
that Jesus lived his earthly life as one of us and understands the joys
as well as the frustrations I have known.

As I read today's scripture, I am exceedingly thankful that I seek to
follow the One who came to earth just as I did, as a mortal human.
How comforting to know that your child Jesus was subjected to all
the temptations, all the frustrations, all the joys and sorrow that I
face. May I be as humble, caring, and loving as was Jesus. May I also
remember that Jesus did not come as an exalted ruler claiming equality with you, Creator, Father and Mother of the universe, but as a
lowly servant. Imprint his story and suffering on my heart.

**MORNING**

As a new day dawns, help me to be aware of all Jesus has done for me.
*(Prayers of Intercession)*

**EVENING**

Divine Spirit, whose presence has been with me this day, accept
those things in which I have exhibited the mind and way of Jesus.
Forgive me when I have not acted as Jesus would have acted.
*(Prayers of Intercession)*

---

**THANK YOU FOR YOUR GIFT OF JESUS CHRIST,
WHOSE LIFE WAS LIVED TO SHOW ME HOW TO ACT, THINK, AND LIVE.**

---

| **MORNING** | **EVENING** |
|---|---|
| Help me to live today in a manner pleasing to you. In the triumphant name of the Christ. Amen. | Tomorrow may I more closely mirror the earthly life of Jesus. In the triumphant name of the Christ. Amen. |

# May 15

*(Read Philippians 2:8–11)*

**MORNING**
Eternal and everlasting God, thank you for exalting Jesus
and making him Sovereign for me and for all who would follow him.

**EVENING**
Eternal and everlasting God, thank you for Jesus, who set an example
for living and for the men and women who have followed in Christ's steps.

I live in a world which, more often than not, does not recognize Jesus as Sovereign. Thanks be to you, loving Creator, for exalting Jesus and making him Sovereign God with you, Divine Being. I remember and am thankful for those through the ages who not only believed in the Messiah and confessed Jesus as Savior, but also went to their deaths rather than deny Christ. Above all, thank you for Jesus, who has become my Savior and Sovereign and lives with you, God, above all others in heaven and on earth, and who loves me.

**MORNING**
May the radiance, joy, and caring that the Christ
brings be manifest in me this day.
*(Prayers of Intercession)*

**EVENING**
Ever-loving God, accept those deeds and words with which
I have exhibited the mind of Jesus today, and forgive me when
I have failed to be a vessel of Christ's love.
*(Prayers of Intercession)*

---

**THANK YOU, DIVINE AND HOLY GOD, FOR THE LIFE OF JESUS,
WHO WAS EXALTED BY YOU AND WHO IS THE CHRIST.**

---

**MORNING**
Spirit of the living God, guide me
this day. In the triumphant name
of the Christ. Amen.

**EVENING**
Dear God, grant unto me peaceful rest
this night, and may my tongue ever
confess that Jesus is the Christ, sent into
the world and exalted by you. In the
triumphant name of the Christ. Amen.

135

# May 16

*(Read Isaiah 50:4–5a)*

**MORNING**

God, morning by morning, you awaken me to live each day joyfully and
with courage. You have created me to bring glory and honor to you, to bless
and be a blessing to all with whom I come in contact.

**EVENING**

God, thank you for the day just over. Thank you for my tongue and the
ability to express my thoughts: thank you for my ears to listen to others.

How wonderful it is to realize anew that you, Eternal One, have created
me with a tongue to speak words of kindness, caring, and love, especially to those who find life difficult and wearisome. I remember, too,
that some of your children have entered this world without the ability
to hear. Grant me, loving God and Creator, the ability to show compassion to such individuals. Grant me the grace to show true love and
help to all those who are differently abled, as did Jesus. Above all, O
God, enable me to listen for your voice speaking to me, and may I then
have the willingness to carry out your will.

**MORNING**

May I begin the day knowing when to use my tongue to speak
and when to use my ears to listen.
*(Prayers of Intercession)*

**EVENING**

Ever-present God, whose love has embraced me this day, grant me a night
of rest and renewal. Accept any kind and helpful thought I have expressed.
Forgive, O merciful God, when I have failed to hear others speak.
*(Prayers of Intercession)*

THANK YOU FOR A TONGUE TO SPEAK AND EARS TO LISTEN.

**MORNING**

I commit myself to being a good
servant of your gifts of speech and
hearing to listen this day. Amen.

**EVENING**

Help me, Divine One, tomorrow to
be a better steward of all my senses,
especially my speech and hearing, that
Jesus may be seen in me. Amen.

# May 17

*(Read Isaiah 50:6–9a)*

### MORNING

Holy God, you are always with me. Thank you for the day
before me. Thank you, too, for the knowledge that no matter what
this day brings—happiness or disappointments—you are present.

### EVENING

Holy God, I have been sustained today by knowing
that you are near. Thank you.

Some of us never have been subjected to physical persecution or verbal insults. Yet I know that the prophets who lived hundreds of years prior to Jesus were persecuted for the stands they took. I am grateful for the stand taken by the early Christian martyrs, "in spite of dungeon, fire, and sword." Most of all, I remember and praise your name for Jesus, who, although completely innocent, went to the cross knowing that it was your will. Enable me to be as true a disciple of Jesus as was Jesus to you, holy God.

### MORNING

Ever-loving God, help me to be a good servant of Christ,
as Christ was the perfect servant to you.
*(Prayers of Intercession)*

### EVENING

For you, O God, have been with me and helped me this day.
Praise be to you. If I have been silent rather than vocal in the face of insults
against the Christian way of life, forgive me. Gracious God,
help me to be a better steward of your gifts tomorrow.
*(Prayers of Intercession)*

---

**THANKS BE TO GOD FOR THE PERFECT MODEL SET BY JESUS.**

---

### MORNING

May my love and commitment to
Christ be genuine. In the triumphant
name of the Christ. Amen.

### EVENING

May my resolve to grow
spiritually increase each day I live.
In the triumphant name of
the Christ. Amen.

# May 18

*(Read Psalm 118:12, 19–29)*

### MORNING

Thank you, gracious God, for you are good and your love
will endure forever. Thanks be to you for another day of life.
May I rejoice and be glad for it.

### EVENING

Thank you, gracious God, for the day that just has passed.
Help me to remember your constant and steadfast love.

I exist in a world that knows both good and evil. May your Spirit, O God, always be with me, that I may face each hour and enter the gates of righteousness and truth rather than those of evil and falsehood. Grant that I may so live that others may know that my life is built on the cornerstone of Jesus Christ. Thank you, God, for sending Jesus into the world to give us a perfect pattern for living. Your love for me and for every human life will never come to an end. Blessing, glory, and honor be unto you.

### MORNING

God, as I begin a new day, may I live in joyful celebration
that I am your child.
*(Prayers of Intercession)*

### EVENING

I give you thanks, O God most high, for light that you
have shed upon my path. Thanks be to you, O God, for your
steadfast love, which will endure forever.
*(Prayers of Intercession)*

---

**THANK YOU FOR THE GIFT OF LIFE AND FOR EACH MOMENT OF THE DAY.**

---

### MORNING

Help me to be a good follower
of Jesus the Christ this day. In the
triumphant name of the Christ.
Amen.

### EVENING

May I remember tomorrow, more
than I have today, to give thanks at all
times for your steadfast and enduring
love. In the triumphant name of the
Christ. Amen.

# May 19

*(Read Luke 19:28–40)*

### MORNING

Everlasting and almighty God, thanks be to you for Jesus Christ.
As I live this day, may I emulate the courage that Jesus exhibited as
he entered Jerusalem, fully aware of the hostility he would meet.

### EVENING

Everlasting and almighty God, thank you for Jesus, who came and
lived among us, setting a perfect example of the way to live.

I thank you, God, that Jesus knew as he entered Jerusalem that the rulers
and chief elders would certainly put him to death. Thank you, too, Holy
One, that knowing the signs of the day, Jesus believed it was your will that
he go to Jerusalem and was obedient. I doubt I would have had such
courage. When being a Christian becomes difficult or unpopular, when life
for me becomes difficult and it would be easier to turn and run away, grant
me courage, O gracious God—a portion of the courage of Jesus. Grant me
strength and unwavering faith to follow in Jesus' footsteps at all times.

### MORNING

Help me, almighty God, to live this day with the boldness
and the caring of Jesus, our Savior.
*(Prayers of Intercession)*

### EVENING

Thank you, merciful God, for your presence and guidance this day. Now grant
me rest this night, that I may awake more determined to be a better disciple.
*(Prayers of Intercession)*

---

THANKS BE TO YOU, HOLY GOD, FOR JESUS AND HIS COMPLETE OBEDIENCE TO YOU.

---

### MORNING

I promise, O God, insofar as I am
able, to be as obedient a follower of
Jesus as he was of you. In the
triumphant name of the Christ.
Amen.

### EVENING

May I more closely follow Jesus
tomorrow with obedience and
steadfastness. In the triumphant
name of the Christ.
Amen.

# May 20

*(Read Luke 19:28–40)*

### MORNING

Great God, new every morning is your mercy. On this day, may my heart sing
for joy as I remember the entry of Jesus into the Holy City.

### EVENING

Great God, thank you for the pageantry and wonder of this day.

I praise you with the multitude of disciples who have blessed you joyfully throughout the ages for all the deeds of Jesus. Enable me to remember, Holy God, that Jesus did not enter Jerusalem as an exalted ruler, riding on a mighty horse, but he deliberately entered the city riding on a lowly colt, a sign of peace. O God, I implore you to help me realize anew that Christ never will force his way into my heart, but comes only as I humble myself and invite him in. Come, Jesus, the Chosen One of God, and live and reign within me.

### MORNING

Spirit of love, Spirit of truth, guide and direct my way this day.
May I feel you once again as the all-embracing power that you are.
*(Prayers of Intercession)*

### EVENING

Accept my gratitude this night, blessed God, for the awe of today.
If I have failed to glean the full impact of this holy day and this
Holy Week ahead, speak afresh to my heart.
*(Prayers of Intercession)*

---

**ALL GLORY AND HONOR FOR THE RICH SPIRITUAL GIFTS OF THIS DAY.
JESUS CHRIST HAS COME ANEW AS A LAMB INTO MY HEART.**

---

| MORNING | EVENING |
|---|---|
| Enable me to find you once more | Because of this day, may I seek you |
| in a fresh way, my God and Sovereign. | and attempt to be a better Christian |
| In the triumphant name of the Christ. | steward tomorrow. And now, grant me |
| Amen. | a night of peaceful rest, I pray. In the |
| | triumphant name of the Christ. |
| | Amen. |

# May 21

*(Read John 20:10–18)*

**MORNING**

Creator God, help me to understand what is hard to understand.
Give me a willing spirit to see what seems unbelievable.

**EVENING**

Creator God, I have seen the power of your witness
in the world through the lives of others. Have I been a witness
this day so that others may know you?

So often in my life, I wonder whether I have been faithful to the power of the resurrection or have been acting only in my self-interest. Mary thought she had lost all that she believed and wept over the loss. Yet it was you, God, through Jesus Christ, who opened her eyes so that she could see life in a new way. I pray you will open my eyes to see you.

**MORNING**

I weep with Mary today because at times I also feel
I have lost all hope for the future. Help me to see what life
is challenging me to see today.
*(Prayers of Intercession)*

**EVENING**

You have been a gift to me this day as you have walked with me.
*(Prayers of Intercession)*

---

**"WOMAN, WHY ARE YOU WEEPING? WHOM ARE YOU LOOKING FOR?"**
*(Sing "I Come to the Garden Alone" or another familiar hymn.)*

---

**MORNING**

O God, be with me this day
so I may bear witness to your holy
name. May the power of your
resurrection give me new life this day.
In the name of Christ I pray.
Amen.

**EVENING**

Thank you, God, for this day.
You have given me energy and hope.
Give me peace this night so I may rest
to serve you tomorrow. In the name
of Christ I pray. Amen.

# May 22

*(Read John 20:19–23)*

### MORNING
O God, help me with my unbelief.
Give me faith that I may believe without seeing.

### EVENING
O God, the peace I have received this day comes with the rich
blessing of knowing you have been with me.

The disciples saw Jesus when Jesus entered the room. They believed because they saw the signs of Jesus' suffering and the power of the resurrection, I find that often I also seek to have visible proof before I can truly believe. God, help me to know your presence even at those times I feel alone and lost. I seek your comforting assurance so that I may serve you in faithfulness.

### MORNING
Be with me this day as I seek to live out your presence in my life while
I engage in my daily activities. This day I pray particularly for . . .
*(Prayers of Intercession)*

### EVENING
Thank you, O God, for your presence as I have lived this day.
I pray I have been faithful to your will and way. Remember this night . . .
*(Prayers of Intercession)*

---

### "Receive the Holy Spirit."
*(Sing "The Strife Is O'er" or another familiar hymn.)*

---

### MORNING
My hope is in you, O God, as I find
my way to witness in your holy name.
May my life be a blessing to all that I
meet and serve this day. In the name
of Christ I pray. Amen.

### EVENING
I sleep this night in the knowledge
that you are with me even as I rest.
You have been with me throughout this
day. May I rise tomorrow with new
energy to serve you. In the name
of Christ I pray. Amen.

# May 23

*(Read John 20:24–31)*

**MORNING**

Comforting God, my doubts seem to overtake my life at times.
Help me this day to see through my doubts and to believe in you.

**EVENING**

Comforting God, thank you for being with me when I have
harbored doubts about your presence with me today.

I feel many times like doubting Thomas because I want clear evidence
that you are with me. There are many ways in which I want to control
other people and even you, O God. I yearn always to believe you are
with me, even when doubts seem to overtake me as I see pain and hurt
in the world. Thank you, God, for revealing yourself through your
Child, Jesus Christ.

**MORNING**

Spirit of God, be with me this day as I seek to be a sign of your
presence in the world. Please remember especially this day.
*(Prayers of Intercession)*

**EVENING**

Thank you, O God, for being present with me as I have lived
this day. I pray you will forgive the things that I should have done
but did not. Remember this night particularly . . .
*(Prayers of Intercession)*

---

**"PEACE BE WITH YOU."**

*(Sing "Peace I Leave with You" or another familiar hymn.)*

---

**MORNING**

I begin this day wondering if I am
able to do what is required of me.
Yet I know all things are possible
through you. In the name of Christ
I pray. Amen.

**EVENING**

I praise your name, O God,
for you have given me strength to live
this day. Give me rest this night.
In the name of Christ I pray.
Amen.

# May 24

*(Read Acts 5:27–32)*

**MORNING**

All-knowing God, help me to obey the way you would
have me live. Give me the courage to speak the truth in love.

**EVENING**

All-knowing God, have I been the kind of person this day
who spoke your Word? Did I witness as a disciple of Jesus Christ?

I am humbled by the way the disciples were able to stand before others
and speak your Word in the midst of danger and disagreement. I want
to do the right thing, but so often I lack the courage and slip silently
away into the shade, I yearn to be able to stand for Jesus in my daily living. Help me to have the courage to be a true disciple.

**MORNING**

As I face the tasks of this day, give me the courage to speak and
live the truth. Remember this day those who feel weak and afraid.
*(Prayers of Intercession)*

**EVENING**

Thank you for standing with me this day when I lacked
the courage to stand up for you. Remember this night . . .
*(Prayers of Intercession)*

---

**"WE MUST OBEY GOD RATHER THAN ANY HUMAN AUTHORITY."**
*(Sing "My Shepherd Is the Living God" or another familiar hymn.)*

---

**MORNING**

Today I look forward to the hope
that I may serve you with faithfulness
and speak with courage your word of
truth in love. In the name of Christ
I pray. Amen.

**EVENING**

I give thanks to you, O God, for the
gift of strength that you have given to
me this day. I ask your presence this
night as I rest to serve you tomorrow.
In the name of Christ I pray. Amen.

# May 25

*(Read Psalm 118:14–29)*

### MORNING

O God, help me be one to witness in your name this day.
Help me be a blessing to those who surround me.

### EVENING

O God, thank you for being with me all this day.
Thank you for helping me know that salvation is through you.

I know in my head that your steadfast mercy and love are with me, but there are times when my heart does not feel them. I want to be glad and rejoice in your name, yet many times I feel alone and without hope. The word of the psalmist gives me courage to see each new day as a blessing from you. Help me find the way to your glorious salvation.

### MORNING

Open me, O God, to the gates of righteousness this day.
Remember especially this day . . .
*(Prayers of Intercession)*

### EVENING

I thank you, O God, that you have come to me and
sustained me so that I may serve you more faithfully.
Please remember this night . . .
*(Prayers of Intercession)*

---

**"GOD IS MY STRENGTH AND MY MIGHT."**
*(Sing "Like a Tree beside the Waters" or another familiar hymn.)*

---

### MORNING

O God, open my heart and eyes to witness in your name this day. I seek your guidance, knowing this is the day you have made. In the name of Christ I pray. Amen.

### EVENING

Thank you for the marvelous way your mercy has been given to me. I know you have made this day, and I rejoice that I have been able to serve you. Give me peaceful rest this night. In the name of Christ I pray. Amen.

# May 26

*(Read Psalm 150)*

### MORNING

Praise God for the day that is before me!
Help me to praise God by the way I live this day.

### EVENING

Praise God for the night that is before me! I pray that every breath
I have taken this day has been filled by God's Spirit.
Let everything within me praise God!

God, this is the day you have made. I seek to serve you with all my being and energy. The beauty of the day is to be lived as a blessing to your great goodness. Help me to know the ways of righteousness and justice for all your people. Give me courage to share the good news of this Eastertide season. Christ has risen!

### MORNING

I sing praises to you, O God, for you have given me life
for another day of your creation. Remember this day those whom
I love and those who are hurting . . .
*(Prayers of Intercession)*

### EVENING

What a glorious day this has been. I have been blessed
by your goodness. Thank you for the signs of your grace and love.
Please remember this night . . .
*(Prayers of Intercession)*

### PRAISE GOD!

*(Sing "I Sing the Mighty Power of God" or another familiar hymn.)*

| MORNING | EVENING |
|---|---|
| I look with great anticipation for this day because I know you have blessed it by your goodness, O God. Help me be the person of faith who lives as Christ would have me live as a disciple. In the name of Christ I pray. Amen. | Thank you for this gift of another day of your creation. Your love and blessing have given me hope for tomorrow. May I rest well this night by your peace. In the name of Christ I pray. Amen. |

# May 27

*(Read Revelation 1:4-8)*

### MORNING
Holy One, you come to give me life for this day and every day.

### EVENING
Holy One, your grace has been a blessing and the hope for another day.

I have learned from Jesus Christ, the firstborn, that the beginning and end come from you, all-knowing God. I seek to live my life in faithfulness, yet know it is possible only by your grace. We learn about you through Jesus' ministry upon this earth, and we are called to bear witness to that ministry by our own ministry. The resurrection of Christ makes all things possible to those who love you. The new world of your creation was made known by your power and love.

### MORNING
I come to the beginning of this day knowing you will be
with me to its very end. I live with that hope and joy.
Please remember this day.
*(Prayers of Intercession)*

### EVENING
Gracious God, your love sustains me even when 1 feel separated
from you and others. By your grace remember this night . . .
*(Prayers of Intercession)*

---

### "I AM THE ALPHA AND THE OMEGA."
*(Sing "Spirit, Spirit of Gentleness" or another familiar hymn.)*

---

### MORNING
I begin this day knowing you are
with me from its beginning to its
ending. Help me be a witness of the
message that Jesus gave to this world.
Christ has risen indeed. In the name
of Christ I pray. Amen.

### EVENING
Thank you, O Creator God,
for fashioning a world where all
beginnings and endings are by your
grace. Thank you for sustaining me
through this day. I offer my praises to
you. In the name of Christ
I pray. Amen.

# May 28

*(Read Acts 2:1–12)*
*Sing "Spirit of the Living God" or another familiar song.*

### MORNING
Holy Power, Love Divine, my eyes open to your wonder
and my lips respond with praise. All night you have kept me and
again this morning touched me with amazing grace.

### EVENING
Holy Power, Love Divine, thank you for a day of joyful surprises.
I have seen you in many faces and felt you in many touches. Thank you for
a day lived in wonder. Forgive my sin and make me one with you.

Holy God, your touch is in every fabric of the world. As flowers begin to bloom, as trees continue to sprout buds and the refreshing rains water the earth, I see your hand. Your power is in every thread of my existence. It connects me in community, it grounds me in relationships, and it keeps me in harmony with you. The Pentecost fire continues to burn within my soul. I pray to be kept in the center of your will and used for your good and glory.

### MORNING
You have called me into community. Today I lift up my community before you.
*(Prayers of Intercession)*

### EVENING
All day long I have sensed your presence. All day I have longed to
bring others into your company through my prayers. Now I leave
them and myself in your care.
*(Prayers of Intercession)*

---

THANK YOU FOR THE GIFT OF THE HOLY SPIRIT'S POWER YET
BEING AVAILABLE TO TRANSFORM THE WORLD.

---

| MORNING | EVENING |
|---|---|
| Today I will live as one empowered by the Holy Spirit! Thanks be to Christ. Amen. | Now I lay me down to sleep. I pray you, God, my soul to keep! Thanks be to Christ. Amen. |

# May 29

*(Read Acts 2:13–21)*

**MORNING**

God of dreamers and visionaries, how good to awake with you!
Thank you for another opportunity to hear your voice.
My heart cries that your name be blessed!

**EVENING**

God of dreamers and visionaries, you have fallen upon me again
today. I praise you for the outpouring of your grace and power,
which has sustained me, encouraged me, and kept me this day.

Calling God, I have experienced love today from many whom you have
called. My day has been greatly blessed by others. For every man,
woman, boy, and girl you have used to make my life better, I offer humble thanks. You use whoever will call upon your name! Thank you for
every respondent!

**MORNING**

All-sufficient One, many need the outpouring of your Holy Spirit's
power today.
*(Prayers of Intercession)*

**EVENING**

Rush of Wind and Breath of Love, you have moved mightily in
your world today. Thank you for all you have done. Forgive me for
all I have left undone. Bless these upon my heart, I pray.
*(Prayers of Intercession)*

---

**THE POWER AND THE GLORY OF PENTECOST IS ALIVE AND WELL TODAY IN ME!**

---

| **MORNING** | **EVENING** |
|---|---|
| Today I will be open to | Speak to me, Holy One, |
| the dreams and visions that come to | in the hours of quiet rest and solitude. |
| me from you, God. Thanks be | Let me hear you clearly in the watches |
| to Christ. Amen, | of the night. Thanks be |
| | to Christ. Amen. |

# May 30

*(Read Genesis 11:1–9)*
*Sing "Halleluja, Halleluja" or another familiar song.*

### MORNING

Creation Builder, I hear you in the silence of this new day.
Let my words be few and seasoned with your grace as I walk with
humility before you in the world today.

### EVENING

Creation Builder, this day I have attempted to imitate you
in my life. I have sought understanding. Forgive my shortcomings
and the many walls I built instead.

God of unity, how awesome to know that you have given unto us the power to re-create our world. Your living Word declares that when we are of one accord we can accomplish anything! Yet I see the many broken places, lost hopes, and wounded spirits among us. Give us understanding. Renew our hope. Bring us into community again, we pray.

### MORNING

Amidst the noises of our world allow me to hear your voice
and to be your voice in the world.
*(Prayers of Intercession)*

### EVENING

I have sought to hear you and to follow your lead today.
Bless now these upon my heart who need to hear from you.
*(Prayers of Intercession)*

---

**NOISE DOES NOT MEAN UNITY. THE PRESENCE OF GOD IS OFTEN IN SILENCE.**

---

### MORNING

Today I will strive to understand
the language of the hearts of my sisters and brothers. Thanks be
to Christ. Amen.

### EVENING

Many times today, I have
become entangled in the many noises
around me. Help me in the stillness of
the night to know you better, I pray.
Thanks be to Christ. Amen.

# May 31

*(Read Psalm 104:24–35)*
*Sing "Morning Has Broken" or another familiar song.*

### MORNING
Wonder-working God, we enter your day with thanksgiving
and begin this day with praise. I honor and adore you. I exalt you
for your goodness and your mercy. I worship you!

### EVENING
Wonder-working God, I pause to offer my sacrifice of praise
for the experiences of this day. Many and great are your marvelous
works, and my soul magnifies you for another day of miracles.

I offer up the meditations of my heart as I ponder the spectacular creation of which I am such a small part. I am amazed at how vast and full
of splendor this world continues to be despite our pollution, misman-
agement, and waste of resources. From the tiny ant, to the fledgling
bird, to the giant redwood forest and enormous mountain ranges, your
handiwork articulates your care! And then you continue to care for me!
With the psalmist I stand in awe.

### MORNING
Again this morning, your new mercies I beseech.
*(Prayers of Intercession)*

### EVENING
For the matchless grace we have received, thank you.
Now again hear the petitions of my heart.
*(Prayers of Intercession)*

---

**I WILL SING THE PRAISE OF MY GOD AS LONG AS I HAVE BREATH!**

---

### MORNING
God, today I will open my eyes
and see your glory in all I meet.
Thanks be to Christ. Amen.

### EVENING
Sleep is a wonder! I commit
myself unto you in all its mystery.
Thanks be to Christ. Amen.

# June 1

(Read Romans 8:14–17)
*Sing "We Shall Overcome" or another familiar song.*

### MORNING

Abba! What joy to awake to a new day of liberty in you!
Thank you for the refreshment of the night. Help me to face the
day with purpose and with confidence in your Holy Spirit's
ever-freeing and ever-living power, I pray.

### EVENING

Abba! Thank you for the gift of being your child today.
I have felt your love. Forgive me for the times I allowed fear to
dictate my actions and did not show love in the world.

Thank you for purpose in my life. Thank you for the gifts of the Holy
Spirit, which operate in me and keep me from being dominated by my
fears. You are the God of power and love, and I have received your
power by adoption into your family. Help me to always remember that
I am an heir to greatness and not mediocrity! Give me clarity of focus
and singleness of heart, I pray.

### MORNING

Many are enslaved today, God.
*(Prayers of Intercession)*

### EVENING

I have tried not to suffer today; forgive me for turning away from
you. Hear the pleas of my heart.
*(Prayers of Intercession)*

### GET PURPOSE! KEEP IT BEFORE YOU!

### MORNING

I will walk in love, courage, and
power today. Thanks be to Christ.
Amen.

### EVENING

The night has great restorative powers.
Embrace me, I pray. Thanks be to
Christ. Amen.

# June 2

*(Read John 14:7–17)*
*Sing "Amen!" or another familiar song.*

### MORNING
Great Amen, I awake with "Yes" upon my lips.
Your claim upon my life calls me to exhibit your loving care in the world.
Walk, talk, and live in me. My heart says "Amen" to your will!

### EVENING
Great Amen, today has been a gift.
I pray that my life has been a gift to you.

It's difficult to believe that I am called to do "greater things" than Jesus. Yet I know that your Word does not lie. I look at the world around me, and my heart is filled with compassion for what I see. There are so many needs, so much hurt, such great sorrow, and such varied cares. And I'm to do greater things? Help me to know what to do. Help me to speak with your authority, to act with your boldness, and to be at one with you, I pray. I will do greater things today because Jesus lives in me!

### MORNING
Greater things begin when I pray.
*(Prayers of Intercession)*

### EVENING
For the great things I have neglected today, I ask forgiveness. For
the great needs upon my heart, I pray.
*(Prayers of Intercession)*

---

## BE BOLD IN JESUS!

---

### MORNING
Greater things are my inheritance!
Thanks be to Christ. Amen.

### EVENING
For the greater things that can
be accomplished in me while I rest,
I now pray. Thanks be to Christ.
Amen.

# June 3

*(Read John 14:25–27)*
*Sing "Jesus Loves Me, This I Know" or another familiar song.*

### MORNING

Jesus, lover of my soul, unto you I lift my spirit.
For the night of rest and the mysteries before me,
I give you thanks.

### EVENING

Jesus, lover of my soul, for enfolding my heart with love and my
day with grace, I lift my voice in exultations of praise.

In this world I have my share of troubles, but in the midst of every
storm I find a place of refuge in you! Thank you for being my anchor.
Thank you for the gift of the Holy Spirit, my comforter, my guide, and
my powerful friend. Thank you for never leaving me alone. Thank you
for the abiding peace that is not simply the absence of confusion and
chaos in my life, but my blessed assurance!

### MORNING

Jesus, everybody ought to know who you are!
*(Prayers of Intercession)*

### EVENING

You have been the lifter of my head!
Lift now the heads and hearts of these, I pray.
*(Prayers of Intercession)*

---

### THERE IS NO SPOT WHERE GOD IS NOT! I AM NEVER ALONE!

---

### MORNING

God, today I am filled with and
possessed by your shalom! Thanks be
to Christ. Amen.

### EVENING

If I should die before I wake, I pray
you, God, my soul to take. Thanks be
to Christ. Amen!

# June 4

*(Read 1 Corinthians 12:12–13)*

### MORNING
Eternal God of creation, I thank you for this day. May I be receptive and responsive to the guidance and power you provide through your Holy Spirit.

### EVENING
Eternal God of creation, I give you thanks and praise for your presence.
Thank you for teaching me the universal language of love.

Loving God, because you chose to be among us and to experience what it is to be human, you know the many challenges we face. Most often it is difficult to demonstrate the love of Christ in a world that judges me by the color of my skin. The diversity of the human family you created is a reality, yet we have allowed it to be a stumbling block to the fulfillment of your domain. Sometimes I want to withdraw and associate only with those who look like me. Help me never to lose the hope of knowing that one day all of your people will hear and speak the common language of love and unity. May your will be done on earth as it is in heaven.

### MORNING
God, anoint my speaking and my hearing,
that I might be a blessing to someone today.
*(Prayers of Intercession)*

### EVENING
Eternal God, help me to realize that while I am a unique creation,
I am also one with all you have created. Give me the courage to act
justly and responsibly toward your creation.
*(Prayers of Intercession)*

MOST GRACIOUS GOD, HELP ME TO REALIZE THAT WHEN I LOOK INTO THE EYES
OF ANOTHER, I WILL SEE A REFLECTION OF MYSELF.

### MORNING
God who is Creator and Sustainer of life, help me never to underestimate the power of the Holy Spirit. In Jesus' name I pray. Amen.

### EVENING
I give you thanks and praise for all I have done that has pleased you, O God; for I can do nothing for you without you. In Jesus' name I pray. Amen.

# June 5

*(Read 1 Corinthians 12:3b–12)*

### MORNING

God of liberation, help me to realize that all things work for the
good of those who love you and are called according to your purpose.

### EVENING

God of liberation, I never cease to be amazed at the
many ways you speak liberating Words. Thank you for looking
beyond our pettiness and jealousy to meet our needs.

God, I'm always puzzled when members of a congregation belonging to a
given denomination do not celebrate with joy and thanksgiving when a
person joins the church. Didn't this person become a part of the body of
Christ in response to the preached Word, ministering community, or
prophetic witness? Should we have the attitude that "we lost one" because
someone did not join "our church"? Or should we have an attitude of joy
because yet another has come to Christ? Do we really believe it when we
read, "For just as the body is one and has many members, and all the
members of the body, though many, are one body, so it is with Christ"?

### MORNING

Loving God, thank you for the many ways your Spirit manifests
itself through persons from every walk of life.
*(Prayers of Intercession)*

### EVENING

God, I give you the praise, honor, and glory because in
and through you all things are possible.
*(Prayers of Intercession)*

---

**WHEN SOMEONE IN OUR FAMILY OF FAITH DOES A GOOD THING,
WE SHOULD PRAISE GOD AND REMEMBER THE MESSAGE, "IT'S ALL GOOD."**

---

### MORNING

God of grace, when and where I see
evidence of the fruit of your Spirit,
help me to give you the praise.
In Jesus' name I pray. Amen.

### EVENING

God of love, in spite of me,
you continue to reach out and draw
me near. Thank you! In Jesus' name
I pray. Amen.

# June 6

*(Read Psalm 104:27–34, 35b)*

**MORNING**

Creator God, this is the day that you have made, and I rejoice and am glad in it.
Truly you are the one and only God. Only you are worthy of my praise.

**EVENING**

Creator God, you are the Potter, and I am the clay. Mold me, God
of creation, so that I might be a vessel of your light. Shape and use
me so that I might live harmoniously with your creation.

God, help me to learn from your children, the indigenous peoples of
Africa, Asia, and the Americas, what many of us who claim to follow
Christ have yet to learn. These people traditionally understood themselves
as not having dominion over the earth. Rather, they saw themselves as in-
timately and inextricably related to the earth and all creation. Theirs was
(and, in many cases, continues to be) a commitment to provide reverence,
respect, and responsible maintenance for the earth and all creation.

**MORNING**

God of liberation, help me to embody those values of my ancestors who tried
to live in harmony with your creation. Help me to love the neighbor who has not
come to understand the responsibility of maintaining the gifts of your creation.
*(Prayers of Intercession)*

**EVENING**

Merciful God, before time was measured, you set into motion the
rhythm of the universe as perfect love. Order our steps that we
might walk in sync with this rhythm.
*(Prayers of Intercession)*

---

**HOLY SPIRIT, HELP ME TO PRAY THE PRAYER OF MY GREATEST ANCESTOR.**
*(Pray the Prayer of Our Savior.)*

---

**MORNING**

Today, loving God, help me to express
my love for you by loving your creation.
In Jesus' name I pray. Amen.

**EVENING**

God of love and justice, all praise,
honor, and glory belong to you.
You and you alone are worthy of such
praise. In Jesus' name I pray. Amen.

# June 7

*(Read John 20:19–23)*

### MORNING

Merciful and gracious God, when I let you down, I often try to run from you.
Thank you for not allowing a place to exist where I can hide.

### EVENING

Merciful and gracious God, thank you for the gift of the Holy Spirit,
which convicts, comforts, challenges, counsels, changes, and cleanses.

God, you are a radical lover. You create and re-create me, rear me, nurture me, feed me, teach me, suffer for me, and even die for me. In return, I have bowed down to other gods, squandered your gifts, done things I had no business doing, and failed to do things I should have done. I even disowned you in your direst hour. Yet, when I was trying to hide from you, you found me and said, "Peace be with you." You love me more than I love myself. Your love has no end. Nothing can separate me from your love. You love me unconditionally. God, you are my radical Lover.

### MORNING

Eternal and gracious God, I don't have to love you or serve you. But because
of your radical love for me, I do love you and seek only to serve you this day.
*(Prayers of Intercession)*

### EVENING

Bless me, God of love, to love others as you have loved
and promise to love me.
*(Prayers of Intercession)*

---

**I AM NOT WHAT I OUGHT TO BE, BUT I THANK THE LIVING GOD
THAT I AM NOT WHAT I USED TO BE.**

---

### MORNING

"Spirit of the living God, fall afresh
on me. Melt, mold, fill, use me.
Spirit of the living God, fall afresh on
me" (Daniel Iverson, 1926).
In Jesus' name I pray. Amen.

### EVENING

Merciful God, you continue to look
beyond my faults and see my needs.
Help me to walk in love such as this.
In Jesus' name I pray. Amen.

# June 8

*(Read Acts 2:1–21)*

**MORNING**

Eternal God and perfect Giver, I give you praise, for you
are a faithful God, a God whose promises are never broken. On
this day, you are the solid rock upon which I will stand.

**EVENING**

Eternal God and perfect Giver, thank you for the perfect gift.
I praise you for whatever good thing I thought, said, or did this day.

Indeed, God, you are the Giver of every good and perfect gift. The greatest
gift you have bestowed upon me is yourself, in Christ Jesus and through
your Holy Spirit. The giving of this perfect gift is what you promised, and
you offer it continually every second of every day. No matter what I do, say,
or think, you extend the perfect gift in perfect love, and you give it unconditionally. Over the years, some have tried to frighten me into believing in
you. But it is not fear that continues to transform my heart; it is your perfect love, as given to me in and through Jesus the Christ and the Holy Spirit.

**MORNING**

God, you are perfect Love. Bless me today to be a vessel through
which the light of your love will shine. Bless me to be a blessing.
*(Prayers of Intercession)*

**EVENING**

O Spirit of the living God, fall fresh upon those who have been known to drift
away. Fall anew upon those who have not known you or your perfect love.
*(Prayers of Intercession)*

---

**WHOM HAVE I LOVED UNCONDITIONALLY TODAY?**

---

**MORNING**

Merciful God, you have saved me,
and now you send me. Help me to
love the least of these, my sisters and
brothers, in the way you have loved
and continue to love me. In Jesus'
name I pray. Amen.

**EVENING**

God of liberation, you died for me.
Help me be clear about what I am
asking of you when I ask for help in
loving my neighbor as you have loved
me. In Jesus' name I pray. Amen.

# June 9

*(Read Psalm 104:24–26, 35b)*

**MORNING**

O God of creation, how great you are! You are the Creator of the
universe and all therein. You are the Giver and Sustainer of all life,
and only you are worthy to be praised!

**EVENING**

O God of creation, thank you for all that you provide
for me in and through your creation. Help me to increase my knowledge
of the healing gifts within your creation.

God, so often I get caught up in the busyness of day-to-day city living.
Days come and go without my taking time to behold the beauty of your
creation. A ride in the country, a picnic in the park, a long walk on the
beach, watching a sunset, and gazing upon a starlit sky from the lights of
the city—these are but a few of the simple and free joys of life of which
I often deprive myself. Your creation is so full of the songs of nature,
which sing your praises. Open my eyes to the beauty of your creation.
Help me to pause and take the time to receive and enjoy your free gifts.

**MORNING**

God of creation, many live in conditions that make it difficult
and impossible to enjoy the beauty of your creation. Help me to be sensitive
and responsive to their needs.
*(Prayers of Intercession)*

**EVENING**

Eternal God, help me to be increasingly aware
of my interrelatedness with your creation.
*(Prayers of Intercession)*

MELODY MAKER, ORDER MY STEPS IN YOUR WORD, SO THAT I MAY WALK
IN HARMONY WITH THE RHYTHM OF YOUR CREATION.

**MORNING**

Have your way with me, most high
God. Today, help me to experience
your creation in new and profound
ways. In Christ's name. Amen.

**EVENING**

Gracious God, help me always
to take time to behold the wonder
and beauty of your creation. In
Christ's name. Amen.

# June 10

*(Read Acts 2:14–21)*

### MORNING

Eternal God, thank you for last night's lying down
and this morning's rising. I give you the praise!

### EVENING

Eternal God, thank you for miracles seen and unseen. On this day,
I give you praise. Help me to receive and be empowered by the Holy Spirit.

God, you work in mysterious ways and have wonders to perform. You never cease to amaze me in the way you move in and through the Holy Spirit: the prophetic word spoken through a friend or stranger; wisdom spoken through a child who seems to transcend his or her years; the friend, family member, or guest who unexpectedly walks down the aisle during worship to profess belief; the empowerment of a disempowered person or group; the healing of an ostensibly terminally ill relative that defies scientific explanation. These are just some of the ways you move, often unexpectedly, in and through your Holy Spirit. Indeed, all things are possible through Christ, who strengthens me.

### MORNING

God of love, help me to be open to the limitless possibilities of your power.
*(Prayers of Intercession)*

### EVENING

Merciful and liberating God, the numbers of the hopeless seem to be increasing.
Pour out your Holy Spirit on those who are forced to the margins of our society.
*(Prayers of Intercession)*

---

THE APPRECIATION OF A GIFT IS MEASURED BY HOW IT IS USED.

---

### MORNING

God of power, help me to walk by faith and not by sight. Help me to demonstrate my belief that all things are possible through you. In Jesus' name I pray. Amen.

### EVENING

God, again you gave me the gift of the Holy Spirit. I stand on your promise of eternal life, which is forever my tomorrow. In Jesus' name I pray. Amen.

# June 11

*(Read Mark 4:35–41)*

**MORNING**

Fearless Savior, travel with me today in my little boat.

**EVENING**

Fearless Savior, I praise you because throughout the day
you stilled my fears and saw to my safety.

Oh, how easy it is to become fearful! How quickly we succumb to the storms around us, as the disciples did on the Galilean lake. We have such a hard time believing that you, Jesus, are with us—fully with us— even though we see you sleeping in the bow. O Christ, strengthen our faith! How often we give in to panic because someone we love is ill, because our society is violent and our children are fearful, because the highway endangers us with reckless drivers, or the creek is rising to our back doorstep. At such times, wake us up and gently chide us, O Christ, to trust that you have not forgotten us for one moment! And then, we pray, say to the storm, "Peace. Be still!"

**MORNING**

May I be absolutely centered in your love today, fearless Savior.
*(Prayers of Intercession)*

**EVENING**

I place in your hands, fearless Savior, the times today
when I forgot to trust that you were taking care of me; and I pray
for those who need to know your care.
*(Prayers of Intercession)*

---

**WITH ALL BELIEVERS I PRAY.**
*(Pray the Prayer of Our Savior.)*

---

| **MORNING** | **EVENING** |
|---|---|
| Fill me with awe, that I too may say, "Who is this that even wind and sea obey?" Thanks be to Christ. Amen. | Fill me with peace that I may rest as trustingly as Jesus did in the boat. Thanks be to Christ. Amen. |

# June 12

*(Read Job 38:1–11)*

**MORNING**
My God, how great you are!
Surround me today with a sense of your glory.

**EVENING**
My God, how great you are!
Remind me that my perspective is not big enough.

Creator God, we read astronomers' descriptions of creation and are surprised to hear even secular scientists say that before space and time began, you existed. We have learned about the earthly eons when stone shifted, continents groaned, and seas learned their places on our planet. We are learning that ours is only one of many planets in the universe! How astounding that the biblical author, who knew so much less than we know about the world's creation, still understood so well your hand in it all. What a gift that the author expressed your perspective in such timeless poetry that three millennia and several translations later, we can still tremble in awe, like Job, before you.

**MORNING**
I thank you, astounding Creator,
for the poets of your word whom I will meet today.
*(Prayers of Intercession)*

**EVENING**
I thank you, astounding Creator, that everyone I met today is part of your plan for creation. I pray for those who don't know they are yours.
*(Prayers of Intercession)*

---

**WITH BELIEVERS ACROSS YEARS AND LANGUAGES I PRAY.**
*(Pray the Prayer of Our Savior.)*

---

**MORNING**
Be with me from the beginning of this day to the end. Thanks be to Christ. Amen.

**EVENING**
Thank you for creating rest time at the end of each day. May I now enter it in peace. Thanks be to Christ. Amen.

# June 13

*(Read 2 Corinthians 6:1–2)*

**MORNING**

God, on a day of salvation you have helped me.
Make today another such day!

**EVENING**

God, it is an acceptable time to rededicate myself to you.
Thank you for today.

It is a warm day in North American climates, a time when most schools are out, graduates have received their diplomas, Sunday school is over, and summer stretches ahead. Loving God, what makes today, or any other day, an acceptable time for your salvation? What was the right day for Paul to be converted or for the Corinthians to own their new life in Christ? What is the right day for my church to need renewal? This day! If we fail to seize the day and move into action, we may have accepted your grace in vain. A sobering thought! But then, loving God, you send another acceptable day for salvation. Will it be today? Tomorrow?

**MORNING**

What I have been waiting for the right day to do, help me do
today, O God.
*(Prayers of Intercession)*

**EVENING**

I pray that my actions show I have not accepted your grace in vain,
O God.
*(Prayers of Intercession)*

---

**WITH BELIEVERS ON EVERY ACCEPTABLE DAY, I PRAY.**
*(Pray the Prayer of Our Savior.)*

---

| **MORNING** | **EVENING** |
|---|---|
| Inviting God, remind me that my living today is not in vain, but given to you in each moment. Thanks be to Christ. Amen. | Inviting God, pull me into my rest at the end of this day, which has not been in vain. Thanks be to Christ. Amen. |

# June 14

*(Read 1 Samuel 17:32–36)*

**MORNING**

O God, you are a great God, Sender of morning sun
and evening shade, Protector of your sheep. Hold me fast today.

**EVENING**

O God, you are a great God, undaunted by challenges
from blustery warriors. May I be likewise undaunted!

We have all been charmed since childhood by the tale of David and
Goliath. The author describes in detail what Goliath wore and the
weapons he carried. Yet David takes a cool look and tells the flustered
Saul, "Let no one's heart fail because of him." Let no one's heart fail?
Please! Do not our hearts fail within us when we hear the taunts of a
secular society that sees the church as weak and outdated? Or when we
hear the taunts of any other strong enemy of the realm of heaven? God,
put your confidence in our hearts, that we may say to one another as
Saul said to David, "Go, and may God be with you."

**MORNING**

Send me out today, living God, unafraid to live,
to challenge, to dare.
*(Prayers of Intercession)*

**EVENING**

Gather me in this evening, strong Shepherd, as you gather in
all of your beloved children who hear your voice and those who
need to hear your voice.
*(Prayers of Intercession)*

**WITH ALL WHO ARE CHALLENGED, I PRAY.**
*(Pray the Prayer of Our Savior.)*

**MORNING**

Thanks! Praise! Joy! Morning has
broken, and I am whole! Thanks be
to Christ. Amen.

**EVENING**

Thanks! Praise! Joy! Evening has
fallen, and I am whole. Thanks be to
Christ. Amen.

# June 15

*(Read Psalm 107:1–3)*

**MORNING**

Astoundingly faithful God, your steadfast love has endured
to this very day. Thank you!

**EVENING**

Astoundingly faithful God, your steadfast love has carried me
through this day. Thank you!

I don't want to say so. I don't like to say so. People would look at me curiously if I walked around saying, as did the psalmist, "Let the redeemed of God say so." That's one of my failings, faithful Savior. All too often I am too timid to say, even in the assembly of the faithful, that I am one of the redeemed whom you brought from the four winds to be your people. But I am! Since the day of my baptism, I have been your redeemed and precious child, called by your name. Teach me, with all the rest of the redeemed, to say so by my life and witness and my actions for justice.

**MORNING**

I am bought for a price, saved for a purpose. Today let that
purpose be clear to me in all that I do, to all whom I meet.
*(Prayers of Intercession)*

**EVENING**

I pray tonight, dear God, for all who do not believe
themselves redeemed or redeemable.
*(Prayers of Intercession)*

**WITH THE GREAT COMPANY OF THE REDEEMED I PRAY.**

*(Pray the Prayer of Our Savior.)*

| MORNING | EVENING |
|---|---|
| O give thanks to God, who is good; whose loving-kindness lasts forever! Let it be so. Thanks be to Christ. Amen. | You redeemed me from trouble and gathered me in. Now set me at rest in your love. Thanks be to Christ. Amen. |

# June 16

*(Read Psalm 9:9–20)*

### MORNING
Sing praises to God, who dwells in Zion,
who dwells among the faithful.

### EVENING
Sing praises to God, who has lived with me all day long.

How wonderful you are, O God, who dwells among the faithful and even among the not-so-faithful. Even the psalmist long ago knew that you are not only this overwhelming God who made heaven and earth, but the indwelling God who walks with us and is mindfully present within our very selves. Teach me to cherish your presence, which I have come to know because you came to live with us in the person of Jesus, whom we call the Christ. There is no part of my life you don't know about, for you have lived it!

### MORNING
Bless me, breathe with me, think with me, love for me
where I cannot love, on this blessed day, living God.
*(Prayers of Intercession)*

### EVENING
As I look back on today, I bless you, living God, for the times
I was aware that you were living with me and directing my ways,
especially as I touched those you sent me today.
*(Prayers of Intercession)*

---

**WITH ALL YOUR BELOVED CHILDREN WHO KNOW CHRIST I PRAY.**
*(Pray the Prayer of Our Savior.)*

---

### MORNING
Thank you, God of nations, for inviting me to trust you, whose name I know. Thanks be to Christ. Amen.

### EVENING
God of past generations and those yet to come, thank you for inviting me to rest tonight in your trusting arms. Thanks be to Christ. Amen.

# June 17

*(Read Mark 4:35–36)*

**MORNING**
Precious Savior, I am grateful you are with me
in whatever storms may arise today.

**EVENING**
Precious Savior, today, like every day, was full of storms and calms.
Thank you for inviting me to trust you throughout all of them.

Those hard-rowing disciples did not seem to know whom they had with them when they climbed into their battered boats to take Jesus across the lake for a rest. Am I wise enough to recognize that I have had your Holy Spirit dwelling in me since my baptism? Am I sharp enough to recognize the new life that accompanies me and all the boats that row alongside mine? Fill me, faithful Christ, with joy and peace in believing.

**MORNING**
Make me strong in your love today and strong in giving that love
to all the hard workers who labor beside me in your vineyard.
*(Prayers of Intercession)*

**EVENING**
Jesus, you are with the weary and with those
whose work is difficult and dangerous. Thank you for seeing them,
and me, through this day.
*(Prayers of Intercession)*

---

**WITH ALL THE WEARY WHO COME TO YOU FOR REST, I PRAY.**
*(Pray the Prayer of Our Savior.)*

---

**MORNING**
I praise you today, O God, that
though I am one of many children,
you know me by name. Thanks be
to Christ. Amen.

**EVENING**
I praise you tonight, O God,
for inviting me to cross to the other
side and rest in your loving care.
Thanks be to Christ. Amen.

# June 18

*(Read Psalm 16:1–6)*

**MORNING**
Almighty God, will I act this day as though you are my God
and I have no good apart from you?

**EVENING**
Almighty God, have I been a reflection this day of the
One in whom I claim to take refuge, or have I taken upon my lips
other gods who will only multiply my sorrows?

Mighty are the idols of the world—idols that promise me wealth, prosperity, and recognition. In the gong and clang of this Internet world, how easy it is be distracted by bread that does not nourish and drink that does not quench thirst. Help me to remember that I have no good apart from you.

**MORNING**
Ever-present One, may those for whom I pray this day
know the mystery and the power of your presence.
*(Prayers of Intercession)*

**EVENING**
O God, I thank you for all who recognized you and
took refuge in you today.
*(Prayers of Intercession)*

**GOD IS OUR EVER-PRESENT STRENGTH AND HELP.**
*(Sing "How Firm a Foundation" or another familiar hymn.)*

**MORNING**
Help me not be distracted
but observant of the presence of your
Spirit in all that I do. Thanks be
to God. Amen.

**EVENING**
I end this day remembering
the signs of your presence, and I ask
that you deliver me through sleep to
the dawn of a new day. Thanks be
to God. Amen.

# June 19

*(Read Psalm 16:7–11)*

**MORNING**

Loving God, today am I ready for you to show me
the path of life that leads to your joy?

**EVENING**

Loving God, how much have I kept you present this day?
How much have I experienced you to be at my right hand?
How steadfastly have I not been moved?

Creator God, how easily I am distracted. You beckon to me, but I can
think only of my plans for the day. You speak to me, but I am smitten
by electronic images and no voices. Help to bring calm to the competing voices of our culture, that I may hear your voice and follow your
path.

**MORNING**

O Ever-present One, may you be at the right hand of those
for whom I pray, and may they know your presence.
*(Prayers of Intercession)*

**EVENING**

Creator and Inspirer, praise be to you for the joyful moments
of your presence this day.
*(Prayers of Intercession)*

GOD IS AT OUR RIGHT HAND; GOD SHALL NOT BE MOVED.
*(Sing "Bring Many Names" or another familiar hymn.)*

**MORNING**

I begin this day to seek in your
presence the path of life that leads to
joy. May you show me the way.
Thanks be to God. Amen.

**EVENING**

As I prepare for rest, I remember that
in the night you also counsel my
heart. May it be so this night, I pray.
Thanks be to God. Amen.

# June 20

*(Read Galatians 5:1, 13–18)*

**MORNING**

O Jesus, our Liberator, will I live today as one who has been set
free or one who is in bondage? Help me to make wise choices.

**EVENING**

O Jesus, our Liberator, how well did I use my freedom today?
Did I use it to care for my neighbor or to take care of myself?

How often, O Holy Comforter, do we use your freedom as an escape
from our responsibilities rather than as freedom for the fulfillment of
your two greatest commandments? Instill in us a hunger to exercise our
freedom this day as a sign of your realm blossoming in our midst. Help
us to be truly free.

**MORNING**

I pray this morning for people I know and people unknown
to me who are enslaved in all manner of ways. O Jesus, may they
experience you and the freedom you offer.
*(Prayers of Intercession)*

**EVENING**

O Jesus, our Deliverer, thank you for reminding me
of my bondage to my own prejudices and for offering me an
alternative this day.
*(Prayers of Intercession)*

---

**IN CHRIST JESUS, GOD HAS SET US FREE.**
*(Sing "Jesu, Jesu, Fill Us with Your Love" or another familiar hymn.)*

---

**MORNING**
Send me forth today with the
courage to make wiser choices than
I did yesterday. Thanks be
to God. Amen.

**EVENING**
For my misuse of freedom today,
forgive me. For the choices I must
make tomorrow, prepare me.
Now, receive me into sleep.
Thanks be to God. Amen.

# June 21

*(Read Psalm 77:1–2, 11–20)*

**MORNING**

O God, help me to perceive your footprints before me this day,
and grant that I might follow you in the ways of righteousness.

**EVENING**

O God, did I see you today when you beckoned
to me to follow you?

When you parted the waters for me, did I recognize you and give you
thanks? You are forever a comfort, almighty God, in times of desolation
and grief. As you were to Abraham, Isaac, and Moses, you make yourself available to us—eternally available. As you did with the Hebrew
people, you offer to part the seas that enslave us and bring us to that
place where our cup runneth over.

**MORNING**

Creator and Healer, may all those who cry aloud and stretch out their hands to
you this day know the calm and consolation of your presence.
*(Prayers of Intercession)*

**EVENING**

For all who called upon you and were consoled by your presence,
I give you thanks.
*(Prayers of Intercession)*

---

**GOD HEARS OUR CRIES AND ACTS TO HEAL US AND SET US FREE.**
*(Sing "God Moves in a Mysterious Way" or another familiar hymn.)*

---

| **MORNING** | **EVENING** |
|---|---|
| Should I know trouble this day, grant that I might reach out to you for your guiding presence. Thanks be to God. Amen. | As I prepare to sleep, may your unseen footprints be about me and deliver me to a new day. Thanks be to God. Amen. |

# June 22

*(Read Luke 9:51–62)*

**MORNING**

Jesus, when you call me to follow you,
where will I put you on my agenda?

**EVENING**

Jesus, what were my priorities today? In my deeds and in my
words was I a reflection of you, or did I mirror the values of my
culture and my own needs?

It is not easy to follow you, Jesus. You keep taking paths we haven't
taken. You don't allow us the comfort of safe places. We keep confronting difficult choices. You do not let us hesitate, but keep us on the
move toward Jerusalem. When we hesitate, when we look back, call us
forward. Do not leave us behind.

**MORNING**

I pray this morning, Jesus, for those who have been left behind,
consumed by their own concerns.
*(Prayers of Intercession)*

**EVENING**

I am thankful, Jesus, for those who joined you today on your on-going journey to Jerusalem.
*(Prayers of Intercession)*

---

**JESUS BIDS US COME AND JOIN THE JOURNEY TOWARD JERUSALEM.**
*(Sing "O Jesus, I Have Promised" or another familiar hymn.)*

---

**MORNING**

Today, when I tarry on my journey,
absorbed in my own needs and
concerns, rebuke me, unsettle me,
and set my eyes toward your realm.
Thanks be to God. Amen.

**EVENING**

O Jesus, bid me rest that tomorrow
I may awake refreshed and be
prepared anew to follow you.
Thanks be to God. Amen.

# June 23

*(Read 1 Kings 2:1–2, 6–14)*

**MORNING**

O God, what problems and old grudges and old hatreds will I,
like Solomon, inherit this day? Grant that I might respond
with wisdom.

**EVENING**

O God, did I act responsibly today when confronted
with the apathy, pettiness, or outright greed and hostility of others?

We inherit from those who have gone before us a tangled web of emotions and aspirations. Lest we should forget, remind us, O God, that sin casts its shadow upon all of us, whether we are King Davids or only pretenders to the throne. Grant that while we seek wholeness, we might also confer our contribution to brokenness this day.

**MORNING**

God of saints and of sinners, help me to pray this day
for those hurt, advertently or inadvertently, by my actions.
*(Prayers of Intercession)*

**EVENING**

I thank you, O God, for all who resisted evil
and who knew not vengeance or revenge this day.
*(Prayers of Intercession)*

**CALL US IN WISDOM, O GOD, THAT WE MIGHT NOT RESORT TO EVIL.**
*(Sing "Lord Jesus, Who through Forty Days" or another familiar hymn.)*

| **MORNING** | **EVENING** |
|---|---|
| Today as I inherit the inequities and injustices of the past, help me that I may act with wisdom. Thanks be to God. Amen. | Receive me now in sleep, forgive me for webs left untangled, and grant that I may act with justice and kindness in the new day to come. Thanks be to God. Amen. |

# June 24

*(Read 1 Kings 19:15–16, 19–21)*

### MORNING

All-inspiring God, how will you cast your mantle upon me today?
What will you call me to do and be?

### EVENING

All-inspiring God, have I been a reflection this day of one anointed
to proclaim your presence by all that I said and all that I did?

How many are the ways, O God, that you throw your mantle upon us
and bid us come? Sometimes we resist; sometimes we hesitate; sometimes we stall, asking to bid our kindred goodbye. But you wait upon
us and invite us to follow. Help us to be servants to you this day.

### MORNING

Hear my prayers, O God, for those not conscious
of your call. Grant that they might know you, hear you,
and follow you this day.
*(Prayers of Intercession)*

### EVENING

For all those Elishas who have experienced Elijah's cloak this day,
I give you thanks.
*(Prayers of Intercession)*

---

### GOD CHOOSES US, CALLS US, AND BIDS US FOLLOW.

*(Sing "God the Spirit, Guide, and Guardian" or another familiar hymn.)*

---

### MORNING

Lest I become too absorbed in my
daily rounds, this day help me to see
when you beckon me to follow at
moments I do not expect.
Thanks be to God. Amen.

### EVENING

Cast your cloak upon me, O God,
that I may rest, and call me forth in
service in the dawning of the new day.
Thanks be to God. Amen.

# June 25

*(Read Mark 5:21–35)*

### MORNING
God, today I trust you to deliver me from all the cares
and difficulties of this world.

### EVENING
God, I thank you for your grace that sets the seal of its amen to
the hopes and prayers of faith by saying, "So be it, and so it shall
be to thee"; and therefore, "Go in peace."

God, if only people would realize that if they reach out in faith, you
would respond to their needs and quiet their fears. They need to know
that you are the God of the impossible who makes all things possible.

### MORNING
God, today I surrender my life soul, mind, and body to you,
like the woman with the issue of blood, realizing that if only I
could touch the hem of your garment I will be made whole.
*(Prayers of Intercession)*

### EVENING
Thank you for your overwhelming goodness to me.
Give me the maturity to trust you more and more, so I can thank
you and my rest will be made perfect.
*(Prayers of Intercession)*

---

### "WHAT A MIGHTY GOD WE SERVE"
*(Pray the Prayer of Our Savior.)*

---

### MORNING
Our God, bless me with a life
that will rise and respond to your
command and rely on your wisdom
that will lead me through this day.
In Jesus' name, I pray. Amen.

### EVENING
What a comfort to lie down knowing
that the One who holds my hand
holds all my nights and tomorrows.
In Jesus' name, I pray. Amen.

# June 26

*(Read Mark 5:36–43)*

**MORNING**

Gracious God, I know that you love me no matter what my
circumstances are. Therefore, I go forth today fully armed.

**EVENING**

Gracious God, I thank you for the ability and boldness to claim
all that you have promised. I can rest in your perfect peace.

Weeping endures for a night but joy comes in the morning. Loving
God, teach your people to know that we can claim victory in you, the
one who has the power over sickness and death.

**MORNING**

Dear God, I thank you and praise you for being
the God who speaks things into being.
*(Prayers of Intercession)*

**EVENING**

Dear God, thank you for your love and patience.
*(Prayers of Intercession)*

**GOD IS ALWAYS FAITHFUL.**

*(Sing "Blessed Assurance" or another familiar hymn.)*

**MORNING**

I wake up happy in the knowledge
that I don't have to travel anywhere
but to my knees to see your presence
in life. In Jesus' name, I pray.
Amen.

**EVENING**

I thank you for inviting me to
"only believe," and by faith I believe.
I can rest knowing that everything
you promise is true. In Jesus' name,
I pray. Amen.

# June 27

*(Read Psalm 30)*

### MORNING

Dear God, I will exalt you for lifting me up, healing me,
and giving me the strength to praise you one more day.

### EVENING

Dear God, I thank you for vanquishing all my foes,
so my focus can be entirely on you and your power in my life.

O Loving God, bless the dedication of this temple (my body). Help me to remember that all that I have comes from you. Help me from getting a puffed-up ego and eliciting your anger because of my disobedience. And when you chastise me, help me to remember that you chastise those you love and your anger is only for a moment and your forgiveness is forever.

### MORNING

What a blessing to wake up knowing I am in your favor.
*(Prayers of Intercession)*

### EVENING

Parent God, I thank you for your protective spirit
that surrounds all your children.
*(Prayers of Intercession)*

### SING "GREAT IS THY FAITHFULNESS."

*(Pray the Prayer of Our Savior.)*

### MORNING

God, this morning I pray for a
spirit of humbleness, thankfulness,
and a grateful heart. In Jesus' name,
I pray. Amen.

### EVENING

Thank you for the blessings
of the day. Bring rest to my body and
soul to prepare me for tomorrow.
In Jesus' name, I pray. Amen.

# June 28

*(Read 2 Samuel 1:1, 17–27)*

### MORNING
Father-Mother God, I thank you for keeping me safe
through my trials and tribulations.

### EVENING
Father-Mother God, comfort and strengthen me in times
of grief and sorrow. Please help me keep my eyes stayed on you.

Thank you, Parent God, for showing us how David was able to forgive
and think well of Saul even after Saul tried to kill him. It reminds us of
our prayer to forgive those who trespass against us. Help us to keep
your commandment to love our enemies as David did with Saul.

### MORNING
I thank you, God, for the wisdom to understand
the lesson learned from the story of Saul and David.
*(Prayers of Intercession)*

### EVENING
Help me to be obedient and to do your will.
*(Prayers of Intercession)*

---

GOD HAS SHOWN US WHAT LOVE AND FORGIVENESS REALLY ARE
BY SENDING GOD'S ONLY BEGOTTEN SON TO DIE ON OUR BEHALF.
*(Pray the Prayer of Our Savior.)*

---

### MORNING
Help me to grow and be
strengthened by the power of love
today. In Jesus' name, I pray.
Amen.

### EVENING
Help me to cast out any grudges
that I have against anyone and to forget
as well as forgive. In Jesus' name,
I pray. Amen.

# June 29

*(Read Lamentations 3:23–27)*

**MORNING**

God, how wonderful it is to awaken to a new day
and new mercies.

**EVENING**

God, tonight as I look back and see how your mercies
and love sustained me, I say thank you.

Today we live in a world where we want instant gratification and we have a hurry-up-and-wait mentality. Let us remember that peace and salvation are found only in you. Teach us to stop, listen, and be quiet in order to hear your voice.

**MORNING**

God, remind me and impress on my heart that it is good
to wait on your salvation. Sometimes I forget that it is through you
that my salvation is guaranteed.
*(Prayers of Intercession)*

**EVENING**

God, help me to remember that by surrendering
to your perfect will, my nights will be blessed.
*(Prayers of Intercession)*

---

**OH TASTE AND SEE THAT GOD IS GOOD.**

*(Pray the Prayer of Our Savior.)*

---

**MORNING**

God, like Jeremiah I know
from personal experience about your
faithfulness in my life. In Jesus' name,
I pray. Amen.

**EVENING**

God, I pray that someone today
saw in me the promise and fulfillment
of your faithfulness. In Jesus' name,
I pray. Amen.

# June 30

*(Read Lamentations 3:28–33)*

**MORNING**

Awesome God, as I arise this morning I will reflect
on what you want from me today.

**EVENING**

Awesome God, I bask in the knowledge that you,
a compassionate God, are watching me as I sleep.

When we are disobedient, remind us that there will be chastisement, because you chastise those you love, but you also promise restoration and blessings when we repent and trust and obey.

**MORNING**

God, allow your Spirit to teach me self-control
in the face of adversity as I face a new day and new trials.
*(Prayers of Intercession)*

**EVENING**

God, thank you for being my portion and my hope.
I pray that I reflected that to some lost soul today.
*(Prayers of Intercession)*

**WHERE YOU GO, I WILL FOLLOW.**
*(Sing "Lead Me, Guide Me" or another familiar hymn.)*

**MORNING**

My prayer today is that I might
lead someone to Christ, but I know
that in order to lead I have to follow
the one true leader. In Jesus' name,
I pray. Amen.

**EVENING**

Tonight I can rest knowing
that there will be new mercies and
new blessings in the morning to
strengthen and guide me.
In Jesus' name, I pray. Amen.

# July 1

*(Read 2 Corinthians 8:7–15)*

**MORNING**

Loving God, fill my heart with love so that I might represent you
to the world as one who gives willingly of time and resources.

**EVENING**

Loving God, thank you for the Holy Spirit,
who directs my path to fulfill your plan for my life.

Creator God, today as I praise and worship you, I ask that you open the
eyes of my heart that I might discern and serve someone's need; and
that they in return will fall to their knees and thank you as the giver of
that gift.

**MORNING**

Jesus, you came to earth that I might have
eternal life with you. Thank you.
*(Prayers of Intercession)*

**EVENING**

Thank you, God, for your Word, which I hide in my heart.
It encourages me to share my resources that others will see
and also share.
*(Prayers of Intercession)*

"NOW I WANT YOU TO EXCEL ALSO IN THIS GRACIOUS MINISTRY OF GIVING. . . .
THIS IS ONE WAY TO PROVE YOUR LOVE IS REAL."

**MORNING**

Most Holy One, let me live as
your ambassador. May the world see
me as a gift and you the giver.
In Jesus' name, I pray.
Amen.

**EVENING**

God, as the door closes on this day,
I pray that you take away my pride so
that I will allow others to help me, so
they, too, can be you to the world.
Also allow me to see you when others
are helping me. In Jesus' name,
I pray. Amen.

# July 2

*(Read Mark 6:1–13)*

**MORNING**

O God, who sent Jesus to teach in his hometown synagogue,
unsettle my tendency to want things to remain as they are and to
reject those who speak your Word in my presence.

**EVENING**

O God, who sent Jesus to teach in his hometown synagogue,
let me be disturbed at my own unbelief, which was so evident in my
unwillingness to speak your name among friends and strangers today.

Astounder of the sitters in comfortable pews, may I not be like the people of the synagogue at Nazareth, the wavering disciples, and Jesus' querulous family. May I not be like those who cannot handle the amazing words of grace that come from the mouth of your Child. Help me, Liberating God, to cast out the demons of racism, sexism, and division and be a voice for unity in our cities.

**MORNING**

When the opportunity presents itself today, may I speak for you,
O God, even if others take offense at my words.
*(Prayers of Intercession)*

**EVENING**

Did I speak a word today that led people to think I uttered wisdom, O God?
*(Prayers of Intercession)*

---

*Sing or read "Won't You Let Me Be Your Servant" or another familiar hymn.*

---

| **MORNING** | **EVENING** |
|---|---|
| O God, Jesus said we would do greater things than he. Anoint me so that I may do powerful deeds today. Thanks be to Christ. Amen. | Forgive the rejection of others that I perpetrated today by not seeing you in them. May I rest knowing that you alone will never reject me or anyone else in this world. Thanks be to Christ. Amen. |

# July 3

*(Read Ezekiel 2:1–5)*

**MORNING**

Sender of prophets to rebellious people, stand me on my feet
and stand before me as I speak truth to power in my nation.

**EVENING**

Sender of prophets to rebellious people, may I know when I sleep
that your Spirit goads me whether awake or asleep.

O God, who stood Ezekiel up on his feet and sent him to the people of
Israel, send prophets to us in our nation. We know we are a rebellious
people and use your name to defend violence. We fail to see how what
we do hurts poor people in other countries struggling with their own
rebellions. We need you to confound our impudence and stubbornness.
As I watch fireworks tonight and celebrate our nation's independence
tomorrow, may it be your spirit that enters into me. May I not be dismayed but hopeful that we will be a people of God in this country.

**MORNING**

May I hear the prophetic words that may be spoken
in my presence today.
*(Prayers of Intercession)*

**EVENING**

May the martial exuberance of fireworks tonight in our nation
turn us from violence as a way to resolve differences.
*(Prayers of Intercession)*

---

*Sing or read aloud "We Would Be Building" or another familiar hymn.*

---

| **MORNING** | **EVENING** |
|---|---|
| May I not be afraid of any briers and thorns that may come to me today because I try to be your prophet. Thanks be to Christ. Amen. | Prepare me for the gatherings, events, and parties that will be part of my holiday tomorrow. Thanks be to Christ. Amen. |

# July 4

### Independence Day

*(Read Psalm 4)*

**MORNING**

O God of the earth and skies, how beautiful for spacious skies,
amber waves of grain, and the majesty of purple mountains
is this nation among nations.

**EVENING**

O God of the earth and skies, may my evening be a time of quiet
recognition that you are the God of our country, forever and ever.

I ponder your steadfast love in our world, O God, you who set before
your people in Jerusalem a place to honor your name. As I go about my
country and look at the homes that line the streets; ride the subways or
fly the airways; squint at the gleaming alabaster cities; admire the gothic
cathedrals and country churches; drive the interstate highways, the
back roads, and the festering city streets, O God, may I never forget
that all this is yours. And may I honor your name by telling all generations that we can be a city set upon a hill when we trust you.

**MORNING**

May I know myself as a citizen of the people
of the covenant brought out of Egypt.
*(Prayers of Intercession)*

**EVENING**

God, help me to remember and confess the times I forgot you
and your ways, and did not do justice to your justice.
*(Prayers of Intercession)*

*Sing or read aloud "America the Beautiful" or another familiar song.*

**MORNING**

May every word I speak today be a
word of steadfastness, love, and strong
testimony to your justice in our
nation. Thanks be to Christ. Amen.

**EVENING**

May I sleep tonight certain that you are
the God of all people everywhere.
Thanks be to Christ. Amen.

# July 5

*(Read 2 Samuel 5:1–5, 9–10)*

**MORNING**

Anointing God, anoint my ears, my eyes, and my lips today,
that I may hear your voice, see you in others, and speak good
words for you.

**EVENING**

Anointing God, may I remember tonight the good words I spoke,
confess the bad words, and be assured of your hand upon me.

God of the tribes of Israel who anointed David king, may your
strengthening hand be with me as it was with David, who served you
faithfully yet failed you miserably, who to the end of his life was still
your anointed, despite his sins. O God, I ask that the leaders of this
country and of all the world know that they can be anointed by you,
learn your ways, and staunchly do what you have set before us for the
good of all humanity. May I keep the promises I have made and be
faithful to the covenants that you have made with all people.

**MORNING**

May I know all people as my bone and flesh today.
*(Prayers of Intercession)*

**EVENING**

Dear God, what things did I do this day that broke my promise to you?
*(Prayers of Intercession)*

*Sing or read aloud "O for a Thousand Tongues to Sing" or another familiar hymn.*

**MORNING**

As I go as one anointed to be
among your people, may I speak and
act for loving justice. Thanks be
to Christ. Amen.

**EVENING**

I know, O God, that tonight
my bed is a refuge, and I seek your
blessing in my sleep, that I may rise
tomorrow anointed by the peace
you give me. Thanks be
to Christ. Amen.

# July 6

*(Read 2 Corinthians 12:2–10)*

**MORNING**

Granter of visions and thorns, may my past experiences of your
presence be daily, living reminders of your vigor in my life.

**EVENING**

Granter of visions and thorns, may I be solaced in coping with
thorns in my flesh, and may this night be a healing time for me.

O God, whose omnipotence humbles us in our boasting, I yearn that
my life may not become so preoccupied in bragging about my accomplishments and my deeds done in your name that I foil the possibilities
to be an effective witness for you. At the same time, may I not become
so despondent about my weaknesses that I am rendered incapable of
fulfilling all that I can do to love neighbors. I know that as I live in the
way of Jesus' weakness I am strong. May weaknesses, insults, hardships,
persecutions, and calamities—to me, to friends, and to all people—
work for good.

**MORNING**

Do not let me become an insufferable boaster
or complainer this day, O God.
*(Prayers of Intercession)*

**EVENING**

I thank you for the times today I focused on others
and not my own problems.
*(Prayers of Intercession)*

*Sing or read aloud "Come, O Fount of Every Blessing" or another familiar hymn.*

| **MORNING** | **EVENING** |
|---|---|
| May I not become too elated today. | May tonight be a time when my own |
| Help me to discover that I have | flesh is restored, and may my dreams |
| thorns that I have not realized. | be filled with visions of paradise. |
| Thanks be to Christ. Amen. | Thanks be to Christ. Amen. |

# July 7

*(Read Psalm 123)*

**MORNING**

My eyes look to you, O Sovereign God, for you regard
the low estate of your people, especially those who bear the scorn
of the proud and the wealthy.

**EVENING**

My eyes look to you, O Sovereign God, so that when I retire tonight
I may know that your mercy has been with me and upon the millions
of your people who suffer and are held contemptible by the rich.

Merciful God, may I be an instrument of mercy in this world, where too many people look to the hands of their masters and mistresses for whatever aid they may deign to give out. May all people be able to live out their own lives with dignity, freed from dependence on the relief of the powerful and mighty. May our nation be a gracious people, merciful in our dealings with the world and open to the independence of others.

**MORNING**

May I be an agent today to affirm the dignity
of poor people and people held in contempt.
*(Prayers of Intercession)*

**EVENING**

Cleanse me of the contemptible ways in which I behaved
today by putting others down.
*(Prayers of Intercession)*

*Sing or read aloud "In Christ There Is No East or West" or another familiar hymn.*

| **MORNING** | **EVENING** |
|---|---|
| I lift up my eyes, | May your mercy rest |
| O you who are enthroned | upon me and upon all who seek |
| in the heavens! | to be at peace this night. |
| Thanks be to Christ. | Thanks be to Christ. |
| Amen. | Amen. |

# July 8

*(Read Mark 6:1–13)*

### MORNING

Sender of your servants into the world, send me into the world
with a consuming mission to call people to repentance.

### EVENING

Sender of your servants into the world, help me to sleep this night
in the peace of knowing that I am trying to live a repentant life.

Provider of all I need to take into my life, wherever I go in this world, whether into the city or countryside, may I go as one sent upon a mission by Jesus himself to preach repentance and to cast out the demons that infest our spirits and our society. May I go without feeling the necessity to avail myself of all of the accoutrements of success, such as expensive electronic devices, lavish meals, large grants, and posh churches. Instead may I meet people face to face and speak a loving word of faith that can cast out the tormenting demons, the unclean spirits, and heal those who are sick.

### MORNING

Prepare me this day for the times when people will reject me
when I try to speak for you and be a disciple of Christ Jesus.
*(Prayers of Intercession)*

### EVENING

If I slammed a door in the face of someone today
who tried to reach out to me, forgive me.
*(Prayers of Intercession)*

---

*Sing or read aloud "Just As I Am without One Plea" or another familiar hymn.*

---

### MORNING

May I be willing to risk the displeasure of those who reject your Word. May I shake the dust off my feet and never quit because of rejection. Thanks be to Christ. Amen.

### EVENING

God of healing and controller of demons, be with me tonight, that I may rest assured that there are many in this world sent on a mission to proclaim your way. Thanks be to Christ. Amen.

# July 9

*(Read John 1:1–6)*

**MORNING**

Holy and Discerning God, how marvelous it is
to comprehend that the light of your love is never overcome.

**EVENING**

Holy and Discerning God, you have guided me this day through
a maze of confusion. Allow me now to ponder the
miracle of your presence in my life.

Divine Redeemer, I find deep assurance in the knowledge that you are the Alpha and Omega. Most importantly, you have always been there from my beginning even though I did not recognize or acknowledge your presence. This day, I want to be bathed in your light, allowing it to search the inmost recesses of my being. Cleanse me and make me more like you.

**MORNING**

Inspired by your presence, I pray for the needs and concerns of
others.
*(Prayers of Intercession)*

**EVENING**

In awe and wonder I reflect on the miracles of this day.
*(Prayers of Intercession)*

---

**WALK IN GOD'S BEAUTIFUL LIGHT. JESUS IS THE LIGHT OF THE WORLD.**
*(Pray the Prayer of Our Savior.)*

---

| **MORNING** | **EVENING** |
|---|---|
| May all who pass my way | As evening shades appear, |
| this day be blessed by your light. | may I rest, assured that your light shines |
| In Christ's name. Amen. | even in the darkness of this night. |
| | In Christ's name. Amen. |

# July 10

*(Read John 1:7–9)*

### MORNING
Loving God, you are truly a lamp unto my feet and a light unto
my path. Allow me to walk in your light this day.

### EVENING
Loving God, there is a blessed assurance that comes from knowing
that I have been following the light.

O Divine One, who came into the world to be our light, our guide, and
our direction, help me to walk in your light today. I do not know where
I am going, but I do know that you are my guide. Armed with that
knowledge, I am able to tread unknown paths and face unforeseen circumstances. Help me to walk boldly under your direction in new pathways of your service.

### MORNING
I lift up to you, Loving God, those who cannot see the light.
*(Prayers of Intercession)*

### EVENING
I thank you for all those whose path I have helped to guide this
day.
*(Prayers of Intercession)*

---

I KNOW WHO HOLDS TOMORROW, AND I KNOW WHO HOLDS MY HAND.
*(Pray the Prayer of Our Savior.)*

---

| MORNING | EVENING |
|---|---|
| This day, I will trust only in your light to guide me. In Christ's name. Amen. | I trust that all I have been able to achieve today was because you were there. In Christ's name. Amen. |

# July 11

*(Read John 1:10–14)*

**MORNING**

God, I am amazed when I ponder your greatness
in the face of our human frailties.

**EVENING**

God, today I have been painfully aware that I, so often,
have not recognized you when I have met you in my daily life.

O God, you have told us that if we receive you, you will enable us to become your children. Help me today to receive you anew, that my life may be an example of your love. Remind me that I am born of you and thus am a new creation.

**MORNING**

For all those who need the power of your presence, I pray.
*(Prayers of Intercession)*

**EVENING**

I thank you today for an infusion of your divine power.
*(Prayers of Intercession)*

**I PRAY AS YOU TAUGHT YOUR DISCIPLES TO PRAY.**
*(Pray the Prayer of Our Savior.)*

**MORNING**
Let me go forth into the day
empowered to be one of your own.
In Christ's name. Amen.

**EVENING**
Tonight, dear God, allow me
a time to rest and renew my spirit
for tomorrow's journey.
In Christ's name. Amen.

# July 12

*(Read John 1:15–18)*

**MORNING**

O God, I want to be a witness for you in all situations.

**EVENING**

O God, your grace has been an abiding presence to me this day.

Redeemer, you have given us both grace and truth to abide with us and to keep us. The contradictions of our lives mandate that we need your grace. The falsehood of who we are requires that we be confronted daily by your truths. Allow me to be bathed in the profundity of your presence. May I be cleansed by your goodness.

**MORNING**

Loving God, your grace is sufficient for all of our needs.
*(Prayers of Intercession)*

**EVENING**

As I reflect on this day, I am astounded by your grace in my life.
*(Prayers of Intercession)*

---

**REDEEMING LOVE HAS BEEN MY THEME AND SHALL BE UNTIL I DIE.**
*(Pray the Prayer of Our Savior.)*

---

**MORNING**
Move me to new heights
of your truth this day.
In Christ's name.
Amen.

**EVENING**
I have been abundantly blessed
by your grace this day. I give you
thanks and praise.
In Christ's name.
Amen.

# July 13

*(Read Psalm 139:12)*

**MORNING**

Caring God, there is no hiding place from your divine gaze.
Help me to live as if I know that you are watching.

**EVENING**

Caring God, you have been with me throughout this day
in every situation. I pause to thank you for the fullness
of your presence in my life.

How awesome are the words that the psalmist speaks of you, O God.
Your wisdom is unfathomable. I cannot keep any part of myself hidden
from you. Empower me, Eternal One, by your Spirit, to be free to live
in the fullness of all that you have created me to be. Remind me always
that, wherever I am, you are with me.

**MORNING**

This day I will disclose the full contents
of my heart to you, Loving God.
*(Prayers of Intercession)*

**EVENING**

This day has been a blessing to me.
Let me count the ways . . .
*(Prayers of Intercession)*

---

**BEING IN YOUR PRESENCE CHALLENGES ME TO GROW IN MY RELATIONSHIP WITH YOU.**
*(Pray the Prayer of Our Savior.)*

---

**EVENING**

With you, I can do all things.
Without you, nothing that I do
is important. Help me to stay
the course. In Christ's name.
Amen.

**MORNING**

May I revere your presence in my life.
In Christ's name. Amen.

# July 14

*(Read Psalm 139:13–16)*

**MORNING**

O God, it is a marvelous thing to know that you have
formed me with your own hands.

**EVENING**

O God, how great it is to know that you have known me
before I knew myself.

OIn the midst of life's complexities, I pause to reflect on the wonder of
your creation, O God. When I doubt myself, I am surprised by what
you are able to do through me. I realize that my body is your greatest
natural resource. I want to protect it and perfect it for your service. Be
my source and my strength, my guide and my protection.

**MORNING**

I offer prayers for the needs of others.
*(Prayers of Intercession)*

**EVENING**

As I lift up to you my evening prayers,
may I be immersed in your Spirit.
*(Prayers of Intercession)*

I AM MADE IN THE IMAGE OF GOD.
*(Pray the Prayer of Our Savior.)*

| MORNING | EVENING |
|---|---|
| I am delighted by the opportunity to be in your service, In Christ's name. Amen. | My hope is to have been used by you this day. In Christ's name. Amen. |

# July 15

*(Read Psalm 139:17–20)*

**MORNING**

O God, make my thoughts more like your thoughts
and my words more like your words this day.

**EVENING**

O God, I have opened myself to you in work and worship.
Grant that all that I have done has been pleasing in your sight.

Creator God, sometimes we find ourselves in the company of those who do not know you and who do not honor your name. This day, I will be in the company of your people. Help me to recognize and rejoice in the difference and to know that our times of mountaintop worship are preparation for our journey to the valley.

**MORNING**

Rejoicing in your greatness, I pray for the needs of others.
*(Prayers of Intercession)*

**EVENING**

I have been inspired by your word this day.
I thank you for your grace and goodness.
*(Prayers of Intercession)*

---

**YOUR WORD IS A STRONG TOWER INTO WHICH I MAY RUN FOR SAFETY.**
*(Pray the Prayer of Our Savior.)*

---

| **MORNING** | **EVENING** |
|---|---|
| I hasten now to worship your name. In Christ's name. Amen. | All good things around me have come from your hand. I respond in humble gratitude. In Christ's name. Amen. |

# July 16

*(Read Colossians 1:15–28)*

### MORNING
Empowering God, I am on a quest, continually seeking answers
to innumerable questions about life and living.
How fruitless this quest often seems.

### EVENING
Empowering God, I have so many unanswered questions
about life and ask your patience with me.

Purposeful God, life has a purpose. And in the living of it, I often question. Searching for its purpose has brought me to the realization that answers to my questions are not what is most important. What is infinitely more important to my well-being is my experience of a centeredness in Christ. A Christ centeredness frees me from pursuing fruitless questioning and frees me to accept what I have decided is inexplicable. This enables me to embrace love, joy, and a passion for living, despite suffering pain and all manifestations of evil.

### MORNING
Holy God, when I experience Christ risen, I know that the
God among us who walked on earth knows the pain of human suffering.
I am then able to embrace life in the midst of setbacks and difficulties.
*(Prayers of Intercession)*

### EVENING
Invisible God, revealed in Christ Jesus, when I am centered in you, resting
in your presence, you infuse me with a serenity that quiets my feverish search.
*(Prayers of Intercession)*

---

**WHAT JOY TO DISCOVER THAT IN CHRIST ALL THE FULLNESS OF GOD
IS MADE AVAILABLE TO US!**

---

### MORNING
I seek the comfort, serenity, and
reassurance that only your presence can
provide. In the name of the life-changing
Christ. Amen.

### EVENING
There is no meaning to my life
apart from you, Divine One. In the
name of the life-changing Christ.
Amen.

# July 17

*(Read Luke 10:38–42)*

**MORNING**

Gracious, living God, I greet this day, fresh with new possibilities.
It offers me an opportunity for renewing my commitment to being your disciple.

**EVENING**

Gracious, living God, thank you for the gift of this day
and its opportunities for discipleship.

Calming God, the world in which I live rewards noise and activity. The phone rings, others need my assistance, and job responsibilities demand my presence. You have given me this day, O Holy One, with its many demands competing for my attention. You call for my undivided attention, but your call is not the loudest. In the midst of the noise of these competing demands, I must make a choice. Only the stillness that comes from centering on you will quiet this frenetic pace, so that I may discern your voice and hear your guidance.

**MORNING**

Listening God, I turn to you for guidance and discernment as to
what is "the better part" for me today.
*(Prayers of Intercession)*

**EVENING**

Holy One, I give you thanks and praise for the opportunities to be
your disciple during the day that has passed. Forgive me for the
times when I failed to discern your call.
*(Prayers of Intercession)*

---

**TODAY I WILL REEVALUATE MY PRIORITIES AND THE INFLUENCES
ON MY THOUGHTS AND TIME.**

---

**MORNING**

Open my heart to hear and receive
these words of the Scriptures with the
freshness and curiosity of a child and
the eagerness of an earnest seeker of
the Word. In the name of the
life-changing Christ. Amen.

**EVENING**

Bless me as I, your disciple,
now turn to renewing rest and sleep.
In the name of the life-changing
Christ. Amen.

# July 18

*(Read Amos 8:1–12)*

### MORNING
God, you are hard on me. I fear your silence and judgment.

### EVENING
God, I hunger for your presence to guide and encourage me.

The ringing of bells may herald an occasion for rejoicing or one of doom. So it is when I turn to your message, O God. I want it to be pealing the good news that you are a God of love who forgives my sins, not a God of judgment. When the message being tolled is that of frightful judgment, I recognize that it is deserved—deserved because of my complicity in accepting unjust and oppressive conditions and in neglecting to speak out against injustices. This warning of judgment is dreadful.

### MORNING
God who cannot be fully comprehended, you always expect justice
and righteousness from your people.
*(Prayers of Intercession)*

### EVENING
God of total and complete judgment, you stand
in solidarity with those who are treated with contempt and malice,
with the poor and the oppressed. Where am I?
*(Prayers of Intercession)*

---

**YES, I WANT TO PARTICIPATE IN YOUR DIVINE PLAN OF JUSTICE FOR ALL.**

---

### MORNING
My complacency is disturbed by
the clanging warning that I must
confront an awful and awe-full hour
of judgment. In the name of the
life-changing Christ. Amen.

### EVENING
I have committed my life
to following you, but I must renew
that commitment daily. In the name
of the life-changing Christ.
Amen.

# July 19

*(Read Psalm 15)*

**MORNING**

God of wisdom, I pause to discern your way among competing
claims for my allegiance and my time. Only you are true.
Only you are deserving of my devotion.

**EVENING**

God of wisdom, guide me in my quest to be your follower.
I thirst for your righteousness in my life.

I am seeking guidance to follow your ways, O God. The directions seem
murky, unclear. You say to love you and to love my neighbor as myself. But
sometimes—often—I fail and find the mote in someone else's eye when
there is a log in mine. I forget your commandments in the cacophony of
the demands and distractions of everyday life. In the comfort of my life, it
is easy to lose sight of my neighbors, persons who live in continual want
and distress. Faithful God, have mercy on me. I ask your forgiveness.

**MORNING**

You show me, O God, what it means to be a righteous person,
a follower of your ways. Guide my steps that I may speak
and live according to your truth.
*(Prayers of Intercession)*

**EVENING**

Gracious, loving, caring God, guide my steps,
that I may speak and live according to your truth.
*(Prayers of Intercession)*

IT IS DIFFICULT TO LIVE ACCORDING TO GOD'S WAYS IN AN UN-GODLY WORLD.

**MORNING**

Guide my steps in seeking
the well-being of all other persons,
my neighbors near and far, in this
world of diversity. In the name of
the life-changing Christ. Amen.

**EVENING**

May your righteousness and your
righteous people infiltrate our global
city, bringing to all love and goodwill.
In the name of the life-changing
Christ. Amen.

# July 20

*(Read Genesis 18:1–10a)*

**MORNING**

God who calls us, the status quo seems so comfortable.
Then you burst in, startling me with new creative prospects.
My preconceived notions of self are called into question.
You instruct me to shake up my life. Is that good news?

**EVENING**

God who calls us, infuse me with courage if I am to confront
the startling news that fruitfulness can replace the barrenness
with which I had grown content.

Abundant, giving God, I have become comfortable with a certain non-productivity, which I have accepted as normal and to which I am accustomed. Now a promise of creativity challenges and startles me. I hear your challenge that I am capable of giving birth in a totally new way. The prospect is both scary and exciting. Can I, will I allow myself to relinquish the familiar in order to embrace the promise of a new possibility?

**MORNING**

You, surprising God, have disclosed the potential for new life.
This revelation leaves me feeling very vulnerable.
What does this mean for my future?
*(Prayers of Intercession)*

**EVENING**

Ingenious God, my preconceptions are shaken, shattered.
You dare me to change.
*(Prayers of Intercession)*

---

**I WILL STEP OUT IN FAITH AND CREATE!**

---

| MORNING | EVENING |
|---|---|
| The newness and challenge of this day bring the delight that you, God, and I are collaborating in a new adventure. In the name of the life-changing Christ. Amen. | Praise be to you, O Christ, for revealing the possibility of fruitfulness and the likelihood of new beginnings. Is anything too hard for me with God? In the name of the life-changing Christ. Amen. |

# July 21

*(Read Genesis 18:1–10a; Amos 8:1–12; Luke 10:38–42)*

### MORNING
Timeless God, praise to you for your Scripture that disturbs
and challenges, sustains and nurtures me. It connects me
with people of faith from earlier times.

### EVENING
Timeless God, praise to you for your Word,
which disturbs and challenges, sustains and nurtures me.

Scripture serves as an icon through which I experience you, Creator
God, Jesus Christ, and the Holy Spirit. Amazingly, I recognize people I
know or know about in the lives of Mary, Martha, Abraham, Sarah, and
the prophet Amos. They come alive when they confront the challenge
to welcome you and your incredible message. They come alive when
they respond to injustice in a world where the powerless and the oppressed suffer, and when they are faced with determining what is "the
better part." This, too, is our dilemma.

### MORNING
God who calls us into relationship, I give praise to you.
The Word lived out in the lives of our spiritual ancestors
is alive in people today.
*(Prayers of Intercession)*

### EVENING
Holy Deliverer, I praise you for the wonderful stories in the Scriptures.
*(Prayers of Intercession)*

---

SCRIPTURE IS A VEHICLE FOR DEVELOPING A RIGHT RELATIONSHIP
WITH GOD AND GOD'S PEOPLE.

---

### MORNING
May my mind be open to your Word.
In the name of the life-changing
Christ. Amen.

### EVENING
Praise to you, O Holy One,
for the inspiration and challenge of
your Scriptures. In the name of
the life-changing Christ. Amen.

# July 22

*(Read Genesis 18:1–10a)*

### MORNING
Welcoming God, what persons with new ideas and insights
may come my way if I am receptive? I struggle with being surprised
by you and those who come in your name.

### EVENING
Welcoming God, help me to show hospitality to your surprises.

God, you challenge me to openness by treating each person sent by you
with hospitality and respect. To toss aside my plans to be hospitable to
others—to stop and share words of welcome and a listening ear, to offer
a cold drink and a comfortable chair to everyone—can be really upsetting.
Then, in addition, when I am confronted with questioning of my
ideas and insights, I'm not sure that I wish to receive your message.

### MORNING
God, how bewildering it is to be hospitable.
Open my closed mind to be what you want me to be, and
open my arms to be welcoming to all persons.
*(Prayers of Intercession)*

### EVENING
Holy God, I thank you for all the ways I have been
offered hospitality. I am astonished to have found myself the
welcomed and honored guest.
*(Prayers of Intercession)*

---

**HAVE YOU COME MY WAY BEFORE AND I HAVE NOT KNOWN?
HAVE YOU SPOKEN WHEN I WAS NOT READY TO HEAR?**

---

### MORNING
I will be open to being surprised
and amazed. In the name of the
life-changing Christ. Amen.

### EVENING
It is with a sense of contentment and
joy that I approach the coming night
of rest. You, hospitable God, make me
feel welcomed and secure. In the name
of the life-changing Christ. Amen.

# July 23

*(Read Psalm 85:1–7)*

### MORNING
Loving God, I give to you this day,
for you are the God of my salvation.

### EVENING
Loving God, as always, you were kind to me as I lived my day.
Thank you for your steadfast love.

Loving God, in times of difficulty I always remember to turn to you for help. But when life is comfortable, I am easily distracted by other pursuits, and I forget you. How foolish I am; but you are full of love, as evident in giving us Jesus Christ, our Savior, to show me the way back to your love. Forgive my ingratitude for your love. Revive me again.

### MORNING
This day will present opportunities to celebrate your steadfast love
and salvation. Open my eyes that I might see signs of your love.
*(Prayers of Intercession)*

### EVENING
Your steadfast love and salvation graced this day, a day I was
privileged to have lived. I have much for which to be thankful.
*(Prayers of Intercession)*

---

### WE BELONG TO GOD. REJOICE IN GOD'S LOVE.
*(Sing "I Am Yours, O Lord" or another familiar hymn.)*

---

### MORNING
It is with eagerness that I
look forward to this day, for in it I
will experience your restoring
presence, which always leads me closer
to you. Glory be to Christ.
Amen.

### EVENING
Now I can rest in blessed peace,
for today I have seen your love,
experienced your forgiveness, and
been revived by your Spirit.
Glory be to Christ.
Amen.

# July 24

*(Read Psalm 85:8–13)*

**MORNING**

Saving God, I turn my heart to you; I long to hear your voice,
for the words you speak are words of peace.

**EVENING**

Good God, you have given to me today what is good:
your steadfast love and faithfulness. Thank you.

Loving God, certain things are important to you: love, faithfulness, righteousness, and peace. They are important to you because they are qualities that describe who you are. Help me to embrace and love these same things, as Jesus Christ, our Savior, showed us to do, that I might live closely with you now and always.

**MORNING**

Good God, I look to you to give me this day what is good:
your steadfast love and faithfulness. Hear my prayers.
*(Prayers of Intercession)*

**EVENING**

Your faithfulness sprang up all around me today and is springing
up even now. Hear my prayers, faithful God.
*(Prayers of Intercession)*

---

**GOD IS A GOD OF JUSTICE AND PEACE.**

*(Sing "O for a World" or another familiar hymn.)*

---

**MORNING**

As I walk through my day,
help me to look down and notice
faithfulness springing from the
ground, and to look up and see
righteousness looking down upon
your creation. Glory be to Christ.
Amen.

**EVENING**

O God, I end my day with joy,
for today I have seen love and
faithfulness meet; I have seen righteousness and peace kiss each other;
and I have heard your voice of peace.
Glory be to Christ. Amen.

# July 25

*(Read Luke 11:1–4)*

### MORNING

Providential God, I can pray; I can talk with you.
You desire to hear my voice as I speak with you in prayer.
What joy!

### EVENING

Providential God, here I am, thankful for the signs of your realm
I have experienced today.

God in heaven, you have taken care of the details of our lives, even seeing to it that we will have instructions for how to pray. May my life be formed by the prayer our Savior taught. May I learn from that prayer to praise your name, to yearn for your realm, and to trust in your gracious generosity.

### MORNING

Heavenly God, there is no aspect of my life for which you are not
concerned. Hear my prayer for such things as daily bread and
strength in temptation.
*(Prayers of Intercession)*

### EVENING

Giving God, you supply my needs, even the forgiveness of my sins.
I now desire to forgive those who have sinned against me.
*(Prayers of Intercession)*

---

### GOD HEARS US WHEN WE PRAY.

*(Sing "Prayer Is the Soul's Sincere Desire" or another familiar hymn.)*

---

### MORNING

God who graces my life with good things, I now set forth on this day you have given, knowing that my daily bread will be provided. Glory be to Christ. Amen.

### EVENING

You have given me signs of your heavenly realm today: food, reconciliation, and strength in trial. I desire nothing but to know the joy of resting in your gracious love. Glory be to Christ. Amen.

---

# July 26

*(Read Luke 11:5–8)*

### MORNING

God, you are my Friend, and day after day as I come to you
in prayer, you are always willing to listen. Thank you.

### EVENING

God, you have been with me today, listening to my prayers.
What a blessing to have such a Friend as you.

God, what a good Friend you are. I can talk with you anytime, and you
will gladly listen to me. If there is any lack of persistence, it is not on
your part, for you are always willing to listen. Any lack of persistence is
my own for not having taken you up on your offer to talk with you. But
now, here I am, and I know you are listening.

### MORNING

I know I am not bothering you, God, for you are always ready
to listen. In your mercy, hear my prayers.
*(Prayers of Intercession)*

### EVENING

You know my needs better than I do, loving God. As I speak
with you, let me know that you have cared for all my needs.
*(Prayers of Intercession)*

---

### JESUS IS OUR FRIEND, ALWAYS READY TO LISTEN.

*(Sing "What a Friend We Have in Jesus" or another familiar hymn.)*

---

### MORNING

During this day, help me
to remember to talk with you in
prayer. Glory be to Christ.
Amen.

### EVENING

Even at midnight, I can come
to you in prayer, and you are not
bothered by my persistence.
What love! What grace!
Glory be to Christ. Amen.

# July 27

*(Read Luke 11:9–13)*

**MORNING**

Generous God, today I will be searching, seeking,
and knocking for your blessings.

**EVENING**

Generous God, I saw them! I saw blessings all around me.
Some were subtle, others obvious, but all of them were from you!

Heavenly God, help me to ask only for what will lead me to love you more. Guide me to search only for the things that will bring me closer to you. Direct me to inquire only about the things of heaven so that I will better know you. Give me your Holy Spirit. That is all I ask for; I need nothing else.

**MORNING**

I am ready to ask, seek, and knock. Help me to trust
in your gentle care, believing in your desire to give me what is good.
*(Prayers of Intercession)*

**EVENING**

I have not finished asking, seeking, and knocking.
I desire more of your presence, for what I have experienced of your
presence today has given me life. Hear my prayers.
*(Prayers of Intercession)*

**IN THIS MOMENT, IN THIS PLACE, GOD IS WITH ME.**
*(Sing "In Solitude" or another familiar hymn.)*

**MORNING**

The day ahead of me is filled not with snakes or scorpions, but with the Holy Spirit. How gracious you are, O God! Glory be to Christ. Amen.

**EVENING**

Can it be that the Holy Spirit lives within me? Yes, the Holy Spirit dwells within. Grace my night, O God, as you have graced my day with the presence of your Holy Spirit. Glory be to Christ. Amen.

# July 28

*(Read Hosea 1:2–10)*

**MORNING**

God of Israel, I humbly come to you this day.
Enable me to hear your voice above all the distracting voices
of this world.

**EVENING**

God of Israel, here I am, without pretense,
trusting only in your unfailing compassion.

God, sometimes you have every right to be upset and angry with your people. We too often think only of ourselves and neglect you and our neighbors. I know I do. But because you are compassionate, you never remain angry; you always offer hope and continue to call us your people, of which I am one by the goodness of your tender mercies.

**MORNING**

Hope—I could not live without it. So it is with hope
in your unfailing love that I now make my requests to you.
Hear my hope-filled prayers.
*(Prayers of Intercession)*

**EVENING**

Yes, God, I neglected you today. I have sinned.
Hear my confession. And in turn, let me hear your words
of acceptance and forgiveness.
*(Prayers of Intercession)*

---

**I AM A CHILD OF THE LIVING GOD.**

*(Sing "Like a Mother Who Has Borne Us" or another familiar hymn.)*

---

**MORNING**

Living God, help me to remember
you today and to serve you by serving
my neighbor. I rejoice in the
knowledge that you will not
forget me. Glory be to Christ.
Amen.

**EVENING**

Thank you, living God,
for being faithful to me today.
Help me to always be faithful to you,
even in my dreams.
Glory be to Christ.
Amen.

# July 29

*(Read Colossians 2:6–15)*

**MORNING**

O Savior, I have begun a new day, full of the promise of new life,
awaiting the unfolding of a day filled with the presence of God.

**EVENING**

O Savior, there were moments today when I was tempted to trust
in myself and my wisdom. But here I am, trusting in you.

God of life, I thank you for the life you have given me. I do not live this life alone; I live with you. What a glorious thing it is to have been buried with Christ in my baptism. And what a wonderful thing, almost too wonderful to behold, to have been raised to new life with Jesus through that same baptism. Thank you for life.

**MORNING**

Jesus, I am joined to you in faith; you are the Ruler of my life.
Hear the prayers I now offer to you in faith,
believing that you will hear them.
*(Prayers of Intercession)*

**EVENING**

Some of this day needs erasing, forgiving God.
Forgive all my trespasses, once again, for I am yours;
you have claimed me in baptism.
*(Prayers of Intercession)*

**I AM ALIVE; I AM BAPTIZED.**

*(Sing "What Ruler Wades through Murky Streams" or another familiar hymn.)*

**MORNING**

Nothing this day will be able
to separate me from you, for I am
alive in you and you are alive in me.
Glory be to Christ. Amen.

**EVENING**

Thank you for this day in which
I have learned to trust even more in
your power. Glory be to Christ.
Amen.

# July 30

*(Read Genesis 29:15–28)*

**MORNING**

Creator, Sustainer, Redeemer, as I open my eyes to the sunlight coming
through my window, keep me ever mindful that I must do only those things
that are pleasing in your sight. I will seek to obey your will at all times.

**EVENING**

Creator, Sustainer, Redeemer, as I close my eyes, I ask for forgiveness
for anything I did today that was not pleasing in your sight. I ask for the peace
that comes from knowing that you always listen to my prayers.

God, you have taught us that patience is a virtue, and each day we feel
your patient love. As Jacob sought Rachel as his love, he remained patient for seven years, only to learn that as his love for Rachel was great,
greater must be his patience. There are times in our lives when we must
exercise great patience. Omnipresent God, only the blessed knowledge
and memory that you have bestowed on us through your patient love
can sustain us. It will bring us to the prayerful conclusion that, without
you, we would be nowhere. Gracious God, all praises be to you!

**MORNING**

Loving God, as I bow my head and lift my heart to you, I implore you to give
me the sustenance so necessary to carry the burdens of those I love.

*(Prayers of Intercession)*

**EVENING**

God, as I kneel before you, help me to be humbled by your healing grace, which I
saw in the individuals who crossed my path today. With renewed patience I pray.

*(Prayers of Intercession)*

**MAY YOUR MERCY AND YOUR GRACE ALWAYS BE PRESENT.**

*(Pray the Prayer of Our Savior.)*

**MORNING**

Loving others and celebrating the joy
that they bring will keep me smiling,
for I am assured that your Spirit will be
present. In Jesus' name I pray. Amen.

**EVENING**

Yes, here I am again, God, knocking at
your door of love, believing as I do that
you will beckon me to enter. Thank
you. In Jesus' name I pray. Amen.

# July 31

*(Read Psalm 105:1–11)*

**MORNING**

Holy One, Maker of heaven and earth, I count it a blessing to awaken with sound mind and body, eager to do your will. Help me to do so with exuberance.

**EVENING**

Holy One, my sound mind and body were tested today,
so I called on your strength and you granted it to me. Thank you.

Dear God, every day we should say, "Thank you for your wondrous works in our lives!" As we look back through the ages on the story of your eternal faithfulness, we see how when Abraham and Isaac and Jacob sought you, you were always there. We thank you, Savior God, for surrounding our ancestors, thereby enabling us to stand tall today. Our gratitude is unending, and so we continually give thanks for your endless giving. We are truly blessed, and we should give your name the praise.

**MORNING**

On this day, help me to appreciate the sights and sounds
that you have placed in this world to remind me of your presence.
*(Prayers of Intercession)*

**EVENING**

Dear God, my cup runs over. Grant me the wisdom
to see how I can help fill the cups of others.
*(Prayers of Intercession)*

**MAKE ME A BLESSING AS I PRAY.**

*(Pray the Prayer of Our Savior.)*

| **MORNING** | **EVENING** |
|---|---|
| Yes, God, here I am again, seeking your strength to buttress me as I attempt to conquer yet another day by doing your will. I ask this prayer in Jesus' name. Amen. | Now, dear God, quiet my mind and still my body as I lie down to sleep with your faithfulness as my cover. I ask this prayer in Jesus' name. Amen. |

# August 1

*(Read 1 Kings 3:5–12)*

**MORNING**

All-wise God, I awaken this morning wishing to be bathed
in your wisdom as I embark upon another day.

**EVENING**

All-wise God, as the night darkens, I am reminded of how
I have been blessed to have my spirit lightened by your presence
with me today. Thank you.

God, Solomon had the nerve to ask, and you graciously granted his request and bestowed wisdom upon him. What a bold request; what an awesome challenge you afforded to Solomon and to us! Loving God, as we grow in your grace and receive more wisdom, we should also pray for more guidance to use that wisdom justly. We should follow Solomon's example and then boldly step out, ever praying that your will be done.

**MORNING**

Grant us wisdom for our journey,
so that we can witness as worthy servants.
*(Prayers of Intercession)*

**EVENING**

Grant us courage to stand reminding others
of how great you are and how overjoyed we are to be servants,
called to do your bidding.
*(Prayers of Intercession)*

---

**LEAD US AS WE PRAY.**
*(Pray the Prayer of Our Savior.)*

---

**MORNING**

Giver of all good and gracious gifts,
I eagerly await your presence and a
new word in which to step out today.
In my Savior's name I pray. Amen.

**EVENING**

My, what a blessing to call
your name and to be known personally by a great and just God. In my
Savior's name I pray. Amen.

# August 2

*(Read Psalm 119:129–136)*

### MORNING

Worthy One, Giver of all good and perfect gifts, joy fills my heart
this morning as I ponder the gifts with which I have awakened—
touch, taste, smell, sound, and sight. I celebrate anew your goodness.

### EVENING

Worthy One, today I jumped over many a hurdle,
buttressed by your everlasting and enduring strength.

When we look up in wonder at how just and fair you are, Creator God,
we become as little children, grateful for so loving a parent. Let us look
to you to feed us, mold us, guide us, use us, and order our steps, for we
are out here on your Word. We know that you will rescue us from the
evils that beset the world and anchor us in your truth. God, in that way
we will become a beacon for others, as your light shines through us. As
we cry out for you to shoulder our burdens, God, please shield us from
harm and look down on us in love.

### MORNING

I beseech you, O God, to rain down blessings on needy families
everywhere today. Give them continual hope in their hunger for you.
*(Prayers of Intercession)*

### EVENING

I beseech you, O God, to rain down blessings on my family
as they retire from a troubled day.
*(Prayers of Intercession)*

---

**WE MUST PAUSE NOW TO PRAY.**
*(Pray the Prayer of Our Savior.)*

---

### MORNING

It is time now to begin anew with
energy and expectancy, dear God.
Go with me as I approach another day.
Thanks be to Christ. Amen.

### EVENING

With energy low and enthusiasm
waning, help me to be silent and to
hear your still, small voice.
Thanks be to Christ. Amen.

\*OPENING HYMN NO. 347 "Let Us Talents & Tongues Employ"

\*INVOCATION
**Catch us, O God, in our aimless scurrying from you and
others and hold us in this Lenten season. Hold our hearts
to the beat of your grace and create in us a resting place,
a kneeling place, a tiptoe place where we can listen for your
whispered summons and be attentive to your healing love.
In the name of the Holy One of Nazareth. Amen.**

\*PRAYER RESPONSE NO. 772 "Nada te Turbe"

ANTHEM "When Jesus Wept"

COMMUNION OF THE LORD'S SUPPER
Invitation to the Table
Hymn No. 330 "Let Us Break Bread Together"
Words of Institution and Prayer of Consecration
Sharing the Bread and Cup (at the table, starting from the front)
Prayer of Thanksgiving
**All: We thank you, God, for abundant gifts given: for
the bread of grace and the cup of joy, for our life together
and a spirit to do the work of love and justice. Refreshed
and nourished at your table, may we be the body of Christ
in the world. Our Father, who art in heaven, hallowed
be Thy name. Thy kingdom come. Thy will be done on
earth as it is in heaven. Give us this day our daily bread.
And forgive us our debts, as we forgive our debtors.
And lead us not into temptation, but deliver us from evil.
For Thine is the kingdom, and the power, and the glory
forever. Amen.**

\*PASSING OF THE PEACE, each to your neighbor
**Saying:** The Lord's peace be with you.
**Replying:** And with you, also.

SCRIPTURE Psalm 25:1-10 Pg. 502
\*Mark 1:12-15 Pg. 35

# Meridian United Church of Christ

*Serving the Community for 130 Years*

Janet Matthews, Interim Pastor
Oralee Stiles, Pastoral Care Associate
Greta Pedersen, Coordinator of Music
Gil Seeley, Choir Director
Kate Tolan, Choir Accompanist

### March 1, 2009
### First Sunday in Lent

THE ORDER OF WORSHIP
(*indicates you are invited to stand)

PRELUDE    Hymn Sing - #186 "Dust & Ashes" -
#223 "What Wondrous Love" - #772 "Nada te Turbe"

WORDS OF WELCOME -   Please sign the friendship book

ANNOUNCEMENTS

INTROIT    "Said Judas to Mary"    (# 210 in hymnal)

*CALL TO WORSHIP
Leader:  Lent is a homecoming.
**People:  Home from weary years,**
Leader:  Home to calm our fears,
People:  Home to dry our tears.
**Leader:  Lent is a homecoming,**
People:  Home to remember our name,
**Leader:  Home to a warm embrace,**
People:  Home to a hopeful place,
**Leader:  Home with Christ, who is one with our journeying.**
People:  Home to prepare again for the last days of the earthly
ministry of Jesus.

# August 3

*(Read Romans 8:26–39)*

**MORNING**

Gracious and loving God, thank you for awakening me and for knowing
my needs as I stretch to meet another day. I don't know what is ahead
of me, but I do know that you are in charge, so I have no fear.

**EVENING**

Gracious and loving God, keep me leaning on your
everlasting arms as I surrender the night to you, faithfully praying
for rest after a blessed yet busy day.

God, your living Spirit falls afresh on us as we come before your throne
once again. May your Holy Spirit anoint our hearts as we trust that all
things that happen to us are for our good. We trust you know that
nothing can separate us from your love. Even when we are unsure, we
merit your love; we are comforted that your love for us never fails. God,
we pray that you will help us to show our love to those whom you love
and for whom you sent your child, Jesus.

**MORNING**

As I move through this day, I shall praise your holy name for loving me. I pray that
your goodness and mercy will continue to surround me. Grant me understanding.

*(Prayers of Intercession)*

**EVENING**

As the evening draws to a close, let me feel your love and grant me
the peace of your closeness.

*(Prayers of Intercession)*

AND NOW I GIVE MY HEART TO YOU, BELIEVING EVER MORE
IN THE PRAYER YOU TAUGHT YOUR DISCIPLES.
*(Pray the Prayer of Our Savior.)*

| **MORNING** | **EVENING** |
|---|---|
| I ask for a closer walk with you today, | May my heart rest satisfied with |
| to draw me nearer to your Holy Spirit | how wonderfully you have blessed me. |
| as I meet my fellow travelers on this | I pray that my night's sleep may be |
| journey of life. In Jesus' name. Amen. | rejuvenating. In Jesus' name. Amen. |

## August 4

*(Read Matthew 13:31–33)*

**MORNING**

Just and righteous God, I come as an eager learner to
understand your way. Teach me, O blessed Savior, teach me.

**EVENING**

Just and righteous God, I come, having learned enough today
to fill only a mustard seed. Yet I know how blessed I am,
and I shall rest in comfort with that thought.

Joy, joy, joy envelops our souls as we contemplate your Word. We know
that the lessons you teach us are designed to create in us an understanding that we must share with the world. Holy God, you pave the
way for us out of the wilderness of darkness. Renewing God, you teach
us that we can start with a tiny mustard seed and begin on the road to
building a realm, so others who see us bursting with your brightness
will be inspired to join us on the road. The majesty of the thought of a
tiny mustard seed becoming a magnificent tree inspires our imagination
as we visualize those who will stand together for Jesus Christ. As we
learn your Word, then we can lead the way.

**MORNING**

Ever-present God, help my unbelief and fortify me with your Word.
*(Prayers of Intercession)*

**EVENING**

I needed to be and I felt fortified today. For this, I gratefully say thank you.
*(Prayers of Intercession)*

**"JUST AS I AM WITHOUT ONE PLEA," I PRAY.**
*(Pray the Prayer of Our Savior.)*

| MORNING | EVENING |
|---|---|
| No, God, I cannot walk alone; | Well, well! It's me, O God, |
| nor do I want to—today or any day. | standing in the need of prayer |
| Walk with me. I ask this prayer in | tonight. I ask this prayer in |
| Jesus' name. Amen. | Jesus' name. Amen. |

# August 5

*(Read Matthew 13:44–52)*

### MORNING

Precious One, as I stare in awe of your magnificence
as shown in the colors of the flowers and in the songs of the birds,
I am eager to discover what today will bring. Be with me.

### EVENING

Precious One, I pray that today I brought some sunshine
into the lives I touched.

God, your precious Spirit permeates our beings and sometimes leaves us speechless. Yet we know that your realm will come. Our prayer should be that we will be found worthy, not only because we are faithful to you but also because we tried to teach others to follow you. God, use us to share your goodness, so that others will see your good works in us and through us and will give your name all the glory. Yes, "your kingdom come." Lead us, "O thou great Jehovah."

### MORNING

Grant to me the reward of the satisfying love of my God.
*(Prayers of Intercession)*

### EVENING

In my eagerness to serve, I pray that even as I falter,
I always will remember to give your name the praise.
*(Prayers of Intercession)*

NOW WE REQUEST YOUR INDULGENCE IN THE LIFE OF THIS HUMBLE SERVANT.
*(Pray the Prayer of Our Savior.)*

### MORNING

Yet another day in which to rest
and declare your infinite goodness.
I pray in Jesus' name.
Amen.

### EVENING

My eyes are heavy, yet my heart
is light, for I know that my
Redeemer lives. I pray in Jesus' name.
Amen.

# August 6

*(Read Hebrews 11:1–3, 8–16)*

### MORNING

God, you always find a way to nudge your people into where they
would not choose to go. Please nudge me into this new day and this new week.

### EVENING

God, as I close this day, I thank you for drawing me into all that it had to offer
and for the way in which it propels me into the days to come.

I have a poster that shows an old-fashioned car floating through space
with a caption that declares, "I can believe anything as long as it's incredible." I like this poster even though it has never really made sense
to me. But, likewise, the basis of faith is beyond reason. Through faith,
we accept even what we can't see. Life is filled with singular events and
material variety, each of which is in reality utterly miraculous. When we
understand this, we understand how the worlds were fashioned by your
word. Then faith really becomes possible as the assurance of things
hoped for and the conviction of things not seen.

### MORNING

O One who opens our eyes to what we do not see, I pray you will continue
to work in my life and will do the same in the lives of those for whom I pray.
*(Prayers of Intercession)*

### EVENING

Revealer of all that is deep and mysterious and wonderful, I thank you for
the subtle ways in which you opened my eyes and enlightened my mind this day.
*(Prayers of Intercession)*

---

**THROUGH FAITH, WE CAN EVEN BELIEVE IN WHAT WE CANNOT SEE.**

---

### MORNING

I begin this day and this week with
an eagerness to see things in new ways.
May I be willing to act on what I see
and open to discover new truths.
In Jesus' name. Amen.

### EVENING

I lie down to sleep, comforted by the
ways in which you have sustained my
faith through all you have revealed to
me: the good news made visible
through Christ. In Jesus' name. Amen.

# August 7

*(Read Isaiah 1:1, 10–15)*

### MORNING

Holy Presence, the morning headlines seem to scream out the bad news:
multiple tragedies of our own making. Guide me to speak truth
to the multiple powers behind the evils we experience.

### EVENING

Holy Presence, whose will is made clear to us in the midst of all
that is wrong, thank you for giving me the ability to assess the circumstances
that affect me and the lives that intersect with mine.

When your people sacrificed to you with their upturned bloody hands, you turned your eyes from them and you closed your ears. So how do our hands look? As the rest of the world looks at us, the judgment seems almost universal. We are a nation that prides itself as the continuation of an errand into the wilderness, the New Jerusalem, yet among the nations of the world, we stand out for the violence that permeates our society. We also rank number one as the provider of weapons to the rest of the world. Can it be the case that nothing we do pleases you because of the blood on our hands?

### MORNING

God, may I be an instrument of the peace Christ modeled for all of us.
*(Prayers of Intercession)*

### EVENING

O One who accepts us even as we are, I thank you for the comfort
and assurance your love and grace grant to all who believe in you.
*(Prayers of Intercession)*

---

**ANY OFFERING IS TAINTED IF IT IS COLORED BY ACTS OF EVIL.**

---

### MORNING

I know that others in the world have
a negative view of how our actions
impact their lives. Help me finds ways
to change what does not have to be.
In Jesus' name. Amen.

### EVENING

Though I may have
struggled with powers much larger
than myself, remind me again that my
struggles are minor compared to
others'. In Jesus' name. Amen.

# August 8

*(Read Isaiah 1:16–20)*

### MORNING

O God, I see many who need to be touched with your love through me.
May I touch someone in your name today.

### EVENING

O God, as I reached out to someone who seemed untouchable, a miracle happened.
I was touched in a new way as well. Thank you for this unexpected gift!

Your Word contains a constant refrain: your preferential option for those who have less, the oppressed, the victims of discrimination, the hungry, the homeless; the sick, and the disadvantaged. The list is so long that few of us fail to appear on it at some point in our lives. Once a person has been on your list, that person may begin to see with new eyes and be motivated to give in new ways. But what if we have never been on your special list? What will it take to move us to care and share? Is this the reason you have inspired us to be the church? Can we name ourselves your church if we fail to understand and act upon the intent of your good news?

### MORNING

There are so many who need our prayers. Remind us, O God,
how our prayers are only the beginning of your expectations of us.
*(Prayers of Intercession)*

### EVENING

Sometimes we truly feel that we can make a difference. O God, compel us
to move beyond good feelings to renewed prayer, intention, and action.
*(Prayers of Intercession)*

---

**IF WE LEARN TO DO GOOD, THEN WE ARE BETTER EQUIPPED TO CEASE TO DO EVIL.**

---

### MORNING

I worked for what I am and have.
Remind me that all I have comes from
you and that I am to sharewith others.
In Jesus' name. Amen.

### EVENING

Thank you for the assurance that
you love me in spite of my blemishes.
In Jesus' name. Amen.

# August 9

*(Read Psalm 50:1–8, 22–23)*

### MORNING

O God, I have so much for which to be thankful: loving family and friends,
challenging and rewarding work, good health, and ample opportunities.
May my sense of thanksgiving truly honor you this day.

### EVENING

O God, my thanksgiving is enlarged by the thanks expressed by those
with whom I have shared. Your Word is lived out: whenever we give, we receive.

An attitude of thanksgiving shifts our focus from self to the other. We
begin by being grateful for what we have received, but the minute we
express our gratitude, we move into a frame of mind in which we become ready to step outside ourselves and encounter you, the One who
receives our gratitude. You are honored when we express our thanksgiving in worship. You are the One who first gave to us, and when we comprehend this, our gratitude becomes the selfless expression you desire.

### MORNING

O generous God, may my gratitude for what you have given me
motivate me to reach out to others in new ways, not only in acts
of giving, but also in the prayers I lift up on their behalf.
*(Prayers of Intercession)*

### EVENING

It's so difficult to move beyond concerns for self. May I absorb in a new way
all that has happened to me this day, and may I be moved to think of the other
as Christ would have me do.
*(Prayers of Intercession)*

**THOSE WHO BRING THANKSGIVING AS THEIR SACRIFICE HONOR GOD.**

### MORNING

May the joy that resides within my
thanksgiving be apparent to everyone
I encounter this day. May my joy be
your joy shared with them.
In Jesus' name, Amen.

### EVENING

O Giver of all good gifts, may today's
accomplishments be received by you as
my expression of thanksgiving to you.
In Jesus' name. Amen.

# August 10

*(Read Luke 12:32–40)*

### MORNING

Creator God, help me begin this day without its being colored by any sense
of worry. Help me be open to the unexpected interruptions and reshaped plans.
Broaden my vision.

### EVENING

Creator God, as the day draws to a close and the sun sets in the west,
may I set aside all that distracts me and focus instead on what you would
have me see and understand.

Worry-free God, worry gets lifted up to you like a prayer asking for a response. But your Word reminds us again and again: worry gets us nowhere; there is no treasure we can bury for a rainy day. You constantly remind us to be ready for the unexpected. Your realm can and will break into our lives when we least expect it. This is the treasure we should desire. Help us to understand and believe so we may truly be worry free!

### MORNING

As I place my thoughts upon the lives of loved ones and those in need, may my
thoughts become the treasure you offer me and those for whom I pray.
*(Prayers of Intercession)*

### EVENING

O Treasure Giver, may your realm break into our lives this very evening
and in all the days to come. Be present now in the prayers we lift heavenward.
*(Prayers of Intercession)*

---

**WHERE WE PLACE OUR HEARTS DEFINES WHAT WE CLAIM AS OUR TREASURE.**

---

### MORNING

Remind me again, O God, that the
alleged treasures we scramble to acquire
are not the treasures you would have us
seek. Help me be open to the new life
you offer through the One who was the
incarnation of your realm in our midst.
In Jesus' name. Amen.

### EVENING

I can rest easy this night, O God,
for now I know what you promise me
and all of your children is not of this
world and is not bound by the finite
nature of the material things we tend
to desire. In Jesus' name. Amen.

# August 11

*(Read Genesis 15:1–6)*

**MORNING**

O God, this is a day to do all the things on my list.
May what I do be pleasing in your sight.

**EVENING**

O God, I have once again addressed this list. Things have been scratched off,
and new things have been added. Help me keep a proper perspective so that
my actions enfold the intentions you have for all of life.

"Covenant" is a word that is often only partially heard. It's too easy for us just to hear your promise of descendants as numerous as the stars. It's too easy to interpret descendants as our own offspring and thus get lost in our possessiveness of family and tribe. Is it possible that by descendants, you mean all those whom we have the possibility to impact by what we say and do? If we truly see all people as your children and thus as our brothers and sisters, then our sense of responsibility for our side of the covenant begins to dawn and grow.

**MORNING**

I used to pray "Now I lay me down to sleep" until I realized the selfishness
of my prayer, so I added words for immediate and extended family,
and everybody else in the world.
*(Prayers of Intercession)*

**EVENING**

It's still difficult to move beyond friends and family when we pray.
Forgive us for our myopia, and lead us to pray for others in such a way that
what we pray governs how we reach out to them.
*(Prayers of Intercession)*

---

**BELIEF IN GOD'S PROMISE IS RECKONED BY GOD AS RIGHTEOUSNESS.**

---

**MORNING**

As we look around the world, we see the results of tribalism. Help us gain such sensitivity so we might move beyond such tendencies. In Jesus' name. Amen.

**EVENING**

I looked at the stars and was reminded of your promise to Abram. Please help all to live in relationship with one another. In Jesus' name. Amen.

# August 12

*(Read Psalm 33:12–22)*

### MORNING

Loving God, this is a special day. It is a day for rest. May we encounter your Word,
and may your Word refashion us just as it first fashioned all that is.

### EVENING

Loving God, our worship is our attempt to give back to you the love you
constantly give to us. It is our attempt to express our gratitude for all that you give.

Our hope is in you, the One who has fashioned our world through the miracle of your Word. Our hope is in you, the One who promises to be in covenant with us. Our hope is in you, the One who expects us to do good and avoid evil. Our hope is in you, the One who chooses our thanksgiving as our sacrifice. Our hope is in you because it is your good pleasure to give us your realm. If we can but believe all of this, then your promise to us becomes abundantly clear: your steadfast love will be upon us!

### MORNING

We place our hope in you, O God, and we lift up others in prayer
so they might know as well the hope you so graciously offer us.

*(Prayers of Intercession)*

### EVENING

The hope we have in you, God, is a hope in which we might experience
the gift of your realm. May that hope be realized by all.

*(Prayers of Intercession)*

### GOD'S LOVE IS UPON THOSE WHO HOPE.

*(Recite Psalm 23.)*

### MORNING

Your Word became known to us in
flesh by the life and death of the One
who was first with you in the creation
of the world. Help us to understand
this Word and to be shaped by it.
In Jesus' name. Amen.

### EVENING

We have placed our hope in you,
O God, and now your promise
unfolds in the very midst of our lives:
you offer us your realm, and your
steadfast love is upon us. Thank you!
In Jesus' name. Amen.

# August 13

*(Read Psalm 111)*

**MORNING**

O God, the words of the psalmist call us to the beginning
of another week. To you we turn for wisdom and guidance for this day.

**EVENING**

O God, night has come and we seek blessings on what has happened
this past day. May your Spirit continue to dwell within us
to give us wisdom for the day.

Creator God, like people in times past, this hymn of praise calls us to ponder the marvels of your creation and the wonders of your work of salvation. We once more commit ourselves to live in covenant with you. Help us to be faithful in the living of this relation so that our lives will show forth your love for all people. May we encourage and support each other as we praise you with our lives.

**MORNING**

Spirit of God, our prayers and concerns this day
are for your people on all the earth . . .
*(Prayers of Intercession)*

**EVENING**

For those on this world who need to experience justice and peace . . .
*(Prayers of Intercession)*

---

**PRAY THE PRAYER OF OUR SAVIOR.**

---

**MORNING**

In thankfulness and in the spirit
of worship, may we live this day.
Though the Sabbath is past, help us not
to confine worship to one hour on
Sunday morning. May it be part of all
our task this day. Send us forth.
In the name of Christ, our Redeemer.
Amen.

**EVENING**

In faithfulness we entrust
to you the labors of this day.
May you bring us rest and refresh us
this night as we prepare for a new day.
In the name of Christ,
our Redeemer. Amen.

# August 14

*(Read Proverbs 9:1–6)*

### MORNING

Caring God, we rise today seeking new insights in the reading of
your word. Open our hearts and minds to hear anew what you
have in store for us.

### EVENING

Caring God, we have tried to let your wisdom guide us this day. In
the quietness of this hour, help us to hear your message.

Sometimes we are lost in a world of conflicting messages. Yet you, O
God, never give up on us. It is we who close our minds, unwilling to
listen. We forget that we are your children, bound by your love and
mercy. If we truly use the gifts you have given us, we will find growth
and new understanding of justice for all. Feed us and we will listen.
Help us to maturity and we will be wiser.

### MORNING

May we choose wisdom over foolishness, life over death.
On this day, we pray to you, gentle and loving God, that we might
make the wise choice as we move on through life.
*(Prayers of Intercession)*

### EVENING

We are offered spiritual food for growth. With thankful hearts,
we come to you seeking your help to make us willing to listen and act upon
your Word. We especially ask that you help each one of us
with our particular needs . . .
*(Prayers of Intercession)*

---

### PRAY THE PRAYER OF OUR SAVIOR.

---

| MORNING | EVENING |
|---|---|
| Give us the wisdom that we need | We ate of the bread and the wine |
| for this day. Send us forth with your | of Wisdom. How great is your name, |
| blessing. In the name of Christ, | O God. In the name of the Christ, |
| our Redeemer. Amen. | our Redeemer. Amen. |

# August 15

*(Read Psalm 34:9–14)*

### MORNING

Listening God, in praise and thanksgiving we come to a new day.
I will listen to you, who teach about abundant life.

### EVENING

Listening God, we come to you with thankful hearts for all
the blessings we have received. Lead us in our search.

God, why is it that so many people interpret "fearing" you as being afraid? Do we believe in a God who punishes without reason? No, I put my trust in you as the one who cares and loves creation. In times of distress, you not only protect us, but teach us to trust. I, and others, must live in right relationship with you, seeking peace and justice, and we will have all we need. Oh, how great is your love, Caring God.

### MORNING

We have been so blessed by your love: God has mercy.
Keep us from doing evil and help us to do good and seek peace.
*(Prayers of Intercession)*

### EVENING

What have we left undone this day? Have we done good?
Have we worked for peace? Our voices rise in prayer so that we
have another chance to continue our tasks.
*(Prayers of Intercession)*

### PRAY THE PRAYER OF OUR SAVIOR.

### MORNING

Morning gives us an opportunity
for new beginnings. Send us into the
world to do good and seek justice.
In the name of Christ,
our Redeemer. Amen.

### EVENING

This day, your gift to us,
has come to an end. With your ever
present love and mercy, watch over us.
In the name of Christ,
our Redeemer. Amen.

# August 16

*(Read Ephesians 5:15–20)*

**MORNING**

Wonderful Creator, morning prayers we raise to you in thankfulness
and praise. The wonder of your creation fills our hearts with awe.

**EVENING**

Wonderful Creator, we have traveled through mountains
and valleys, and we have proclaimed the wonders you have done
for us. Quiet our hearts so that our minds can also hear you.

You have given us bread and wine to feed the spirit. You have filled our hearts with poetry that has touched us deeply. Yet we have heard loud and clear "do not get drunk with wine." Are you calling us to be wise in using the gifts of the spirit? Are you reminding us that we need also to search our minds and be wise in our response? Help us, God, to find the ways of the wise. May we make the most of this day as we live it in faithfulness to you.

**MORNING**

Our prayers are for those who need to be reminded of how fragile life can be.
Through prayer may we find the strengthening power for our daily lives.
*(Prayers of Intercession)*

**EVENING**

Grant us another night of rest. May the prayer of Jesus give us the
wisdom to know better how to live.
*(Prayers of Intercession)*

**PRAY THE PRAYER OF OUR SAVIOR.**

| **MORNING** | **EVENING** |
|---|---|
| We have been fed by the spirit. | We took refuge in God, |
| May we live this new day to the | and the reward has been great. |
| fullness that only God can give us. | With thankful hearts we rest this |
| In the name of Christ, | night. In the name of Christ, |
| our Redeemer. Amen. | our Redeemer. Amen. |

# August 17

*(Read John 6:51–58)*

**MORNING**

Loving God, we are seeking bread for the journey.
It is in you that we find the living bread we seek.

**EVENING**

Loving God, you know what we seek and you have given it to us,
but we need to be willing to receive it.

The bread of Holy Communion. The body of Christ. The living bread.
Each time I take the bread and wine of communion, I remember that
day when I stood by the bedside of my life companion and best friend.
We shared together our last communion. We strongly felt your presence
in the bread we received. My husband was a gentle and loving person,
who faced death knowing that Jesus' gift of living bread was for eternal
life. I received it knowing that it was the bread for the journey ahead.
Thank you, God, for showing us the way to live life to its fullest.

**MORNING**

Bread of life given for us all, you are a gift to share with others
who travel, seeking to live by God's purpose on this world.
*(Prayers of Intercession)*

**EVENING**

Jesus, you have fed our hunger even when we did not know how hungry
we were. We entrust to you all those who have not even begun the search.
May they find in you the food to nourish their souls.
*(Prayers of Intercession)*

---

**PRAY THE PRAYER OF OUR SAVIOR.**

---

**MORNING**

Go in peace to live this day in love.
Remember the words, the face, and
the touch of Jesus, who called us to be
family to one another. In the name
of Christ, our Redeemer. Amen.

**EVENING**

May the forgiving grace of God enfold
us and uphold us. We hope for a day
when all people will sit down at the
table of friendship to dine in joy. In the
name of Christ, our Redeemer. Amen.

# August 18

*(Read 1 Kings 2:10–12)*

### MORNING

Blessed Savior, guide us today to live as you intended. Do not let us
fall prey to power struggles, but help us to be true ambassadors of your love.
Help us today to find ways to listen to the powerless people of this city.

### EVENING

Blessed Savior, bless the closing of this day.
Grant us pardon for our mistakes and lead us to restoring rest.

The aged ruler charges his son to walk in God's way. From David to Solomon power passes on. It was a choice of wisdom. O God, it was your divine providence that moved David to select the one who was to be responsible for the chain of historical events that resulted from it. You not only create but set the chain of events in life. We, your children, need to be wise as we walk in your ways.

### MORNING

God, we have honored you with our words and songs,
but not always with our hearts. We need to be touched by you
so that we can receive the wisdom needed to discern more clearly
what we should be about in this world. Help us to use power
for the sake of justice and peace.
*(Prayers of Intercession)*

### EVENING

Today, our prayers are lifted for those whom we have hurt
by misuse of power . . .
*(Prayers of Intercession)*

### PRAY THE PRAYER OF OUR SAVIOR.

### MORNING

May we be strong and courageous
as we deal with principalities and
powers. In the name of Christ,
our Redeemer. Amen.

### EVENING

We rededicate ourselves to be
instruments of God's love and peace.
In the name of Christ,
our Redeemer. Amen.

# August 19

*(Read 1 Kings 3:3–14)*

### MORNING

O God, on the days set apart for worship, as we gather to sing praises,
help us to hear your words of wisdom and inspiration.

### EVENING

O God, search our souls and illumine our hearts and minds
that we may respond better to your call.

God, have we learned the true meaning of wisdom? Too many times we
equate it with knowledge acquired through academic education. We
praise those who have the highest scores and a PhD behind their name.
We stand in awe of them and do not dare contradict them because we
think they know more than we do. We are reminded, once more, that
wisdom comes from you. Like Solomon, in humbleness we ask that
you give us an understanding mind.

### MORNING

Spirit of the living God, come into our lives and the lives
of our brothers and sisters. As we prepare ourselves for the beginning
of another school year, help us to learn more about you,
so that we may live with true wisdom.
*(Prayers of Intercession)*

### EVENING

Help us to embrace the cross of Christ and to grow in understanding.
*(Prayers of Intercession)*

### PRAY THE PRAYER OF OUR SAVIOR.

### MORNING

Send us to proclaim the crucified
Christ, who embodies your power and
wisdom. In the name of Christ,
our Redeemer. Amen.

### EVENING

May the words of God's mouth
be in our ears and the power of love
in our hearts and actions. In the name
of Christ, our Redeemer. Amen.

# August 20

*(Read Psalm 103:1–12)*

**MORNING**

Creator God, I know that storms come in life and that the rain of trial and
temptation will fall, even on me. But as I meet the new day, I do so with great
faith that you will walk with me, not letting me drown in the midst of the storm.

**EVENING**

Creator God, thank you for being with me today.
No matter where I went, you were there and I felt strong.

Creator God, sometimes I feel as though I am in the midst of a quiet
storm. Nevertheless, I know that I must hold on because help is on the
way. God, when you forgive my iniquities, I am forgiven. When you
heal me from all my diseases and transgressions, I am healed. When you
redeem me from the pit of problems, I am crowned with love and
mercy. No matter what storm is raging in my life, you forgive me. Your
anger will cease and you will be merciful to me. Thank you for calming
the quiet storms.

**MORNING**

O God, help me to start this new and wonderful day, assured that if I hold
my peace and let you fight the battle, you will say to my storms, "Peace, be still!"
*(Prayers of Intercession)*

**EVENING**

Loving God, thank you for being with me today.
Forgive me if I, at any time today, doubted your ability to protect
me from the storm. Let me sleep the sleep of renewal in you.
*(Prayers of Intercession)*

**THANK YOU FOR YOUR WORK OF VINDICATION AND JUSTICE FOR ALL.**

**MORNING**

I pledge to develop a great faith
in you and in your mighty power.
In the matchless name of
our Savior. Amen.

**EVENING**

O God, let me awaken tomorrow with
a strong conviction to meet whatever
and whomever knowing that you are
with me and in me. In the matchless
name of our Savior. Amen.

# August 21

*(Read Psalm 103:13–22)*

**MORNING**

Problem-solving God, I need you today more than I ever have needed you.
I come to you because there are situations in my life that are raging. I need strength
for this day, and I know that you are the only one who can make me strong.
Thank you, God, for being God all by yourself.

**EVENING**

Problem-solving God, thank you for always reminding me that you
are in charge of everyone and everything and that you are in complete control.
I rest easier because your throne is everlasting.

God, as a child I would exclaim, "Just wait until I become an adult;
then I will be in charge!" One of the most interesting things about
being an adult, however, is that when storms rage I often wish I could
run to my parents for protection and comfort. But while I cannot run
to my parents, you, Protector God, are the Great Parent who always has
compassion for me. You know me and love me. God, help me always
to remember that I can run to you for shelter from the storm.

**MORNING**

O God, may I start this new day with the blessed assurance of knowing
that if I need to run to you for comfort, you will be there.
*(Prayers of Intercession)*

**EVENING**

Thank you, God, for continuing to prove yourself to me. Every time I get weak,
you are there to comfort me. Every time I doubt your love, your love lifts me.
Let me sleep assured that you will never leave me or forsake me.
*(Prayers of Intercession)*

**THANK YOU FOR YOUR ANGELS, WHO WATCH OVER ME. BLESS GOD, O MY SOUL.**

| **MORNING** | **EVENING** |
| --- | --- |
| I pledge to witness to the world your love for me, as a parent loves a child. In the matchless name of our Savior. Amen. | O God, let me awaken tomorrow assured that while I am frail like the flowers and the grass, you make me strong. In the matchless name of our Savior. Amen. |

# August 22

*(Read Jeremiah 1:4–10)*

### MORNING

O God, you have richly blessed me. You have seen me through many storms, but today I face a problem that I am not sure I'm strong enough or seasoned enough to handle. Be my guide today.

### EVENING

God, thank you for calming my fears of inadequacy. I did not believe that I would be able to meet the challenge, but you are the one who promoted me and put me in such a high place. I should have known that you would not lift me up just to let me down.

God, I can remember the first time I was in charge of something, and while first all was going well, problems developed. I felt that I was not good enough to meet the challenge. But then I remembered that I was chosen by you for such a time as this. What you did for me yesterday, you will do again for me today. God, thank you for reminding me that you are with me to deliver me.

### MORNING

God, touch my mouth with your hand of guidance and wisdom, so that your words and will might be spoken through me.
*(Prayers of Intercession)*

### EVENING

Thank you, God, for speaking to me and through me today. I know that I must constantly submit my will to yours so that you might be glorified through me. Grant me a rest that will not only refresh me but encourage me to serve you even more.
*(Prayers of Intercession)*

---

THANK YOU FOR CHOOSING ME TO BUILD AND TO PLANT.
THANK YOU FOR YOUR DIVINE GUIDANCE.

---

### MORNING

Today, I pledge to do the very best I can for others and to use wisely the gifts that you have given me. In the matchless name of our Savior. Amen.

### EVENING

O God, let me awaken tomorrow determined to make a difference where I live, so that your light will shine from me. In the matchless name of our Savior. Amen.

234

# August 23

*(Read Isaiah 58:9b–14)*

**MORNING**

O God, I continue holding on in the midst of this storm in my life. Help me to move away from my problems, so that I might minister to someone else who is in greater need. Help me to minister to others even in the midst of my pain.

**EVENING**

O God, thank you for helping me to move away
from my problems and help another find joy and meaning in life.

God, there have been times when I have felt totally immobilized. All was very bleak. But during those times, a knock on the door or a call on the telephone broke through my despair. It was a cry for help from someone else. I disregarded my troubles and went to assist another. God, you remind me that if I make myself available to others, you will guide me and make me strong. You will enable me to endure and overcome.

**MORNING**

God, help me to be determined to get the most out of my worship
experience this week at church.
*(Prayers of Intercession)*

**EVENING**

Thank you, God, for helping me take my mind off of my troubles by giving me the opportunity to serve others in their hour of need. As I go to sleep tonight, anoint me so I am able to discern when another is in need.
*(Prayers of Intercession)*

THANK YOU, GOD, FOR YOUR GIFT OF WORSHIP. I WILL STRIVE EVER TO DELIGHT
IN YOU AND YOUR GLORY. O GOD, REPAIR THE BREACHES IN MY LIFE.

**MORNING**

Today, I pledge to be open to your Spirit, so that if you send someone for me to serve, I will do so with gladness. In the matchless name of our Savior. Amen.

**EVENING**

O God, should I awaken tomorrow, give me the yearning to worship you more and more. Help me to give you the honor and glory tomorrow. In the matchless name of our Savior. Amen.

# August 24

*(Read Psalm 7 1:1–6)*

**MORNING**

O God, I'm stepping out on your promise of deliverance.
Today I leave my home trusting in you, because I know that if I
run into trouble, you will be there to protect me.

**EVENING**

Caring God, thank you for looking out for me today. When I had to take
time out and regroup, you made it possible for me to take shelter in you.
I regained my balance, despite the storm winds blowing upon me. You became
for me a rock of refuge. I survived the day and was victorious.

Storms in life come, and storms in life go. But you, O God, remain
constant during the time of trauma and trial. Even from our birth, we
have depended upon you. God, you delivered us at birth, and you will
continue to deliver us from the storms in our lives.

**MORNING**

Protector God, as I face a new day, deliver me from anyone or anything desiring to do me harm. Be my fortress and my rescue from
the storm. Give me the strength to meet this day.
*(Prayers of Intercession)*

**EVENING**

Thank you, God. I was not sure how the day would turn out,
but you let me lean upon you. In you I placed my trust, and because
of this I was delivered. As I leaned upon you today, let me sleep
in you tonight and rest assured that you are with me.
*(Prayers of Intercession)*

THANK YOU, GOD, FOR PROTECTING ME TODAY. MY PRAISE IS CONTINUALLY OF YOU.

**MORNING**

I pledge today to put my trust in you.
Be my strength and my guide; let me
ever lean on you. In the matchless
name of our Savior. Amen.

**EVENING**

O God, as I prepare to retire for the
night, thank you for protecting me.
Keep me as I sleep and encourage me to
do better tomorrow. In the matchless
name of our Savior. Amen.

# August 25

*(Read Hebrews 12:18–29)*

### MORNING
Reassuring God, I realize that without you I would be lost.
Thank you for your son, Jesus Christ. In Jesus I find my direction and
am coming to know my purpose in life. In Jesus I am steady and focused.

### EVENING
Reassuring God, thank you for your precious grace.
Without your grace I could not have accomplished all that I did today.
I embrace you and look forward to one day being with you in your heavenly realm.

God, sometimes in this life I am called upon to sacrifice something of great importance to me. Your Child Jesus, through the shedding of his blood, brought into being a new covenant between you and humankind. Because of Jesus' sacrifice, I have the opportunity for eternal life. Jesus experienced a storm that cost his life. But because Jesus sacrificed his life, I gained mine. When I sacrifice myself, I actually gain more than I have lost.

### MORNING
Dear God, if I am faced with the opportunity to make a sacrifice for someone
else, help me to do so cheerfully so that my gift will be from my heart.
*(Prayers of Intercession)*

### EVENING
Sacrificing God, today you called upon me to make a sacrifice. Thank you
for helping me work through my difficulty in making it. Help me to rest in you
and learn from you, so that I might better serve and love you.
*(Prayers of Intercession)*

---

**GOD, YOU ARE WORTHY, AND YOUR REALM IS FOREVER. LET ME BE WORTHY OF IT.
IN YOU I STAND STRONG AND FIRM, NO MATTER WHAT IS ASKED OF ME.**

---

### MORNING
Jesus, I thank you for your sacrifice.
Let me hear your voice today.
In the matchless name
of our Savior. Amen.

### EVENING
Now, God, as I lie down to sleep,
help me to be worthy of your promise.
I will trust in you to face tomorrow.
In the matchless name
of our Savior. Amen.

# August 26

*(Read Luke 13:10–17)*

### MORNING

Parent God, I was in the midst of a terrible storm last week.
My life was in trouble, and I sought you. You heard my cry. I trusted in you,
and you healed me. I awaken to stand tall and strong again because of you.

### EVENING

Parent God, thank you for your concern. I rest tonight assured that because I claim
Jesus as my Sovereign Savior, no matter what might happen, you will deliver me.

God, your work cannot be confined to one specific time or place. My
mission in life is to daily serve you. There will be times when I must
stop what I am doing because there is a greater demand placed on me.
I cannot be worried when, to some, what I am called to do appears to
be strange or different. I cannot let ceremony get in the way of healing.
I must be Spirit-led. When I operate under your power, my service becomes anointed and healing occurs.

### MORNING

Dear God, give me the ability today to discern when you need me
to do something for another. Help me to place in proper perspective what I should do and when I should do it.
*(Prayers of Intercession)*

### EVENING

Thank you, God, when you made an opportunity for me to assist someone
today in their healing. As I go to sleep, be with me. Should I awake to see the
morning sun, help me to be a blessing to someone else.
*(Prayers of Intercession)*

---

GOD, YOU ARE MY HEALER, MY SUSTAINER, AND MY LIFE. I SUBMIT MY DREAMS TO YOU.
NEVER CEASE FROM CALMING THE STORMS IN MY LIFE.

---

### MORNING

Jesus, you have been my salvation
from the beginning of my life.
Help me to do good. In the matchless
name of our Savior. Amen.

### EVENING

O God, as another day ends,
thank you for being with me. Even when
I fell short, you were still there. In the
matchless name of our Savior. Amen.

# August 27

*(Read Exodus 1:8–2:10)*

**MORNING**

Creator God, thank you for the gift of this day. Help me to make
the most of the opportunities and challenges.

**EVENING**

Creator God, for the energy you have provided for the living of
this day, I now give you my thanks. Thank you for the courage to
meet the challenges and the grace to face the obstacles.

God, you always find a way. The midwives had the courage to outwit
Pharaoh with the wisdom of their trade. They knew what was right and
what was wrong. You can almost hear them saying, "You know, Pharaoh,
those Hebrew women are just too quick for us. They are not like the
Egyptian women; for they are vigorous and give birth before the mid-
wife comes to them." God, you blessed the midwives and gave them
families. Their "fear" of you strengthened them to do the extraordi-
nary—to stand against the political system that destroyed life. These
women were ordinary people who risked their own lives to save others.

**MORNING**

O God of compassion, your care for us is more than we can imagine.
*(Prayers of Intercession)*

**EVENING**

Tomorrow is a new day. Thank you, God,
for your care through this long day.
*(Prayers of Intercession)*

---

GOD, HELP US BE CREATIVE AND BOLD IN OUR RESPONSE
TO THE INJUSTICES IN OUR WORLD.

---

**MORNING**

Each new day, I know you are
with me, O God. I am grateful!
In the name of the Christ. Amen.

**EVENING**

God, my Companion, be present
with me even in my rest.
In the name of the Christ. Amen.

# August 28

*(Read Psalm 124)*

**MORNING**

O God, Guardian of lives, help me be aware today that
you are in charge, not me. You are on my side even when life may seem
against me. My help is in you, who made heaven and earth.

**EVENING**

O God, Guardian of lives, I have felt your presence with me
this day. Help me put to rest all the worries and concerns of the
day, so that my spirit will be refreshed by dawn.

How often we try to do things on our own! How often we want to be
in control! We would do well to be reminded to relinquish control and
trust in you, loving God! Like the psalmist, we sing out, "Blessed be
God, who has not given us as prey to our enemies. We have escaped like
a bird from the snare of the fowlers; the snare is broken, and we have
escaped." Indeed, our help is in you, who made heaven and earth.

**MORNING**

O God, who has faithfully created the dawn,
may the light of this day give fullness and strength to my life.
*(Prayers of Intercession)*

**EVENING**

God, you are a refuge for those who trust in you!
At the close of this day, be my refuge and strength.
*(Prayers of Intercession)*

**WITH GOD ON OUR SIDE, ALL THINGS ARE POSSIBLE.**

**MORNING**

God is good and gracious,
our help when the storms of life rage.
May I be reminded of this as I live out
the day. In the name of the Christ.
Amen.

**EVENING**

Thank you, God, for your
constancy in a very busy day!
In the name of the Christ.
Amen.

# August 29

*(Read Isaiah 5 1:1–6)*

**MORNING**

O God of light, this day has the possibilities of joy and gladness.
Help me find the joy and sift away the bad.

**EVENING**

O God of light, I have tried to listen to you in all the voices
I have heard today. Now in this evening time, I listen again for
your comfort, so that my rest may be peaceful.

God, you promise joy and gladness if we but listen. "Listen to me, my people, and give heed to me, my nation; for a teaching will go out from me, and my justice for a light to the peoples." Yes, God, how we yearn for the waste places in our world to be comforted and the desert of olives to be turned into a garden. Your words are our joy, our light, and our hope!

**MORNING**

O God, bring me comfort today as I seek to discern your will
for my activities. Help me listen to your voice
and your teaching in all that I do.
*(Prayers of Intercession)*

**EVENING**

Thank you, God, for the light you bring to all.
*(Prayers of Intercession)*

---

**"LISTEN TO ME, MY PEOPLE, AND GIVE HEED TO ME, MY NATION;
FOR A TEACHING WILL GO OUT FROM ME, AND MY JUSTICE FOR A LIGHT TO THE PEOPLES."**

---

**MORNING**

O God, I give you thanks today for
the gift of the dawn. In the name of
the Christ. Amen.

**EVENING**

O God of light, the sun is fading,
and so is my energy. You have been
present in all the moments of this day,
giving comfort and courage.
May this night of rest restore me.
In the name of the Christ. Amen.

# August 30

*(Read Psalm 138)*

**MORNING**

I give you thanks with my whole heart, O God.
I sing your praise and give thanks to your name for your
steadfast love and faithfulness.

**EVENING**

I give you thanks with my whole heart, O God.
I sing your praise and give thanks to your name for your
steadfast love and faithfulness.

"Though I walk in the midst of trouble, you, God, preserve me against the wrath of my enemies; you stretch out your hand and your right hand delivers me." So what do I fear? What holds me back from speaking the truth in love? What holds me back from being courageous and bold when wrong clashes with right? "God will fulfill God's purpose for me," the psalmist proclaims! God will fulfill God's purpose through ordinary persons. God, you are an awesome God!

**MORNING**

O God of steadfast love, I give you thanks with my whole heart.
Use me for your purpose this day.
*(Prayers of Intercession)*

**EVENING**

I sing God's praises with my whole heart and give thanks
for God's steadfast love and faithfulness.
*(Prayers of Intercession)*

**GOD'S PURPOSES MAY BE FULFILLED THROUGH US!**

**MORNING**
Let me be filled with
thanksgiving this day. In the name
of the Christ. Amen.

**EVENING**
I have called upon you this day,
O God, and you have increased my
strength of soul, In the name
of the Christ. Amen.

# August 31

*(Read Romans 12:1–8)*

**MORNING**

O inexhaustible God, as I face this new day, be present with me
as I try to use those gifts with which you have blessed me.

**EVENING**

O inexhaustible God, thank you for the many gifts
you have given me. Thank you, God, for the gifts of so many people,
which have been used to enrich this day.

Thank God that we have many gifts. Wouldn't it be a dull world if only
one gift were present? As a community, how rich we are because of one
another. "We have gifts that differ according to the grace given to us."
Honoring the gifts of one another enriches us all.

**MORNING**

O God, I consecrate the living of this day to you.
*(Prayers of Intercession)*

**EVENING**

Be with me now, O God, as I reflect upon the ways that I have
used the gifts with which you have blessed me.
*(Prayers of Intercession)*

---

I AM AWARE THAT I DON'T ALWAYS USE GOD'S GIFTS AND THAT I DON'T ALWAYS
CELEBRATE THE GIFTS OF OTHERS. I HOPE I WILL BE MORE AWARE.

---

**MORNING**

Thank you, God, for the dawn.
I know you are with me as I face the
new day. In the name of the Christ.
Amen.

**EVENING**

O inexhaustible God,
I am exhausted. Thank you for being
with me always. In the name
of the Christ. Amen.

# September 1

*(Read Romans 12:1–8)*

**MORNING**

Merciful God, I approach this new day hoping to do
what is good and acceptable in your sight.

**EVENING**

Merciful God, this day has been filled with challenges.
I pray that my actions have been in keeping with your will.

The world is so demanding! How easy it is to be conformed to the
world, rather than transformed by God's will.

**MORNING**

Renew me today, O God, to do your work.
*(Prayers of Intercession)*

**EVENING**

Transforming God, you have blessed me
with the gift of your presence throughout this day.
Hear my prayers for . . .
*(Prayers of Intercession)*

**GOD'S LOVE IS TRANSFORMING.**

| **MORNING** | **EVENING** |
|---|---|
| God of wonders, | God of holy love, |
| you have given me the gift of another | thank you for this day. |
| day. Help me do your work graciously. | Renew me with this evening of rest. |
| In the name of the Christ. | In the name of the Christ. |
| Amen. | Amen. |

# September 2

*(Read Matthew 16:13–20)*

**MORNING**
Faithful God, I am awakened to new possibilities that this day holds.
Help me make the most of my time today.

**EVENING**
Faithful God, you have been with me each step of the way today.
Thanks.

When asked the tough questions, it is always easier to defer to others. But Jesus did not let the disciples get away with that! "Who do you say that I am?" And impetuous Peter proclaimed, "You are the Christ!" And Jesus said to Peter, "Blessed are you. . . . You are Peter and upon this rock I will build my church." God, when confronted with naming the Christ in my daily activities, I pray that I, too, can proclaim, "You are the Christ!"

**MORNING**
O God, our Rock and our Guide,
hear the prayers for the church and for others.
*(Prayers of Intercession)*

**EVENING**
You have been present today in so many ways, O God.
I have been challenged and comforted by your presence in all I
have said and done. Be with me now in my resting, that I may be
renewed for the new day. Hear my prayers of intercession now.
*(Prayers of Intercession)*

---

**ON THE SOLID ROCK OF CHRIST I STAND; ALL OTHER GROUND IS SINKING SAND.**

---

**MORNING**
The sunrise ushers in the new day!
May God's peace and presence
surround me today. In the name
of the Christ. Amen.

**EVENING**
The sunset marks the ending
of the day. As evening falls, be
present, God, in my resting.
In the name of the Christ. Amen.

# September 3

*(Read Exodus 14:19–31)*

**MORNING**

O God, be with me as I seek to increase my trust
in your Word and my faith in your presence.

**EVENING**

O God, I give thanks to you
for abandoning neither me nor the world.

There are those moments when I doubt. It is especially true when I observe the pain and struggle in the world. Then I am reminded, God, that you move in human history in ways that amaze me. You make a way out of no way. When I am fearful and filled with anxiety, I begin to see evidences of your hand and your footprints changing the very course of events. Praise be to you, Savior God.

**MORNING**

God, when I am cast down, lift me up,
so that I may feel and see your presence in the world.
*(Prayers of Intercession)*

**EVENING**

Today I reaffirmed that you have the world in your hands.
*(Prayers of Intercession)*

GOD DOES STEP INTO THE HUMAN CONDITION.
WE MUST BE OPEN TO GOD'S ACTIONS.

| **MORNING** | **EVENING** |
|---|---|
| O God, how good it is | Touch me and touch all peoples |
| to know that you are God! | in the world. Make a "way" |
| In Jesus' name. | for all of us. In Jesus' name. |
| Amen. | Amen. |

# September 4

*(Read Exodus 14:19–31)*

**MORNING**
O God, I will sing praises to you all the day long.

**EVENING**
O God, thank you for all you have done.
I thank you with my whole body.

God, when I think of you and remember how you reach into life and save us from the dangers of conflict, I can only exclaim your praise. Loving God, I praise you with my lips, with my hands, with songs and shouts. Let me never forget you, O God, or forget to give thanks. You are my strength when I have no strength. You are my way when I have no way.

**MORNING**
Today I will sing your praise with my whole being.
*(Prayers of Intercession)*

**EVENING**
Even as the night falls,
I will continue to give you praise.
*(Prayers of Intercession)*

**NEVER FORGET TO SING GOD'S PRAISES.**

**MORNING**
I awaken to your presence
with songs of praise on my lips.
May they remain throughout this day.
In Jesus' name. Amen.

**EVENING**
As the night falls and
I close my eyes, let me do so with
songs of praise on my lips.
In Jesus' name. Amen.

# September 5

*(Read Psalm 114)*

**MORNING**

Holy, holy, holy God, you are the Holy Other.
I tremble in your presence.
You are in heaven and earth.

**EVENING**

Holy, holy, holy God, I bow before your presence—
you, who are before me and behind me.

Worship is a wondrous experience. I can worship while I work, while I play, when I am sitting down, and when I am standing up. When I think of you, God, and your creative genius, I am touched that I can call upon you, my personal God. I do so in awe and wonder. I tremble when I think of you, who created the universe, and yet you know me by name. Let us all praise you, omnipotent God.

**MORNING**

God, you never fail me or anyone
who calls upon your name in faith.
*(Prayers of Intercession)*

**EVENING**

God, you are a great and good God.
I tremble in your presence, but I do not fear you.
*(Prayers of Intercession)*

**GOD IS AWESOME YET LOVING.**

**MORNING**

Let me come into
your presence, God, with joy and
thanksgiving. In Jesus' name.
Amen.

**EVENING**

You have been with me
all the day long. Let me rest myself
in you. In Jesus' name. Amen.

# September 6

*(Read Genesis 50:15–21)*

**MORNING**
God, may I have a forgiving heart this day.
Jesus calls us to forgive seventy times seven.
May I live up to this counsel today.

**EVENING**
God, you have forgiven me.
I pray that I have forgotten the slights
and forgiven others this day.

I must always remember that what others mean for evil, God, you mean for good. I must always pray not to return evil for evil, but to learn to forgive. I know how to forgive because I have been forgiven by you, forgiving God, and by others. I must remember that at the heart of the Christian life in relation to others is the quality of my forgiving spirit.

**MORNING**
A forgiving and contrite heart is what God requires of me today.
*(Prayers of Intercession)*

**EVENING**
Have I helped someone today by forgiving him or her?
*(Prayers of Intercession)*

**GOD CAN CHANGE EVIL INTO GOOD.**

**MORNING**
God, you have shown us
the way to forgive. May I also forgive?
In Jesus' name. Amen.

**EVENING**
May I not close my eyes
this day without forgiving someone.
In Jesus' name. Amen.

# September 7

*(Read Psalm 103:8–13)*

**MORNING**
God, I have awakened once again to the truth
that through Christ my life has been redeemed.

**EVENING**
God, I pray that I have proclaimed this day,
in thought, word, and deed, that you can and do redeem us all.

God, you are a redemptive God. You judge, you forgive, and you redeem. Of all the names ascribed to you, none is more important to me than knowing that you are the Redeemer. Loving God, you do not deal with us according to our sins. I am, at times, overwhelmed that you—who know my down-sitting and my up-rising, my sins of omission as well as my sins of commission—do not deal with me according to my weakness. God, you redeem me!

**MORNING**
God, you have redeemed me with your love.
Let me never forget you.
*(Prayers of Intercession)*

**EVENING**
Again I end my day as a redeemed person.
I have been redeemed by God.
*(Prayers of Intercession)*

**TOUCH ME, O REDEEMING GOD!**

**MORNING**
As your child,
I thank you for saving my life.
In Jesus' name. Amen.

**EVENING**
Let me rest this night
with the knowledge that God has
been good to me. In Jesus' name.
Amen.

# September 8

*(Read Romans 14:1–12)*

**MORNING**
God, I pray that I will not be judgmental today.

**EVENING**
God, may I remember as night comes that only you judge.

God, we live in a world of conflicting opinions. We often differ with one another. We must remember to differ with love. I have come to realize that in differing with another, I need not pass judgment. Whoever differs with me, I have come to understand that we are one in Christ. As brothers and sisters in Christ, there is no place for judgment.

**MORNING**
I pray this day that I will see my brothers and sisters in Christ
as objects of my love, not as objects of my judgment.
*(Prayers of Intercession)*

**EVENING**
I have left my differences with others at the altar of God.
*(Prayers of Intercession)*

---

**DELIVER ME FROM BEING A PERSON
WHO JUDGES MORE THAN LOVES.**

---

**MORNING**
God of love and hope,
hear me when I pray to be delivered
from being judgmental.
In Jesus' name.
Amen.

**EVENING**
As Christ has taught,
I now pray the Prayer of
Our Savior . . .

# September 9

*(Read Matthew 18:21–35)*

**MORNING**

Forgiving God, it is not enough for me
to forgive with my lips.
I must forgive from the heart.

**EVENING**

Forgiving God, I pray
that I have been forgiving this day.

Forgiving God, why is it that I say I forgive and yet continue to remember the slights and the offenses caused by others? Why do I seek forgiveness while, at the same time, I do not forgive others? If I remember the slights and the perceived offenses, then I have not forgiven with my heart. Truly it is not enough to forgive with my lips. I must forgive with my heart.

**MORNING**

Forgive us our sins as we forgive the sins of others.
*(Prayers of Intercession)*

**EVENING**

I pray that no one can say of me
that I have been unforgiving this day.
*(Prayers of Intercession)*

**HELP ME TO BE A FORGIVING PERSON.**

**MORNING**

Dear God, you have taught
me how to forgive by forgiving me
in Jesus Christ. In Jesus' name.
Amen.

**EVENING**

Wash me thoroughly, O God,
so that I might sleep this night with a
clean and forgiving heart.
In Jesus' name. Amen.

# September 10

*(Read Proverbs 1:20–33)*

**MORNING**

Gracious God, as the sun rises to proclaim the dawn of this new
day, I awake to a renewed awareness of your presence.
Guide me in my walk today.

**EVENING**

Gracious God, for those times today when I did not hear
your voice or when I did not heed it, forgive me.
Help me to be a better listener tomorrow.

God, this world you have created is a world of choices. You have given
us the freedom to make daily choices for better or worse, for right or
wrong. Too often we do not choose wisely because we do not listen attentively to the counsel you offer. Today slow me down, God of
Wisdom. Strengthen the bond between you and me that I may be more
eager to discern your will and more open to your direction.

**MORNING**

All-caring God, many people will face difficult choices today.
I pray you will give them your gift of discernment and the courage
to choose what is good, right, and life-giving.
*(Prayers of Intercession)*

**EVENING**

O God, forgive our failure to choose always what is best,
and bring life out of our less-than-perfect choices.
*(Prayers of Intercession)*

---

TODAY I ASK GOD TO PERMEATE MY LIFE,

THAT ALL MY CHOICES WILL REFLECT GOD'S LOVE AND GRACE.

*(Pray the Prayer of Our Savior.)*

---

**MORNING**

Today, give me a clear mind,
a loving heart, and helping hands.
In Jesus' name. Amen.

**EVENING**

Tonight, O God, look with compassion
upon today's failures and grant me the
joy of serving you more faithfully
tomorrow. In Jesus' name. Amen.

# September 11

*(Read Psalm 19:1–6)*

### MORNING
Creator God, the magnificence of your created universe fills
me with awe and wonder. In thanksgiving for your marvelous artisanry,
help me walk through this day with a grateful heart.

### EVENING
Creator God, as the sun sets and the curtain of night falls, I lay before you
my thoughts and acts of this day. I trust that they have been pleasing in your sight.

The wordless, majestic display of sun, moon, and stars speaks silently
and universally of you, Creator God, with greater eloquence and power
than any words ever could. We are so accustomed to speech—TV,
radio, telephone, and general conversation—that all too frequently, the
words uttered fall on unhearing ears. Yet often we seem to fear silence.
Give me, O God, the wisdom to discern times for speech and times for
silence, so that in both, I may offer you praise and glory.

### MORNING
Teach me, O God, to speak pleasingly today so that people may
listen, and teach me to hear with empathy when others speak.
*(Prayers of Intercession)*

### EVENING
In the quiet of this evening hour, accept my flawed efforts of this day,
I pray. And strengthen me as I continue my faith journey tomorrow.
*(Prayers of Intercession)*

---

STILL ME, QUIET ME, THAT I MAY CENTER ON YOU AND HEAR YOUR VOICE
ABOVE THE NOISE AND CLAMOR OF THE WORLD.
*(Pray the Prayer of Our Savior.)*

---

### MORNING
Guide me today so that through
silence and speech alike my life will
glorify you. In Jesus' name. Amen.

### EVENING
Thank you, gracious God, for
walking with me through this day.
Enfold me in the shelter of your love
tonight. In Jesus' name. Amen.

# September 12

*(Read Psalm 19:7–14)*

**MORNING**

God of my life, as I greet this day, I pray your love
will guide what I think, do, and say. May my actions be pleasing
to your Child, Jesus Christ, my Pattern.

**EVENING**

God of my life, look with mercy on my business today.
Forgive when I have failed to recognize your presence. Help me
to be a more faithful disciple tomorrow.

Today is the first day of the rest of my life. Today I must choose whether
to do right or wrong. God, the future is your secret. But what I decide
today may help to shape my future as well as that of my family and community. Obedience to your precepts is the key. Only by giving you my
allegiance, making your law my law, and taking your plan for my plan
will my life truly be worth living. Help me, O God, to choose correctly.

**MORNING**

For everyone who faces hard choices today—choices with far-reaching
consequences—I pray, O God, for your counsel and wisdom.
*(Prayers of Intercession)*

**EVENING**

Merciful God, forgive my errors in judgment today and intensify
my desire to follow you more intentionally tomorrow.
*(Prayers of Intercession)*

WE ARE RESPONSIBLE FOR WHAT OUR MINDS THINK,
WHAT OUR HEARTS RESOLVE, AND WHAT OUR HANDS DO.
*(Pray the Prayer of Our Savior.)*

| MORNING | EVENING |
|---|---|
| Holy God, help me to make | Loving God, thank you |
| good use of the gift of this day. | for your presence and direction today. |
| In Jesus' name. Amen. | Knowing you love me, I shall rest in |
| | peace. In Jesus' name. Amen. |

# September 13

*(Read Psalm 116:1–9)*

### MORNING

Wondrous God, as the radiant sun warms the earth this morning, so may the warmth of your love radiate through me to those whose lives touch mine today.

### EVENING

Wondrous God, bless me through the night with the gift of your renewing strength, and wake me in the morning refreshed and eager to do your will.

Before the days of antibiotics and the wonders of modem medicine, a four-year-old child was declared dead by the attending physician. The ravages of diphtheria had taken their toll. The mother requested permission to pick up the child in a final gesture of good-bye. As she cradled her child in her arms, she saw the child's eyelids flutter faintly, and she quickly summoned the doctor. He detected a faint pulse. The child lived! Praise be to you, Loving God! I was that child. Many years later, I, like the psalmist, walk humbly and gratefully before you in the land of the living.

### MORNING

Caring God, let all who are experiencing pain feel your healing touch today.
*(Prayers of Intercession)*

### EVENING

Merciful God, if I have carelessly caused any of your children pain today, forgive me and teach me to pray with renewed understanding the prayer our Savior taught.
*(Prayers of Intercession)*

LET US WALK GRATEFULLY EACH DAY IN THE LIGHT OF GOD'S LOVE,
AWARE OF GOD'S LIVING PRESENCE.
*(Pray the Prayer of Our Savior.)*

| MORNING | EVENING |
|---------|---------|
| As I greet this morning, I greet you, | Grant a night of revitalizing rest, |
| my God, and praise your holy name. | a prelude to renewed energy for service |
| In Jesus' name. Amen. | tomorrow. In Jesus' name. Amen. |

# September 14

*(Read James 3:1–12)*

### MORNING

God of wisdom, let me not interrupt you with my chatter today.
Rather, help me listen attentively to your still, small voice.

### EVENING

God of wisdom, as the evening rays color the sky, I pray that my words today
have lent encouragement to one discouraged, have offered hope to one suffering,
and have expressed gratitude for kindness shown.

It has been said that a spoken word, a sped arrow, and a lost opportunity can never be recalled. Pondering this truth, I have become acutely aware of the power of words both to hurt and to heal. Angry, hateful words may be forgiven, but their scars remain forever. By our words we are known, for they are a mirror to our character. By our words we also honor or dishonor you, O forgiving God. Guard, I pray, my tongue from evil; let the words of my mouth be acceptable to you.

### MORNING

Merciful God, let me not be dismayed by the mistakes
I made yesterday. Let me think ahead with joy to today.
*(Prayers of Intercession)*

### EVENING

I pray that I lived today well, both in word and in deed,
in a manner pleasing to you, my Savior and Redeemer.
*(Prayers of Intercession)*

FOR THE POWER YOU GIVE US TO USE OUR VOICES FOR GOOD, THANK YOU, GOD.
*(Pray the Prayer of Our Savior.)*

### MORNING

Loving God, much is expected
of those to whom much is given, and
I have been given much! Keep me
alert to opportunities for serving you
by serving others today.
In Jesus' name. Amen.

### EVENING

Now I lay me down to sleep.
Keep me in your watchful care, and
wake me in the morning light to do
what's right with all my might.
In Jesus' name. Amen.

# September 15

*(Read Mark 8:27–38)*

**MORNING**
Almighty God, I thank you for the gift of this day.
Help me draw closer every hour to your Child, Jesus, that in our Savior's
presence, I may know more fully the abundance of your grace.

**EVENING**
Almighty God, as twilight falls and I reflect upon the day just ending,
I pray that my life today has affirmed Jesus Christ as my Example and my Redeemer.

God, how easy it is to sing about the cross of Jesus, the cross of sorrow
and pain, and to vow to stand beneath that cross. It is much more difficult to embody those sentiments in day-to-day living. How often our
actions contradict our words! The Jesus of Easter is so much easier to
follow than the Jesus of Calvary. The joy of discipleship is much more
inviting than is its cost. To choose deliberately to put ourselves unre-
servedly in Christ's service, sharing the burdens of other lives and
unashamedly professing Jesus as Savior, is the mark of true discipleship.

**MORNING**
Loving God, walk with me through this day.
Where I am weak, make me strong so that I may better serve you.
*(Prayers of Intercession)*

**EVENING**
Bless, O God, the labors of this day now ending
and grant your peace in the quiet of rest.
*(Prayers of Intercession)*

---

**THE WAY OF THE SUFFERING SAVIOR LEADS TO THE PAIN
AND GLORY OF THE CHRISTIAN GOSPEL.**
*(Pray the Prayer of Our Savior.)*

---

| MORNING | EVENING |
|---|---|
| Guiding God, let your will be my will today. In Jesus' name. Amen. | If I have disappointed you today, O God, forgive me and grant me now your loving benediction. In Jesus' name. Amen. |

# September 16

*(Read Isaiah 50:4–9a)*

### MORNING

Eternal God, be in this day. Be in my broken prayers
and the exultation of my heart. Be in my voice, mind, and hands
as I seek to share your love with all I meet.

### EVENING

Eternal God, in gratitude I praise you with joy
for your constant presence, nearer to me than the air I breathe.
Forgive my shortcomings. Bless me to be a blessing to others.

God, you have a plan for each of us, but you will never force that plan
on anyone. It is our task to seek your will by prayerful listening, and to
implement it. The scope for fruitful activity in this world is wide and
varied, furnishing a place for service and a use for every talent. By the
inspiration of the Holy Spirit, we can discern the role we should play
in helping to bring your realm of justice, righteousness, peace, and love.

### MORNING

Gracious God, who stands at the door of our lives,
let me listen for your voice today and open the door for you to enter.
May my listening spur my action in obedience to your will.
*(Prayers of Intercession)*

### EVENING

Look with love, compassionate God, upon my attempt
to live in harmony with your will today. Let me be an
even more faithful servant tomorrow.
*(Prayers of Intercession)*

---

To THE LISTENING EAR, GOD SPEAKS; TO THE WAITING HEART, GOD COMES;
THROUGH WILLING HANDS, GOD MINISTERS.
*(Pray the Prayer of Our Savior.)*

---

### MORNING

Dwell in me, O God, and make me
an instrument to reach out in love to
someone today. In Jesus' name. Amen.

### EVENING

In the stillness of the night, renew my
strength as in your blessed love I rest.
In Jesus' name. Amen.

---

# September 17

*(Read Matthew 22:1–14)*

**MORNING**
Thank you, God, for this day.
I will embrace it with confidence and faith.

**EVENING**
Thank you, God, for your enabling and your guidance
through the day. By your grace I have done my work today.

Too long have I stood on the margins looking in, powerless, voiceless, watching others making decisions about me. Too long have I simply accepted the order of things, never reaching for changes or asking, "Why?" Then I heard God calling my name and I saw the angels setting a place for me at the banquet table. And I knew that I am a child of God. I have a right to be here. Thanks be to God.

**MORNING**
Give me the grace, dear God,
to know and embrace your love today.
*(Prayers of Intercession)*

**EVENING**
Thank you, dear God, for you have shown me
your love in many ways today.
*(Prayers of Intercession)*

**THERE IS A SPECIAL PLACE FOR YOU AT THE BANQUET TABLE.**
*(Pray the Prayer of Our Savior.)*

**MORNING**
Dear God, to whom I have completely surrendered my life, make me an instrument of your love and grace toward the people I meet today.
In Jesus' name, I pray. Amen.

**EVENING**
Most gracious God,
who causes all things beautiful to grow, may the seeds of love and compassion planted today blossom.
In Jesus' name, I pray. Amen.

# September 18

*(Read Exodus 32:1–14)*

**MORNING**

Dear loving God, I commit myself to your will
in everything I do today.

**EVENING**

Dear loving God, thank you for your blessings upon me today
and for your grace that enabled me to fulfill your will.
Where I have fallen short, forgive me.

But for your grace, Caring God, I am always in danger of committing idolatry. How easy it is to venerate the symbol, to worship the image as if it is your essence. For it is with good intentions that we stray. The path to idolatry is paved with a passion for truth, but passion misguided. How easy to take the symbol for Truth. Thanks to you, O God. By your grace I have been saved.

**MORNING**

Guide me through the day, O God,
that I may not stray from your will today.
*(Prayers of Intercession)*

**EVENING**

Loving God, you have revealed yourself to me in many ways today.
Give me your grace to worship you and you alone.
*(Prayers of Intercession)*

---

**BLESSED ARE THEY WHO WAIT UPON [GOD].**
*(Pray the Prayer of Our Savior.)*

---

**MORNING**

Most compassionate God,
who in Jesus Christ has provided a
way of forgiveness, have mercy on me
as I start another day. I am weak, yet
by your grace I will overcome.
In Jesus' name I pray. Amen.

**EVENING**

Gracious God, by whose compassion
our sins are forgiven, deliver me from
my idolatrous ways by the revelation
of your true self, through Jesus Christ
our Savior, in whose name I pray.
Amen.

# September 19

*(Read Psalm 106:1–6)*

**MORNING**

Loving God, I pray that today I may be among your people
who exude blessedness and release your love.

**EVENING**

Loving God, I have sensed your presence in my life all day today.
I place myself in your secure hands for the night.

When I take the time to reflect on your blessings upon us, I am overwhelmed by your immeasurable love. It does not only come in the form of the great things you do to keep the universe in its place and amazing equilibrium; it also comes in the minute details of my life. You understand my insecurities. You remember my fears and lift me out of my anxieties. I trust you without reservation, in small and great things, because you know who I am.

**MORNING**

Remember me, dear God, as I seek to fulfill your will today.
*(Prayers of Intercession)*

**EVENING**

I give thanks to you, God. You have been good to me
and your love is eternal.
*(Prayers of Intercession)*

---

I LOVE YOU, GOD. YOU UNDERSTAND THE MINUTE DETAILS OF MY LIFE.
YOU KNOW ME MORE THAN I KNOW MYSELF.
*(Pray the Prayer of Our Savior.)*

---

**MORNING**

Loving God, in whom we trust and have the courage to live, help me to keep my faith in you today and to continue trusting in your promises. In Jesus' name I pray. Amen.

**EVENING**

Dear God, thank you for the people whom you have sent to enrich my life today. Thank you for the community around me. Give me the strength to keep on serving you. In Jesus' name I pray. Amen.

# September 20

*(Read Psalm 106:19–23)*

### MORNING
Dear God, guide me through the day,
that I may not fall into temptation.

### EVENING
Dear God, give me grace to worship you and you alone.

All Scripture is inspired by you, dear God, and it is useful in guiding me to spiritual growth. But Scripture is not the totality of you. In it, you are revealed but not contained. God, you are greater than your word in Scripture. To elevate Scripture to your totality is idolatry. To do so is to exchange your immeasurable glory for the image. Words give us but a snapshot of your glory. God, you are the Great Spirit. In Jesus Christ, we experience and develop a relationship with you. But we can never contain the Great Spirit.

### MORNING
Praise God, for God has set me free.
*(Prayers of Intercession)*

### EVENING
Praise God, who has called me by name.
*(Prayers of Intercession)*

---

### "THEY FORGOT THE GOD WHO SAVED THEM!"
*(Pray the Prayer of Our Savior.)*

---

### MORNING
Gracious God, who has given us freedom to explore your wonderful creation and for whom we have a yearning to worship, give me the wisdom to know my weaknesses, the will to embrace your transforming power, and the faith to wait for your promises.
In Jesus' name I pray. Amen.

### EVENING
God of mercy, who in Jesus has given me a second chance, forgive my idolatrous ways and help me to walk in accordance with your will.
In Jesus' name I pray. Amen.

# September 21

*(Read Isaiah 25:1–9)*

**MORNING**

Loving God, the day ahead of me is littered with challenges.
Give me the faith and the courage to face them.

**EVENING**

Loving God, thank you. I felt your presence in my life today.
I triumph because of your love. You are my strength.

Sometime it looks as though bad people are winning. I look out and everything seems to be falling apart for those who strive to do the right thing. At such times I pause to wonder why—God, why won't you intervene? When will justice be done? When will the just be vindicated? But you have shown me that justice will be done in your own time. In your time you turn the tables and set the oppressed free. In your time the song of the ruthless is stilled. This is my testimony.

**MORNING**

God, in you I have the courage to embrace another day.
*(Prayers of Intercession)*

**EVENING**

God, you gave me the strength to face today's challenges.
*(Prayers of Intercession)*

**IN GOD'S OWN TIME JUSTICE WILL BE DONE.**
*(Pray the Prayer of Our Savior.)*

**MORNING**

Almighty God, in whom we have
refuge in our distress, lift up a shelter
for your people in need, a shade for
those with various kinds of pressure,
that today may be a day of triumph
for those who love you.
In Jesus' name I pray. Amen.

**EVENING**

Almighty God, who provides
for our every need and more, teach us
to appreciate one another and the gifts
we share among ourselves.
In Jesus' name I pray.
Amen.

# September 22

*(Read Psalm 23)*

### MORNING
Loving God, I place myself in your hands today, trusting that you
are my shepherd and will guide me in the right path.

### EVENING
Loving God, thank you, for you have allowed me to rest in fields
of green grass today and you have led me to quiet pools of fresh water.

I look back at some of the most trying times of my life and wonder: how
did I survive that? How is it possible that I was not crushed by the weight
of so much suffering? How is it that I was not afraid? How did I overcome? Then I remember that all along, in the middle of my most trying
moments, you were there. My spirit was securely wrapped into yours and
I was safe. Why should I be afraid? Your goodness and love will indeed
be with me all my life and your house will be my home as long as I live.

### MORNING
You are my loving God.
There is nothing of which I should be afraid.
*(Prayers of Intercession)*

### EVENING
You are my loving God. Whenever I call your name, you answer.
*(Prayers of Intercession)*

MY SPIRIT SECURELY WRAPPED INTO YOURS, THERE IS NOTHING TO FEAR.
*(Pray the Prayer of Our Savior.)*

### MORNING
Almighty God, who in Jesus Christ
delivered us from the sting of death,
give me the faith to trust in you that I
may not be afraid any more.
In Jesus' name I pray. Amen.

### EVENING
Most gracious God, in Jesus Christ
you have forgiven us our sins.
Renew us that we may walk in accor-
dance with your will. In Jesus' name
I pray. Amen.

# September 23

*(Read Philippians 4:1–9)*

**MORNING**

Dear God, I pray that I may be joyful in union with you this day.

**EVENING**

Dear God, thank you for all the people you brought into my life
today and for using me as a channel of your blessings to some.

We are what we allow our minds to feed on. If I fill my mind with violence, anger, and hatred, I will have nothing worthwhile to share with the people around me. Caring God, I will be a curse rather than a blessing upon your people. I will therefore fill my mind with things that are good, deserving, and praiseworthy. I will fill my mind with things that are true, noble, right, pure, lovely, and honorable. Then out of me shall flow your blessing upon the community.

**MORNING**

Loving God, today we rejoice in the gift of being your children.
*(Prayers of Intercession)*

**EVENING**

Dear God, help me to get along with the people
in my life who disagree with me.
*(Prayers of Intercession)*

**REJOICE IN THE UNION WITH CHRIST.**

*(Pray the Prayer of Our Savior.)*

**MORNING**

Gracious God, in whom are good
and praiseworthy things, give us the
grace to fill our minds with things that
are true, noble, pure, and honorable,
that our lives may glorify your name.
In Jesus' name I pray. Amen.

**EVENING**

God of mercy, who in Christ
has provided a way for us to confess
our sins and be forgiven, forgive us
our sins. In Jesus' name I pray.
Amen.

# September 24

*(Read 2 Timothy 1:1–7)*

**MORNING**
Good morning God! I awaken this day
with the promise of life that is in Christ Jesus!

**EVENING**
Good evening, God! The day is spent. I am tired and weary.
Rest cannot come soon enough. My prayer is that I lived this day
in its entirety in your will; if not, please forgive me.

God, I am grateful this day for those who saw something in me years ago that I did not see in myself. Those persons believed in me and taught me how to believe. They encouraged me and never stopped praying for me. I am grateful for their continued prayers. There are days when I forget who I am and whose I am. When faced with the challenges of life and ministry, it is easy to become timid or fearful. Thank you, God, for reminding me at those times that you did not give me a spirit of timidity or fear, but a spirit of power, love, and self-discipline.

**MORNING**
Giver of every good and perfect gift,
help me to fan into flame the gift that you have placed in me.
*(Prayers of Intercession)*

**EVENING**
As I prepare to retire for the evening, I do so remembering
those with whom I share the joy of loving relationship.
*(Prayers of Intercession)*

**IN FAITH, I PRAY TO YOU, O GOD.**

**MORNING**
As I enter the day, may I do so
with a sincere faith—the faith of one
who accomplished great things for
you, O God. For the sake of Jesus,
I pray. Amen.

**EVENING**
May the promise of life
be renewed in me as I sleep, O God.
For the sake of Jesus,
I pray. Amen.

# September 25

*(Read 2 Timothy 1:8–14)*
*Sing "Evening Prayer" or another familiar hymn.*

### MORNING

O God, renew in me this morning a sense of your purpose for my life
and for this day. I don't want to waste a minute of the life you have given me.

### EVENING

O God, it was a tough day. Fulfilling your purpose for my life and
living up to your holy calling is not easy.

I'm really not ashamed of you, God. I just don't like conflict. Being in places every day with persons who question whether or not you are real is a challenge for me. I want to defend you, but at times I'm not sure what to say. I suppose I should just tell them my story. It is only by your grace that I am who and what I am. The grace that was revealed to me in Christ Jesus has made me who I am. You have called me with a holy calling to share with others the good news of grace found in your Child Jesus. I am ashamed. I will tell everyone I have an opportunity to tell who Jesus is even if they shun me.

### MORNING

Give me the words to say that will bring honor and glory to you!
*(Prayers of Intercession)*

### EVENING

What a wonderful day this was! I claimed your power
to speak boldly on some pretty tough issues. I pray for those who will
claim the power of a new life in Christ and boldly witness.
*(Prayers of Intercession)*

---

**I AM PRAYING TODAY WITH RENEWED CONFIDENCE IN THE POWER OF PRAYER!**

---

### MORNING

I know I believe in you, O God,
and I know you will guard what I entrust to you this day. For the sake
of Jesus, I pray. Amen.

### EVENING

If I have wounded any soul today,
if I have walked in my own willful way,
if I have caused one foot to go astray,
dear God, forgive me. For the sake
of Jesus, I pray. Amen

# September 26

*(Read Lamentations 3:19–26)*

**MORNING**

Reassuring God, what a joy to wake up this morning
with the assurance of your love and mercy.

**EVENING**

Reassuring God, thank you for keeping me safe this day!

I was tempted to give up today, God. I had lost all hope. I thought about all that I have already been through, and at times it looks like things are getting worse and not better. I didn't know how much more I could take. I wasn't sure I wanted to take any more until I remembered how loving and compassionate you are. You know what I am going through. You have been faithful to keep me thus far, and I know that you will continue to be faithful. My hope has been restored. I will be delivered. All I have to do is wait for you.

**MORNING**

You are so good to me, God! Your Word says that you are good
to those whose hope is in you. I will live this day in anticipation
of your goodness and your love.
*(Prayers of Intercession)*

**EVENING**

I am still waiting for you, Compassionate One.
I know that you know what I need.
*(Prayers of Intercession)*

**WAITING FOR YOU, MY STRENGTH IS RENEWED.**

| **MORNING** | **EVENING** |
|---|---|
| Every morning, your love for me is renewed. I feel brand new in the fullness of your love for me. For the sake of Jesus, I pray. Amen. | I can lie down and rest secure knowing that I am loved by you. For the sake of Jesus, I pray. Amen. |

# September 27

*(Read Habakkuk 1:1–4, 2:1–4)*

**MORNING**
Creator God, this is the day that you have made.
I will rejoice and be glad in it.

**EVENING**
Creator God, rejoicing in you this day gave me the courage
to see it through.

God, I know that it seems like I am always complaining, but I have some concerns about the way things are going in the world. Violence has never been so prevalent. Young people make plans for their funerals rather than their graduations. It is not safe for children to walk the streets. Some of them are not even safe at home. How long must I cry to you about the injustices in the land? Isn't it time that we dealt with racism, sexism, classism, and ageism? Why are you tolerating these wrongs? Say something, God!

**MORNING**
I lift up to you this day all those who work for and practice peace with justice.
I pray for myself, that I may be a part of the solution and not the problem.
*(Prayers of Intercession)*

**EVENING**
I bring to you all those who have been the perpetrators
and victims of violence.
*(Prayers of Intercession)*

**I AM WAITING PATIENTLY FOR AN ANSWER FROM YOU.**

**MORNING**
Your Word makes clear to me
that the righteous shall live by faith. I
have faith this day that those things
that concern me are of concern to you
as well. For the sake of Jesus,
I pray. Amen.

**EVENING**
I don't always understand your
timetable, but I know that you are
always on time and in time. Your
timing is always perfect—I trust that!
For the sake of Jesus, I pray.
Amen.

# September 28

*(Read Psalm 37:1–9)*

**MORNING**

Sustaining God, trusting in you I am safe.
Delighting in you I have the desires of my heart.
What can anyone do to me?

**EVENING**

Sustaining God, I had another day of rest in you
and your love for me. I am so blessed!

Today, I am clear that I am not to fret, even when evil persons succeed in their plans or when they carry out their wicked schemes. Their plans and schemes soon come to nothing, just like them. But the righteous flourish and your just cause will overcome the wickedness of those who are unjust. You see to that, God, in your own time and in your own way.

**MORNING**

One day the wicked will cease from troubling and the weary will
be at rest. Thank you, O Giver of Rest, for this blessed promise.
*(Prayers of Intercession)*

**EVENING**

God, give me the strength not to want to seek revenge
or to get even when folks mess with me.
*(Prayers of Intercession)*

**I WILL LIVE EACH DAY IN PEACE WITH MY NEIGHBOR.**

**MORNING**

As I begin this new day,
I commit everything to you, God: all
my hopes, dreams, and desires.
For the sake of Jesus, I pray.
Amen.

**EVENING**

As I end this day. I commit to you,
God, all my hurts, disappointments,
fears, and frustrations. I will lie down
in peace. For the sake of Jesus,
I pray. Amen.

## September 29

*(Read Luke 17:5–6)*

**MORNING**

God, I have only one request of you this morning:
Increase my faith!

**EVENING**

God, I believe you. It is by faith that I find myself
in relationship with you. Help my unbelief.

God, you keep challenging me to trust you more, to take you at your word and step out on your promises. I keep asking myself, "What have I got to lose?" It's not like you are asking a lot of me. If I had faith the size of a mustard seed. . . . A mustard seed isn't very large; it is quite small, and it doesn't take a whole lot of faith to do great things for you. You can take nothing and make something of it. If I can conceive it, I can achieve it. Help my unbelief.

**MORNING**

I have faith in you to help me accomplish the following tasks
or to help me achieve victory in the following areas of my life . . .
*(Prayers of Intercession)*

**EVENING**

I have faith in you to do great and small things
in the lives of the following persons . . .
*(Prayers of Intercession)*

**WITH FAITH, NOTHING IS IMPOSSIBLE TO ME!**

**MORNING**

Faith sees the invisible,
claims the unreachable, and does the
impossible. Faith can conquer anything! For the sake of Jesus, I pray.
Amen.

**EVENING**

Without faith it is impossible to
please you, God. I want to please you.
For the sake of Jesus, I pray.
Amen.

# September 30

*(Read Luke 17:5–10)*

**MORNING**
God, I ask so much of you, what is it that you
would have me do for you today?

**EVENING**
God, I am not worthy of all that you do for me.
I give you the best of my service. I owe it to you.

God, I am so fortunate that you would even let me serve you. I know
that I am not worthy. Whatever I give is my duty. I need to remember
this, because sometimes I want to act like I am doing you a favor. I really don't mean to be so arrogant. Forgive me when at times I tend to
think of myself and my gifts more highly than I should.

**MORNING**
I offer this prayer with thanksgiving
for all those who serve you faithfully.
*(Prayers of Intercession)*

**EVENING**
God, I offer this prayer with thanksgiving
for those who fulfill thankless duties for you.
*(Prayers of Intercession)*

**THANK YOU, GOD, FOR THE GIFT OF FAITH.**

**MORNING**
Prepare me this day, O God,
for another day of meeting the needs
of persons on your behalf and in your
name. For the sake of Jesus, I pray.
Amen.

**EVENING**
I want to hear you say one day,
"Well done, good and faithful servant."
For the sake of Jesus, I pray.
Amen.

# October 1

*(Read Luke 15:1–10)*

### MORNING
Most compassionate God, stir in me the sensitivity
to see people not as the world sees them but as those
who are precious in your sight.

### EVENING
Guide my steps, O God, that I may walk in the steps
of those who are considered expendable in this world.

God, your love is inclusive and seeks out especially those who are least able to do for themselves. The woman in the parable must be someone with limited means, or else she would not have searched so carefully. A rich woman could have decided easily that the lost coin was not worth bothering about.

### MORNING
Loving God, grant me wisdom,
so that I may see the faces of my brothers and sisters
in all people and not just those who are like me.
*(Prayers of Intercession)*

### EVENING
Ever-present God, let me not forget that when I am lost,
you are present. Help me to be in touch with you.
*(Prayers of Intercession)*

---

**"JESUS IS EASILY SEEN AS THE GOOD SHEPHERD
BUT SELDOM SEEN AS THE GOOD HOUSEWIFE."**

(John Dominic Crossan)

---

### MORNING
God, in whom there is rest,
calm my spirit, so that I may go to
sleep and awake refreshed
in the morning. Amen.

### EVENING
Most compassionate God, help me
to see and feel the expansiveness
of your love for those who seem least
important in ordinary life.
Through Jesus Christ, our Lord.
Amen.

# October 2

*(Read Jeremiah 4:11–12)*

### MORNING
O God of righteousness, I feel the heat of your anger
when people stray from your ways,
and I want to shield myself from your judgment.

### EVENING
O God of righteousness, you are angry
because your people do not listen to you.

When the war in Kuwait was ending and the Iraqis were fleeing to their own country, they set fire to all the oil wells. The scene looked as though a hell had been created on earth. God of creation, when human beings resort to wanton destruction of other human beings and the earth's resources, how deep your anguish must be.

### MORNING
Anger is very often a cover-up for hurt and disappointment.
Help me, caring God, to understand my anger and teach me
to listen to the anger of others.
*(Prayers of Intercession)*

### EVENING
O God, I confess that I am sometimes angry at you
for what seems to be unfair in this world. Help me to work
through my anger so I may feel your compassion.
*(Prayers of Intercession)*

---

**"FOR I HAVE REDEEMED YOU; I HAVE CALLED YOU BY NAME, YOU ARE MINE."**

---

### MORNING
Let not the anger of others blind me
to the possibility of understanding
and compassion for what lies beneath
the anger. Through Jesus Christ,
our Lord. Amen.

### EVENING
When the heat of my anger has
spent itself, help me, O God, to look
within and view my relationship to
you. Grant me rest for the night that I
may awaken to a new day. Through
Jesus Christ, our Lord. Amen.

# October 3

*(Read Jeremiah 4:22–28)*

**MORNING**

Creator God, the signs of your presence in this world
are everywhere. Open my eyes and tune my ears so I may see
and hear more keenly.

**EVENING**

Creator God, you gave us a good creation
and placed your people as stewards. Guide me in my ways
so that I might be a worthy steward.

Creator God, your presence is everywhere, in Scripture and in your land. Like your Word, all things become new when your spirit abounds. In the midst of your destroyed creation, the signs of your presence are coming forth in places like Kaho'olawe. Restoration returns.

**MORNING**

I pray that restoration and conservation of the earth's resources
will prevail. May I do my part to make it so.
*(Prayers of Intercession)*

**EVENING**

O God, pour your healing into the devastated places
of the earth and let your people correct their destructive ways.
*(Prayers of Intercession)*

**"HAVE REGARD FOR YOUR COVENANT, FOR THE SHADOWY PLACES
OF THE LAND ARE FULL OF THE HAUNTS OF VIOLENCE."**

**MORNING**

O God, signs of your presence
in this world are everywhere.
Through Jesus Christ, our Lord.
Amen.

**EVENING**

O God, you know that all things
need rest. May the stars and the moon
keep watch while the earth sleeps in
your care. Through Jesus Christ,
our Lord. Amen.

# October 4

*(Read Psalm 14)*

**MORNING**
O God who is the refuge of the poor,
keep me alert to see the signs of your presence, even as the world
tries to convince me that you are absent.

**EVENING**
O God, bless all those who call on your name.

Omnipotent God, when cynics say you do not exist, they do not know what they are saying. All forces of evil, sloth, pride, and destruction could be unleashed and no one made accountable if your realm did not exist. The hearts and minds of human beings would be cold and calculating, and no one would care for their neighbor. Save us, O God, from such a fate.

**MORNING**
O God who gave human beings the freedom to choose
either good or evil, guide my thoughts and actions, so that I
may seek that which is right in your sight.
*(Prayers of Intercession)*

**EVENING**
God of mercy, may the poor seek refuge in you tonight.
Grant them the Spirit that will kindle hope.
*(Prayers of Intercession)*

**"WHERE GOD IS, EVERYTHING IS POSSIBLE."**

(Walter Brueggermann)

**MORNING**
God who is with the righteous
and the poor, do not count me among
the cynics who say there is no God.
Through Jesus Christ, our Lord.
Amen.

**EVENING**
Grant me rest, O God,
as I go to sleep, knowing that you are
with me. Through Jesus Christ,
our Lord. Amen.

# October 5

*(Read Exodus 32:7–14)*

### MORNING

O God, whose compassion is greater than your wrath,
I am thankful that you can change your mind—even with people
who may have offended you.

### EVENING

O God, grant me the humility to know when I have been
too harsh and unyielding with others. Help me to be supportive
of those who have had a change of heart.

God, when a Canaanite woman asked Jesus to heal her daughter who
was tormented by demons, he at first refused. He said he was sent "only
to the lost sheep of the house of Israel." Later, however, he changed his
mind and healed the daughter because of the woman's great faith. Great
is your faithfulness!

### MORNING

O God, whose realm overcomes distinctions of race, color,
or creed, keep me open to receive and respond to different
expressions of faith.
*(Prayers of Intercession)*

### EVENING

O God, help me to know that your love never fails those
whose hearts are repentant.
*(Prayers of Intercession)*

---

"AS OFTEN AS I SPEAK AGAINST HIM, I STILL REMEMBER HIM.
THEREFORE I AM DEEPLY MOVED FOR HIM; I WILL SURELY HAVE MERCY ON HIM."

---

### MORNING

Most compassionate God, your people
are easily led astray by the attractions of
false gods. Let not your wrath consume
them. Grant them wisdom and courage
to change their ways. Through
Jesus Christ, our Lord. Amen.

### EVENING

Most compassionate God,
it has been a demanding and
perplexing day. Grant me rest for the
night and fresh energy when I awake.
Through Jesus Christ, our Lord.
Amen.

# October 6

*(Read Psalm 51:1–10)*

**M O R N I N G**

Most merciful God, you know me better than I know myself.
Help me to begin the day with the gift of a clean spirit within me.

**E V E N I N G**

Most merciful God, you have known me since I was in my mother's womb.
What evil I have committed, knowingly or not, that was my doing and
mine alone. Forgive me that I might start anew.

God, forgiveness is a gift from you. It is seen in your Scripture and in
times of pain. When families fight and tragedy strikes, you are an in-
termediary. Your love can rise above all evil and unrest. You are always
transforming lives.

**M O R N I N G**

Help me, O God, to understand that when I mistreat
my neighbor or consider my neighbor to be less important than myself,
I am sinning against you. Forgive me and help me to correct my ways.
*(Prayers of Intercession)*

**E V E N I N G**

O God who forgives and makes new, enfold me in your Spirit
like a wind that blows through and around me,
so that I may be clean and fresh again.
*(Prayers of Intercession)*

---

**"THE SACRIFICE ACCEPTABLE TO GOD IS A BROKEN SPIRIT;
A BROKEN AND CONTRITE HEART, O GOD, YOU WILL NOT DESPISE."**

---

| **M O R N I N G** | **E V E N I N G** |
|---|---|
| I thank you, God, for being ever watchful over me and demanding that I be true to you. Through Jesus Christ, our Lord. Amen. | You have called forth in me, O God, my deepest loyalty, which is to you. And now I go to rest with thank-fulness and peace. Through Jesus Christ, our Lord. Amen. |

# October 7

*(Read 1 Timothy 1:12–17)*

**MORNING**

Most merciful God, immortal and invisible yet most patient
and forgiving, I thank you for giving me life and turning me
around when I have not heeded your ways.

**EVENING**

Most merciful God, immortal and invisible, you call us
into your service even if we have done evil things. If we repent and turn
to you, you are gracious and eager to receive us. Thank you.

God, your grace and mercy sustain me. When we run away from our
faults, you are there; when we steal, you are there; when we are imprisoned, you are there. Your Child, Jesus, came into the world to save us
from sin. Thank you for your mercy and for those who are merciful.

**MORNING**

It is easy for me, O God, to condemn those who break
human laws and hurt their families. Teach me wisdom in my
heart, that I may know your mercy.
*(Prayers of Intercession)*

**EVENING**

O God, teach me not to judge others' failings.
I, too, am a failure when I turn away from you. Temper my pride
so I can ask for your forgiveness.
*(Prayers of Intercession)*

**"SO IF ANYONE IS IN CHRIST, THERE IS A NEW CREATION."**

**MORNING**

O God, often I do not understand
the motives of people I know, but you
do. And for those who truly repent,
your mercy is abundant. Thank you,
God. Through Jesus Christ,
our Lord. Amen.

**EVENING**

Most merciful God, I lay before
you all that I have thought and done
this day. Grant me rest for the night
and a fresh start when I wake in the
morning. Through Jesus Christ,
our Lord. Amen.

# October 8

*(Read Job 38:34–41)*

### MORNING
How could I have lost you? Signs and symbols of your presence
are with me everywhere! I am open again to hear and see.

### EVENING
For all you have given and the insights that came,
now I remember who presides and provides. Thank you, my God.

God, you placed wisdom in these autumn colors of my life and season. Help me to reflect on Job's experience with my own. Like trees blown bare, an ordering of my life becomes clearer. I forsook Wisdom—she who for so long inspired my life when you brought her to me as a gift. Earth's rhythms and hidden cadences show me an order so profound that I am returning to her and to you. You came in mutuality with Job to recall him to faith. I would like answers to your plan for my life. God, are you telling Job and me that there is no plan, but that there is an ongoing ordering of my life, which is a part of your creating?

### MORNING
I am going to rage and rave with you today, God.
I will need courage to do so, but I need you to come forth
from hiding and speak with me for this season of my life.
*(Prayers of Intercession)*

### EVENING
My God, we did it! I shouted; you pronounced.
Such freedom and release.
*(Prayers of Intercession)*

---

### AND NOW IN YOUR GRACE I ENTRUST MY PRAYER.

---

### MORNING
My life is in your hands.
I thrive in your orderings
of my journey. In the name
of the Christ. Amen.

### EVENING
Thank you for your Word
unto this day and through this night.
In the name of the Christ.
Amen.

**281**

# October 9

*(Review Job 38:34–41; read Psalm 104:1–9, 24, 35c)*

**MORNING**
All glory, honor, and awe be to God! In you, my God,
I will be refined this day by the fire and flame of my daily routine.

**EVENING**
All glory, honor, and awe be to God! Rendered to ash
were my guilt and shame by confession and fire; I let go of judgment.

God of judgment for justice, cleanse me by your fire and flame so that I leave judgment to you. I am caught by the psalmist's words, that fire and flame are your ministers. The ending of the song "Amazing Grace" uses the injunction "Let sinners be consumed from the earth, and let the wicked be no more." Does this mean that I, and we, who forget to honor the fullness of your creation, are the sinners and the wicked? Every day I start the morning by building a fire; it is part of my survival. Let it remind me that fire and flame are your ministers. Perhaps my confessions to you are like the logs in my stove. They become ash as I am warmed by their heat. Does your fire and flame minister to me by rendering my confessions into heat, which warms me to life and becomes balm for my day?

**MORNING**
God, be fire and flame to my soul so that I may be warmed
this day by the rendering to ash of my confessions.
*(Prayers of Intercession)*

**EVENING**
Let my sin flee by your Word as the waters fled by your rebuke.
*(Prayers of Intercession)*

---

CLEANSE ME TO KNOW YOUR MEANING, GOD OF MY SALVATION.

---

**MORNING**
Be balm to my heart
by the warmth of your flame.
In the name of the Christ.
Amen.

**EVENING**
Keep me warm through the night,
that my spirit may be cleansed afresh
until the morn. In the name
of the Christ. Amen.

# October 10

*(Read Isaiah 53:4–12 and Psalm 91:9–16)*

### MORNING

Caring God, to be partners with you in creating is an
awesome responsibility! I accept with joy in my spirit. I stand in
awe to know that I am a partner and steward of your mysteries.

### EVENING

Caring God, to be partners with you in creating is an awesome responsibility!
I accept with joy in my spirit. What a joy and task to have the job of protecting
you. My call is to answer and obey. I trust that I have been and done so this day.

God, your prophet Isaiah and your psalmist call me back to know that
the time is fulfilled. I am Eve; I am Adam. I am nature and history.
Named by you, I am partners with you. Imbue me with the will to serve
you fully. Isaiah knew the freedom that comes from cleaving to you.
Cleaving seems more personal—I like it. I have been teased for being
Christian and scorned for being a minister. Usually I feel defensive and
spiteful. How good, how released I have felt the few times I have
cleaved to you and simply said yes. I want to learn more about cleaving
and to be your partner in loving and creating in the world. Teach me
more, God. I commit myself this day to cleaving.

### MORNING

When you call, God, I will answer. Awed but not afraid, I will cleave to you.
*(Prayers of Intercession)*

### EVENING

To deliver you to life is freedom and release,
salvation in immanence even when reviled.
*(Prayers of Intercession)*

GOD, MY BURDEN IS LIFTED, AND MY HEART IS FULL OF LOVE FOR YOUR REVELATIONS.

| MORNING | EVENING |
|---|---|
| I am called to succor you. I will be succor as I open to this new understanding of who I am. Thanks be to Christ. Amen. | Thanks beyond belief for the experience of knowing you, my God, as a partner. Thanks be to Christ. Amen. |

# October 11

*(Review Isaiah 53:4–12; read Hebrews 5:1–10)*

### MORNING

God, teach me more of what it means to be a priest—
your ministry of all believers. Made anew by you, I cease my search
and answer my call to community. I rejoice in new life.

### EVENING

God, teach me more of what it means to be a priest—
your ministry of all believers. Appointed by your Spirit, I have given
myself this day. And I am your servant.

Angel messengers at dawn break into our lives and give us resolutions we cannot make ourselves. Insights, revelations, the Word. They are imps, troublemakers, for they change us into your greeters and servants. And so we serve, take stands, listen, and often forget how to receive as well as give. I am one of these so favored. But I am afraid—not with the fear provoked by danger but with the awe evoked by wisdom, the wisdom that makes me know I will suffer. So I will try to stop and understand rather than leap to fix the suffering—my own and that of others. Jesus' call is not my call. However, fulfilling my call, as he fulfilled his, is being made perfect in you.

### MORNING

I remembered those vague images and felt the deep breathing release
of resolution as I awoke: an angel messenger at dawn! Thank you.
*(Prayers of Intercession)*

### EVENING

I am pondering the meaning of my message and my suffering.
I am begotten to fulfill your ordering.
*(Prayers of Intercession)*

---

**KEEP ME, THAT I MIGHT KNOW MORE FULLY MY FULFILLMENT.**

---

### MORNING

Out of my suffering, my loss, my
chaos, come a new day, a new order,
and a new covenant with God.
Thanks be to Christ. Amen.

### EVENING

Grace infuses me from the learnings
of this day. Thanks be to you, my God,
for fulfilling me in your eternal covenant.
Thanks be to Christ. Amen.

# October 12

*(Read Mark 10:35–45)*

### MORNING
God, you really are right in our midst. Keep coming and waking me.
What is my preparation, my serving you on my path of fulfillment? I am ready.

### EVENING
God, you really are right in our midst. Keep coming and waking me.
These were my experiences . . . My preparation was . . .
My fulfillment is . . . I give thanks for . . .

Parent God, what made your Child was his knowing and cleaving to you. Christ Jesus fulfilled to perfection his call. How do I follow his norm? Each of us is prepared for our own fulfillment in you. I remember that Jesus said he came to fulfill the law, not to destroy it. The word he used for "fulfill" means to fill a cup to overflowing. Is this what you intend for me too? I may share in baptism and the cup with Jesus, but my fulfillment is not to be the Christ. It is something else: what? What are the clues, the obvious characteristics? How am I fulfilling these now? Perhaps I am still fighting being a Christian, for I have not yet given myself up fully. It does mean leading and accepting full responsibility for all I am given. In this day, how shall I lead and minister as your servant?

### MORNING
God, make me responsive to your call for my service.
Help me to see and hear the fullness you intend.
*(Prayers of Intercession)*

### EVENING
God, I tried to be flexible and allow you to transform me.
I feel . . . I learned . . . I know now . . .
*(Prayers of Intercession)*

---

**BEING FORMED AND FULFILLED CAN SEEM OVERWHELMING. THE GIFT IS TO LET GO IN GOD.**

---

### MORNING
God, lead me into my community
as a servant this day. Thanks be
to Christ. Amen.

### EVENING
Your peace is mine. Thank you,
God, for fulfillment. Thanks be
to Christ. Amen.

# October 13

*(Read Isaiah 53:4–12 and Mark 10:35–45)*

### MORNING

God of all creation, what a gift you have given us!
For this morning, I want to reflect on who I am and what being Christian
means, through this poem in each of my meditations.

### EVENING

God of all creation, what a gift you have given us!
For this evening, I want to reflect on who I am and what being Christian
means, through this poem in each of my meditations.

God of all creation, what a gift you have given me! To be born in a time
of one globe, one people, one economy, of mixed genes. Cross-fertilized
by rituals and food, faith and art, music and media, trade and politics,
even terror, war, and death. What chaos, what creativity. Whose am I?
You are my God, and I am your person. Alleluia!

### MORNING

Help me to see the plank in my own eye, shared with all people
who refuse to see and hear anew.
*(Prayers of Intercession)*

### EVENING

Open me to your unconditional love so I may love my neighbors
near and far, here and now.
*(Prayers of Intercession)*

---

**AS ONE CALLED TO LEAD IN THE WAY OF CHRIST,
CATCH ME AND GUIDE ME TO YOUR WISDOM AND WORD.**

---

### MORNING

Dear God, wake me to really
understand the person who seems
most different in my life this day.
Thanks be to Christ. Amen.

### EVENING

Cleanse my spirit through
the night, with dreams configured for
my light to see and hear anew.
Thanks be to Christ. Amen.

# October 14

*(Read Psalm 91:9–16 and Hebrews 5:1–10. Reflect on the week's readings.)*

**MORNING**

God, through the Christ, I come to you. On this Sabbath day,
I submit myself to your Word through Christ's spirit.

**EVENING**

God, through the Christ, I come to you.
Night is folding 'round me, settling all the day.
Gently let me know how I have been the way.

In my faith community, I will know more fully your Word and the way of Jesus. Through the seeing and hearing of my neighbors, my faith will be enriched. Sometimes I wonder about the church; then I remember that my faith community is found in and through the church. Jesus' way is the way of which I have so much more to learn. He is the one in whom I have placed my trust. Not the media, not my political party's platform, not my teachers or my workplace, not even my family. The focus is Christ Jesus, the mark is God, and I will keep returning to faith in and through all I experience in my faith community.

**MORNING**

God, remind me of my baptism and the words I spoke,
so that their meaning becomes fresh this day.
*(Prayers of Intercession)*

**EVENING**

I know that my gifts, life experiences, joys,
and sufferings are from you in the way of the Christ.
*(Prayers of Intercession)*

---

**FOR SCRIPTURE THAT LEADS ME TO REMEMBER AND TO PONDER,
I GIVE THANKS AND AM HUMBLED IN FAITH AND COMMUNITY.**

---

| **MORNING** | **EVENING** |
|---|---|
| God, when I share the cup, | Obedience to your Word and way |
| infuse me with a focus for my faith. | is becoming my freedom and faith. |
| In Christ and in the world. | For this gift, I rest in peace and trust. |
| Thanks be to Christ. Amen. | Thanks be to Christ. Amen. |

# October 15

*(Read Proverbs 22:1–2, 8–9)*

MORNING

Bountiful God, I breathe in the first breaths of this new day.
This breath, my very life, is a gift from you. My first words to you
this morning are "Thank you, loving God. Thank you for life."

EVENING

Bountiful God, the pulse of my breath and heart calms
as I begin my evening rest in you. Thank you for your abiding
and generous care throughout the day.

Abundant God, in poverty or wealth, keep me near you. In my poverty, you are my bread, my shelter, my only hope. In my wealth, you are the source of all my gifts. Without you, far from you, I hunger and despair. Even when I am rich in silver and gold, if I am without you I desire only more of that which neither fills nor shelters me. Loving God, give me a bountiful eye, to see all the gifts that surround me. Teach me your ways, that I may live with a grateful and generous heart. Come to the aid of all who without food, home, or hope call out to you.

MORNING

Keep me alert to the needs of those around me.
Be their sustenance, shelter, and joy.
*(Prayers of Intercession)*

EVENING

Help me to recall those in need today. Bountiful God, whom did I see
and where did I witness those who need your nourishment and care?
*(Prayers of Intercession)*

YOU ASKED YOUR FOLLOWERS TO PRAY THIS PRAYER.
WITH ALL YOUR CHILDREN, RICH AND POOR, I PRAY.
*(Pray the Prayer of Our Savior.)*

| MORNING | EVENING |
|---|---|
| Send me into this day, God, | Let me rest in you, sheltered, fed, |
| serving you and my neighbor. | and assured of your eternal care. |
| Thanks be to Christ. Amen. | Thanks be to Christ. Amen. |

# October 16

(Read Psalm 125)

### MORNING

Strong God, you held me through the night.
Awaken me to your ways today.

### EVENING

Strong God, you looked on me today with a watchful gaze.
Listening God, hear me now as I call upon you this evening.

When I am surrounded by you on all sides, O God, I am not afraid. Many forces threaten your people: relationships, work, finances, violence, change, political realities, and the terror of our own hearts. But when I imagine you as a mountain range, sheltering me in your valley, these forces are held at a distance. Guarded by your mountain strength on the north and south, the east and west, your people know great assurance and joy. Help me to live with such confidence in your care that I may live justly. Ground me in such strength that my heart and life declare your goodness. Bring all your people into your care. Keep them safe.

### MORNING

God, guard those who are under attack
by violence, injustice, and disease.
*(Prayers of Intercession)*

### (EVENING

Strong, Loving God, I saw, heard, and read of those
in need today. Help me to remember their faces. Come to them
with your strength and comfort.
*(Prayers of Intercession)*

---

### I JOIN WITH ALL YOUR CHILDREN WHEN I PRAY.

*(Pray the Prayer of Our Savior.)*

---

| MORNING | EVENING |
|---|---|
| With you, I confidently journey into your world to love and serve. Thanks be to Christ. Amen. | With the release of a deep breath, I rest in you, God. I sleep in your mountain arms. Thanks be to Christ. Amen. |

# October 17

*(Read James 2:1–10, 14–17)*

**MORNING**

Persistent, ever-working God, wake me to your work
in this world. Do not let me grow sleepy, but keep me always
ready to act on my faith in you.

**EVENING**

Persistent, ever-working God, I call upon you at the end
of the day, when my work ceases. Hear my prayers even in the night.

God, your Word says, "So faith by itself, if it has no works, is dead."
These are hard words. I wonder how much I hide my faith in only being
nice and in saying prayers? You call for more from your people, from me.
Enliven me so that when I see or hear your people suffering, I will act.
Replace any hesitation to serve with a passion born of authentic faith.

**MORNING**

God, today I will be cautious of my prayers.
When shall I pray, when shall I act? Move me to love
and serve those for whom I pray.
*(Prayers of Intercession)*

**EVENING**

God, forgive me for not having responded to all of the needs
I witnessed today. I pray for those in need.
Teach me how you would have me minister to those needs.
*(Prayers of Intercession)*

---

YOUR PRAYER WAS MORE THAN WORDS.
IT WAS A LIFE LIVED FAITHFULLY. TEACH ME TO PRAY.
*(Pray the Prayer of Our Savior.)*

---

| **MORNING** | **EVENING** |
|---|---|
| God, today make my life show absolute love and faith in you. Thanks be to Christ. Amen. | My work is done today. Forgive what I did not do. Only in your grace can I rest. Thanks be to Christ. Amen. |

# October 18

*(Read Psalm 146)*

**MORNING**

Steadfast God, you saw me through the night.
If I am wise, I will trust you through this new day.

**EVENING**

Steadfast God, at the end of this day, I come before you.
Help me to recall your presence throughout the day.

Whom should I trust? I wonder about that sometimes. Just when things seem so certain, so rock-solid, people and situations change. Your Word, God, reminds me that people and their best-made plans last only a little while. What keeps us, keeps me, from despair? Am I to trust you, God? You have been present and faithful since the beginning. You have created and continue to create. You remain. No one else shows such compassion for the poor and downtrodden. You inspire our best acts of compassion and justice. O God, I want to trust you, your justice, your consistent love for this world. Trusting you, I seem to trust humanity a bit more. Am I right? God, in your grace, reveal your trustworthiness.

**MORNING**

Gracious God, I name those who are on my heart this morning.
I entrust them to your watch and care.
*(Prayers of Intercession)*

**EVENING**

Abiding God, please watch over these persons,
to whom you have given your breath. I entrust them to your care.
*(Prayers of Intercession)*

**WITH THE CONFIDENCE OF THE CHILDREN OF GOD I PRAY.**
*(Pray the Prayer of Our Savior.)*

| **MORNING** | **EVENING** |
|---|---|
| God, today I trust in you. I will live in the assurance of your steadfast care. Thanks be to Christ. Amen. | Eternal God, tonight I rest in you, trusting in your care. Thanks be to Christ. Amen. |

# October 19

*(Read Isaiah 35:4–7a)*

### MORNING
Restoring God, I am awake.
You bring me and this world to life again.

### EVENING
Restoring God, at the end of today's journey, I come to you.
Hear these prayers.

Welcoming God, I have been exiled before, far from home. At times, this world is an inhospitable and uninhabitable wilderness. You seem so far away. There have been times, as well, when I exiled others. I am the one who kept others away and made their lives difficult. Your Word promises renewal and a welcome return: fear will cease; sightless eyes will see again; water will flow over the hardened desert floor; grass will grow green and tall. God, in your grace replenish our world. End all places of exile—those we live in and those we create for others. Return us to you, our fertile Home.

### MORNING
God, this morning welcome these persons into your tender care.
*(Prayers of Intercession)*

### EVENING
Loving God, these persons and situations come to my mind
this evening. In your mercy, bring healing and renewal.
*(Prayers of Intercession)*

JESUS PRAYED FOR A NEW WORLD. MAY GOD'S REIGN COME.

IN CONFIDENCE, I TOO PRAY.

*(Pray the Prayer of Our Savior.)*

| MORNING | EVENING |
|---|---|
| When I go about this day, God, bless me with your vision of a welcome and just world. Thanks be to Christ. Amen. | God, as I sleep, grant me your vision of a wilderness renewed and people healed. Even as I rest, show me your ways. Thanks be to Christ. Amen. |

# October 20

*(Read Mark 7:24–30)*

**MORNING**

Creating God, who knows and desires the depths of my heart,
bring me to full life today.

**EVENING**

Creating God, before I rest, I want to tell you my heart.

Intimate One, will you hear me? You are a brave and vulnerable God. Through your Word, you introduce us to the Syrophoenician woman. She was also brave and vulnerable. When Jesus rejected her and her child, she talked back with faithful wisdom. God, be intimate. Wrap me in you so that I may challenge with confidence preconceptions about you and your people. Enrich our mutual love so that we may speak the truth to one another, even in heartbreak and disappointment. Let the woman teach me to declare your justice and acceptance, even when you are silent.

**MORNING**

Mysterious God, bring to my heart and imagination
all those who are disregarded because of their race, culture,
nationality, health, orientation, ability, age, or gender.
*(Prayers of Intercession)*

**EVENING**

God, I bid you to care for those whom so many disregard.
Do not forget these, your children.
*(Prayers of Intercession)*

---

**WITH THE CONFIDENCE OF THE CHILDREN OF GOD I PRAY.**
*(Pray the Prayer of Our Savior.)*

---

**MORNING**

Send me, God, to listen for your truth in the words of those who have been forgotten. Send me, God, to speak passionately a truth that demands life for your children. Thanks be to Christ. Amen.

**EVENING**

Mysterious and intimate God, let me know you even better as I rest in you tonight. Thanks be to Christ. Amen.

# October 21

*(Read Mark 7:31–37)*

**MORNING**

Healing God, may the first words I think or speak today
be thanks to you.

**EVENING**

Healing God, may the last words I think or speak today
be thanks to you.

Before I speak, teach me to think about you, God. Before I talk, touch my mouth with your hand. Heal my mouth with your salve of wisdom, compassion, and justice. Let me gaze into your eyes long before I open my mouth. Teach your people, your church, to carefully discern the word you would have us say today. And when you are ready, when we are ready, declare, "Ephphatha, be opened!" Heal our speech. Forgive us when we silence others. Forgive us when our words destroy or deceive. Forgive us when we are silent, even when you call us to proclaim a word. May we utter the miracle of your Word, because we first heard the Word from you.

**MORNING**

God, help me name those who long for your healing touch and Word.
*(Prayers of Intercession)*

**EVENING**

Healing God, bring to my mind those persons who today,
in silence or speech, desire your presence.
*(Prayers of Intercession)*

IN SIMPLE WORDS, PLAINLY SPOKEN, I PRAY WITH ALL YOUR CHILDREN.
*(Pray the Prayer of Our Savior.)*

| **MORNING** | **EVENING** |
|---|---|
| Wise God, open me to your Word spoken today. Thanks be to Christ. Amen. | Compassionate God, speak to me in the silence of my sleep. I rest in you. Thanks be to Christ. Amen. |

# October 22

*(Read Joshua 3:7 –17)*

**MORNING**
God of difficult crossings, I arise, rejoicing
that you exalt my precious humanity.

**EVENING**
God of difficult crossings, I rest, thankful that you held back
this day's concerns and troubles from swamping me.

God of Purpose and Direction, guide me as you guided Joshua and the people of Israel, through transitions: birth or death; new jobs or retirement; the first months of kindergarten, college, or a nursing home; marriage, divorce, or the death of a spouse; new towns, new churches, new colleagues, new goals. Each of these frightens me. Help me to stand still, clutching my faith, as the Israelites did the ark, and expecting the way to be clear.

**MORNING**
I pray for those, particularly adolescents,
who need a sign to believe in their possibilities for going forward.
*(Prayers of Intercession)*

**EVENING**
I pray for those who need your protection "going over Jordan"
into death this night.
*(Prayers of Intercession)*

---

**WHEREVER WE GO, YOU GUIDE OUR PATHS AND STEADY OUR FEET.**

---

**MORNING**
Holy God, for myself and for others,
I pray that this day will be filled with
large and small transitions.
May they become opportunities for
your blessing. In the name
of the Christ. Amen.

**EVENING**
Holy God, restrain the flood
of my confusions, yet bathe me
in the river of sleep. In the name
of the Christ. Amen.

# October 23

*(Read Psalm 107:1–7)*

**MORNING**

Loving God, open my mind, heart, spirit, and body to thankfulness,
so that everything I do today may be rooted in gratitude
for creation's wonder and the intimacy of your saving presence.

**EVENING**

Loving God, as I prepare for sleep, let me count out thanks
for the particular blessings of this day.

Your song is found in the rhythms of the psalmist, in the heartbeat of
an infant, and in thousand-year-old light pulsing from a distant star.
And yet you know each one of us. You have always been, you are now,
and you always will be a source of limitless caring. However faint, lost,
needy, or frightened your people are, you sustain them. Forgive me
when I don't remember your love for me. Forgive me when I don't vol-
unteer to be a love-sharer with others.

**MORNING**

I pray for the thirsty, and I pray to be empowered
to give the living water.
*(Prayers of Intercession)*

**EVENING**

I pray for the hungry, and I pray to be empowered
to give physical sustenance.
*(Prayers of Intercession)*

---

**I KNOW WHAT IT IS TO BE LOST. SEEK THOSE WHO ARE LOST THIS DAY.**

---

**MORNING**

Send me, one of your found children,
out into this day willing to share my
faith and your love. In the name of
the Christ. Amen.

**EVENING**

As one of your found children,
I relax secure in your grace and
expectant of the blessing shadow
of the night. In the name of
the Christ. Amen.

# October 24

*(Read Psalm 107:33–37)*

**MORNING**

God of river blessing, soak into the parched desert soil
of my life today, so that I may be an oasis to all who pass my way.

**EVENING**

God of river blessing, I give you thanks for the fruitfulness
of my day in work, friendship, family, community, and church.
Now I am thirsty for the deep drink of silence.

Justice-seeking God, some of the parched, barren, desert places in our society are the results of human wickedness. I confess that sometimes I wait to ride the wave of some miraculous ever-flowing stream when I could be planning an irrigation system with pipelines through school boards, town meetings, ballot boxes, community centers, urban gardens, youth outreach, prison visitation, and my own congregation.

**MORNING**

I pray for those whose experience is life as a salty waste
because of discrimination based on race, age, ability, gender,
sexual orientation, or ethnic background.
*(Prayers of Intercession)*

**EVENING**

I pray for the small settlements where justice is bubbling up
in secret this night. Some of them are churches.
*(Prayers of Intercession)*

---

**WE ALL "FOLLOW THE DRINKING GOURD" AS WE TAKE YOUR PATH TO FREEDOM.**

---

**MORNING**

Today I am wet with love of you,
love of all your children, and love
of myself. Splash me. In the name
of the Christ. Amen.

**EVENING**

Tonight I am wet with love of you,
love of all your children, and love of
myself. Let my surface reflect your
face. In the name of the Christ.
Amen.

# October 25

*(Read 1 Thessalonians 2:9–13)*

**MORNING**

Voice in my heart, Word of God, I awaken and know
you have been speaking in my dreams.
I turn to Scripture, expecting you again.

**EVENING**

Voice in my heart, Word of God,
I reflect on this day and know you have spoken in nature,
friend, and event. I turn to scripture, expecting you again.

Day and night, light and darkness, creatures and breath—all are your words. The Christ child of Mary, Wisdom of creation, Healer, Bread-breaker, and Star-namer are your words. Teach me to listen. Teach me, as well, to trust my own fragile words to share your love, even when I know they are imperfect. And teach me, like Paul, not to burden with my gospel words but to witness, lift up, and encourage.

**MORNING**

I pray for those who have been damaged because your Word
was enslaved by bigoted, judgmental, or fanatic human words.
*(Prayers of Intercession)*

**EVENING**

I pray for those who have lost interest because your Word
was masked by boring, trivial, or repetitious human words.
*(Prayers of Intercession)*

YOUR WORD IS A LAMP TO MY FEET; LET ME BE A WISE KEEPER OF OIL.

**MORNING**

Open my lips, that I may praise you.
Let your Word work in me today, that
I may be worthy of the life you have
given me. In the name
of the Christ. Amen.

**EVENING**

Hear my prayers and then
close my mouth, so that I may listen
to your whisper before I speak.
In the name of the Christ.
Amen.

# October 26

*(Read Micah 3:5–12)*

### MORNING
Prophet-maker God, I rise this morning willing to face
my situation with honesty. Confront me with what I should do and say.

### EVENING
Prophet-maker God, I rest the struggles of this day in your care.
As you have stirred my spirit, now ease my weariness.

You call me to unflinching evaluation of my political, social, and economic environment. I confess that sometimes I avoid challenging the injustices that create a society in which I am silent when others are harmed, unless I or someone close to me is threatened. Shake me with your Spirit and pour into me your call for justice, so that I may never be tempted to murmur a false "peace" instead of an uncomfortable prophecy.

### MORNING
I pray for journalists, preachers, and politicians,
all in their own ways called to be prophets.
*(Prayers of Intercession)*

### EVENING
I pray for elementary-school teachers, lawyers, and artists,
all in their own ways entrusted with the preservation of truth-telling.
*(Prayers of Intercession)*

---

TEACH ME TO LIVE WITH HONESTY AND JUSTICE IN MY OWN HOME AND FAMILY
BEFORE I CONFRONT THE LARGER WORLD.

---

### MORNING
Open me to your will this day,
Creator of true peace, Christ of the
dispossessed, Spirit of urgent answers.
In the name of the Christ. Amen.

### EVENING
Let the sun go down on false prophecy,
compromise, and faithlessness. May I
discover your clarity under the night
wings. In the name of the Christ.
Amen.

# October 27

*(Read Psalm 43)*

### MORNING
Light-sender, Hope-sealer, Morning Joy, I praise you with the harp
of my soul-strings, and I dance to the altar of your dwelling in my heart.

### EVENING
Light-sender, Hope-sealer, Evening Refuge, I praise you again
for the plucked tunes of this day's music. I climb the holy hill
of your nightfall.

Ubiquitous God, sometimes I am unsure of your presence, particularly when I am buffeted by the opinions of others. I defend you against arguments and indifference. When I do not feel your constant warm assurance because of personal suffering and grief or the random violence and oppression of the world, I am resentful and petulant. Help me to welcome you into the depths of pain as well as good fortune, so that I can understand your love of me. With joy and sorrow, teach me to be more fully human.

### MORNING
I pray for those who will face this day the diagnosis of an illness,
the death of a spouse, the loss of a job.
Give them strength for their mournful walking.
*(Prayers of Intercession)*

### EVENING
I pray for those who are depressed this evening, especially those
tempted to end their lives. Be their dwelling place of safety.
*(Prayers of Intercession)*

---

"WHY ARE YOU CAST DOWN, O MY SOUL, AND WHY ARE YOU DISQUIETED WITHIN ME?"

---

### MORNING
Send out your light and your truth,
and let them lead me through this day.
In the name of the Christ. Amen.

### EVENING
So assure me of your love that my doubt
may melt away and my hope may shine
brightly enough to be seen by others.
In the name of the Christ. Amen.

# October 28

*(Read Matthew 23:1–12)*

**MORNING**

Creator God, I awaken humble before sunshine and rain, humble before
the magic of time and the treasure of space, humble before the bounty of
human diversity and the kaleidoscope of human behavior.

**EVENING**

Creator God, I lay down the burdens other people have pressed on me today
and those I foolishly have chosen for myself. I lay down the burden of sinfulness
and that of self-righteousness. I float into your embrace.

You, Creator God, are all the authority I need. Protect me from religious doctrines and observances that squeeze the joy out of faith. Shut my ears to self-appointed judges, and help me recognize my own tendency to place obligations on others. Save my faith community from being stifled under committees, traditions, insider groups, deadening liturgy, or endowment funds. Let us travel light.

**MORNING**

I pray for surgeons, psychotherapists, CEOs, foster parents,
who are given authority and may choose to be servants.
*(Prayers of Intercession)*

**EVENING**

I pray for fast-food handlers, assembly-line workers, and nursing-home aides,
that within their servant roles they may discover a deep authority.
*(Prayers of Intercession)*

---

"ALL WHO EXALT THEMSELVES WILL BE HUMBLED,
AND ALL WHO HUMBLE THEMSELVES WILL BE EXALTED."

---

| **MORNING** | **EVENING** |
|---|---|
| Christ, stern and gentle Teacher, remind me that I am called to be a servant. In the name of the Christ. Amen. | Christ, stern and gentle Teacher, I am exalted by your love. Nothing I have ever known compares to the sheer exaltation of resting in your grace. In the name of the Christ. Amen. |

# October 29

*(Read 1 Samuel 1:4–20)*

### MORNING

Ever-present God, my heart is open before you this new day,
trusting in your compassionate presence.

### EVENING

Ever-present God, for remembering me this day,
I thank you with my whole heart.

With an open heart I praise you for your eternal and compassionate remembrance of me. In her deep and silent distress, enduring alone the
"shame" of barrenness, the pain of ridicule, and the guilt of apparent
worthlessness, Hannah presented herself to you at the temple. As bitter
tears flowed from an anxious and vexed heart, she prayed for a child . . .
for worth . . . for happiness. Upon receiving words of promise, which
she knew in her heart to be true, she returned to her quarters, filled
with hope and trust. For God, you would remember her and honor her
life with the child named Samuel.

### MORNING

I welcome this day, trusting that all in my soul is known to you,
my dear God.
*(Prayers of Intercession)*

### EVENING

For a day of light and shadow and your goodness in it,
I give you a heart filled with the deepest of gratitude.
*(Prayers of Intercession)*

---

### "THE BEST NAME FOR GOD IS COMPASSION."

(Meister Eckhart)

---

### MORNING

In anticipation of tears and laughter,
pain and happiness, I thank you, for
in them my soul finds your healing
presence. Through Jesus Christ,
I pray. Amen.

### EVENING

For the wiping of my tears and
the healing of my troubles, I worship
and adore you, O God, this night.
Through Jesus Christ, I pray.
Amen.

# October 30

*(Read 1 Samuel 2:1–10)*

**MORNING**

Merciful God, may I sing a new song of praise to you this day,
with a glad and adoring heart.

**EVENING**

Merciful God, for a day lived in and through your strength, I give thanks.

I will sing to you Hannah's song, making her prayer and proclamation mine. Caring God, with a heart filled with gladness, Hannah, being thankful for your strength and victory, knowledge and judgment, celebrated in poem and song your remembrance of her in the day of her deep distress. In poem, she recognizes and proclaims with her whole life that you not only remembered her but remember also the feeble, hungry, poor, low, needy, and faithful ones. Loving God, you know their needs and respond with generosity, raising up those who have been forgotten and neglected. You break the bows of the mighty. You raise the poor from the dust. You lift the needy from the ash heap. God, you will judge the ends of the earth.

**MORNING**

In this day I will rejoice in your strength, knowledge, and judgment, O God.
*(Prayers of Intercession)*

**EVENING**

In your goodness I will rest this night, assured of your presence
with me, even in my sleep.
*(Prayers of Intercession)*

---

**WITH A HEART OPEN TO NEW LIFE, PLACE INTO YOUR OWN WORDS HANNAH'S SONG.**

---

| MORNING | EVENING |
|---|---|
| In my waking, I celebrate your goodness for all, especially the downcast, the poor, the needy. And with you, I commit my life to their raising up. Through Jesus Christ, I pray. Amen. | Now I rest in you, knowing that you will raise me up to new life and commitments. Through Jesus Christ, I pray. Amen. |

# October 31

*(Read Daniel 12:1–3)*

**MORNING**
God of new mornings, upon awaking this day,
I remember that you are my salvation.

**EVENING**
God of new evenings, in my sleep, may my whole being and all
who put their trust in you rest in the promise of your salvation.

God, you have promised to be with us always. In suffering and crises,
you are the salvation of all people. God, your promise of everlasting life
extends to all who walk in the way of right relationships, even in times
of increased evil and oppression. Protection and deliverance from evil
will come from you. Shame and everlasting contempt will come to
those who do evil. Yet the doers of justice—the lovers of righteousness—will shine like the brightness of the sky and the stars, which are
forever and ever. This is your promise, sealed with truth. Let us run always to these words of life, for in you is our salvation.

**MORNING**
You are my protector and deliverer. This day I will trust
in your protection and deliverance. I will look to you.
*(Prayers of Intercession)*

**EVENING**
As I come to the end of this day, I thank you for
leading me into the way of righteousness, of right relationships.
*(Prayers of Intercession)*

**AND JESUS SAID, "I WILL BE WITH YOU UNTIL THE END OF AGE."**

**MORNING**
May each moment of this day be filled
with the brightness of eternal life. May
eternity be near to me and to all who
love your ways of true justice and peace.
Through Jesus Christ, I pray. Amen.

**EVENING**
In the hours of my sleep, seal in me
and in all your people everywhere
your words of life. Through Jesus
Christ, I pray. Amen.

# November 1

*(Read Psalm 16)*

### MORNING
Awesome God, how wonderful you are! In you I will take refuge this day.

### EVENING
Awesome God, this night while I sleep, I trust that your counsel will continue
to instruct my heart in your ways of goodness and life.

God is the shepherd of my life and all my ways. God, you feed and lead
us. You restore and renew us. You watch over us and wake us up to new
life each morning. You walk with us. You prepare for us the cup of
wholeness and the path of life. I will bless you. I will keep you before
me always. I will be glad and rejoice in you. I will delight in all your
pleasures. I will know the fullness of the joy you give to all the faithful
ones who live with one another as you live with us. We shall not be
moved from this path of life.

### MORNING
Your goodness this day will be my fill. You are my inheritance;
in you my life is made whole and blessed. Thank you, O God.
*(Prayers of Intercession)*

### EVENING
I now rest my body in the wonderful security
of your presence throughout the night.
*(Prayers of Intercession)*

---

SING A SONG OR HUM A TUNE THAT STIRS IN YOUR SOUL
THE WATCHFUL PRESENCE OF GOD OVER YOUR LIFE.

---

### MORNING
Upon waking, I delight in your
counsel, path of life, and pleasures.
Today I will follow in these, knowing
that in you I am secure. Through
Jesus Christ, I pray. Amen.

### EVENING
I give thanks for the pleasures of
your divine presence stirring in me as
I prepare for a night of restoring rest
and peace. O God, you are good, and
my soul knows this. Through Jesus
Christ, I pray. Amen.

# November 2

*(Read Hebrews 10:11–14 [15–18])*

### MORNING
O Loving Holy Spirit, this life of Jesus make mine today.

### EVENING
O Loving Holy Spirit, be the presence this night
that sanctifies my heart, soul, mind, and body.

Prepare me now, O Spirit of the Living One, for these words of life and true meaning. In vain we look for ways of living that leave us empty and without meaning. Yet this need not be how we live. There was a life lived with integrity that is now the way of life for all. This life is Jesus! Jesus, you offered your life, heart, soul, mind, and body. Before they came to take it and nail it to a tree, you gave it back to God. You laid it down in love for us, with the power that comes from above—the power of love, of compassion, of fearlessness, of forgiveness, and of a holy life. Nothing can remove sins and make whole as this life can; yes, this way of life, the only way to live. I know this life and power to be also in you.

### MORNING
This morning I pray, O God, for a clean heart, a heart cleansed
with Jesus' life. Make me one with you, as he was.
*(Prayers of Intercession)*

### EVENING
I will rest this night in your right hand,
for in it I am set apart for your way of life and love.
*(Prayers of Intercession)*

---

**ALL DAY, CONTEMPLATE ON THE WAY OF LIFE JESUS SHOWED THE WORLD.**

---

### MORNING
Today may my life sanctify and set apart for you all that I touch and all that touches me. Through Jesus Christ, I pray. Amen.

### EVENING
May the meditations of my heart and the thoughts of my mind, even now as I lay down, be made whole by your Spirit. Through Jesus Christ, I pray. Amen.

# November 3

*(Read Hebrews 10:19–25)*

### MORNING

Care-giving God, this morning I praise you
for your faithfulness with me and the whole world.
You do not waver with us. Thank you.

### EVENING

Care-giving God, for a day filled with your faithfulness,
I now thank you. This night I will rest secure in it.

May we approach you, O God, and one another with friendship, confidence, intimacy, Christ's life, openness, a true and sincere heart, full assurance, faith, a cleansed conscience, confession, hope, love, togetherness, courage, and with all that comes from the fiber of your being. For you have a great priest in your house, whose name is Christ Jesus.

### MORNING

You give me confidence, O Spirit, to enter into your presence.
I worship you with my whole being.
*(Prayers of Intercession)*

### EVENING

Cleanse my conscience and heart of all that is not pleasing in your
sight this night, and sprinkle me with your purifying presence.
*(Prayers of Intercession)*

### PRACTICE LOVE AND GOOD DEEDS TODAY.

### MORNING

Sprinkle my heart clean
this morning, and make the
confessions I now declare true
and pure in your presence.
Through Jesus Christ, I pray.
Amen.

### EVENING

For the strength to persevere this day
and this night, I give you my deepest
thanks, offering to you my heart,
mind, soul, and body, for your service
of deeds of justice and kindness.
Through Jesus Christ, I pray. Amen.

# November 4

*(Read Mark 13:1–8)*

**MORNING**

Loving God, teach me this new day what really is great and glorious in your sight.

**EVENING**

Loving God, as the end of this day arrives, draw me again to you
and your purpose for me.

Open my eyes, O God, and show me what lives forever. What will survive when all is said and done—when the end appears? What has eternal value? "Not one stone will be left here upon another; all will be thrown down." Stones and buildings do not have eternal permanence. But there is a temple that when destroyed is raised up again in three days. Oh how wonderful it is when our bodies are restored, built up again, by your power and presence, O God. When war, enmity, strife, earthquakes, famines, destroy life and shatter all hopes, your divine purpose still remains. In the end, neither evil nor the might of the nations will prevail. You will judge all things, destroy what makes for rubbish, and save what makes for eternal life.

**MORNING**

I awake to you and your greatness. Keep me from being led astray
from your truth: My life is your temple; all of life is holy.
*(Prayers of Intercession)*

**EVENING**

The wars I heard about today have worn me down. O God,
have mercy upon us and bring to an end all that destroys life.
*(Prayers of Intercession)*

**GOD IS THE ALPHA AND THE OMEGA, THE BEGINNING AND THE END.**

**MORNING**

Give birth to me anew today and teach
me not to fear the might of the nations
and what makes for war. Teach me your
divine purpose: respect for all who
breathe the breath of life. Through
Jesus Christ, I pray. Amen.

**EVENING**

When all of life fades, may I come
to you filled not with shame but with
confidence in your eternal love.
Through Jesus Christ, I pray.
Amen.

# November 5

*(Read Matthew 22:15–22)*

**MORNING**

God over all commerce, may I honor you as I enter today's work.

**EVENING**

God over all commerce, may my life and my life's work
be an offering to you.

It is so easy, O Provider God, to lose sight of purpose, integrity, your teaching, and your truth. We often are trapped and swayed by the systems of trade, commerce, and currency. But Jesus, our example, made no distinction between common living and the reign of your sovereignty. Help us to offer, as Jesus did, all our lives, all our doings, as a praise to you. Help us to give wholly our work in the world of commerce as worship. May even our "daily grind" be made holy by your presence.

**MORNING**

Provider God, help me to work with your intentions in sight.
Give me the courage of integrity.
*(Prayers of Intercession)*

**EVENING**

Provider God, as I review my day, forgive my failures to trust you
or to walk in integrity. Give me grace for the next opportunity.
*(Prayers of Intercession)*

---

**"RENDER EVEN TO CAESAR AS UNTO GOD."**
*(Pray the Prayer of Our Savior.)*

---

**MORNING**

It is so easy to work for work's sake. Teach me, O God, to work with your reign in view. Remind me that jobs and civic responsibilities are merely places in which I may serve you better. In Jesus' name. Amen.

**EVENING**

As I rest in your provision of sleep, O God, may I rest knowing that all that I am and all that I do are in your care. Remind me that jobs and civic responsibilities are merely places in which I may serve you better. In Jesus' name. Amen.

# November 6

*(Read Exodus 33:12–23)*

**MORNING**

Great God of glory, I wake to experience your presence anew.
Throughout this day, may I know your grace and favor.

**EVENING**

Great God of glory, thank you for your presence,
which has attended me today, and for the rest you now give.

Leadership is hard, gracious Leader. While it is sometimes a lonely job, none of us is able to lead alone. In all our endeavors, we need at least two things: able helpers to ensure that the tasks of life are done, and the assurance that your own presence will be our guide and aid. How else can we be assured that the tasks of parenting or pastoring, supervising or supporting, will be done with your favor? We do not want only to get the job done by brute force or human effort. But, gracious Leader, we want the wind of your compassion and mercy, your glory, to be the power in all we do.

**MORNING**

God of goodness, declare your name and presence in my life today.
May I be a conduit of your glory in the earth.
*(Prayers of Intercession)*

**EVENING**

God of goodness, shelter me safely in your care, covering me
with your loving hand. May I know the afterglow of your presence.
*(Prayers of Intercession)*

---

"**MY PRESENCE WILL GO WITH YOU, AND I WILL GIVE YOU REST.**"
*(Pray the Prayer of Our Savior.)*

---

**MORNING**

This day I long for your glory, the assurance that you are with me, and the faith and confidence that you are pleased with me, O God of mercy and compassion. In Jesus' name. Amen.

**EVENING**

As I yield my mind and body to your care in the night, thank you for your steadfast loving-kindness, your mercy and compassion, O God of glory. In Jesus' name. Amen.

# November 7

*(Read Psalm 99:1–5)*

*(Read Psalm 99:1–5)*

### MORNING

Sovereign Creator, give us your perspective on the governments and leaders of the earth. You are the ultimate authority. May we bow to your awesome and holy name.

### EVENING

Sovereign Creator, we exalt you as governor of our lives and of the life of all your people. Indeed, you are the ultimate authority who loves justice and equality.

Almighty God, in whose presence the natural order gives reverence, we praise you for your great and awesome name. Especially we praise you for the characteristic of holiness, by which you measure justice and establish equality. Sometimes, O God, we cannot see what is just and right. All around us are famine and poverty, chaos, and war. Nations and their leaders do not acknowledge your presence in the affairs of all people. Often we are guilty of the same. Help us to live with the perspective of exalting you and bowing humbly at your feet as we share the stewardship of all creation.

### MORNING

God, exalted over all the nations, teach me what is just and right,
then enable me to live my life governed by your justice.
*(Prayers of Intercession)*

### EVENING

I rest tonight on the footstool of your mercy, Holy God.
Be enthroned in my life, and be ruler of my heart and actions.
*(Prayers of Intercession)*

---

**LET US PRAISE GOD'S GREAT AND AWESOME NAME, FOR GOD IS HOLY.**
*(Pray the Prayer of Our Savior.)*

---

### MORNING

As the morning dawns to new
responsibilities and possibilities, help
me experience the day in your holiness.
In Jesus' name. Amen.

### EVENING

Sleep comes to my eyes, O God
of all creation, as to all creatures.
Yet you do not sleep. Watching over me
is your care. In Jesus' name. Amen.

# November 8

*(Read Psalm 99:6–9)*

### MORNING

Choosing God, as you chose Moses, Aaron, and Miriam to represent you in the world, choose me. May I be as Samuel and Huldah, who called on your name.

### EVENING

Choosing God, thank you for giving me the opportunity
to be your emissary in the world.

The world is such a busy and noisy place. We can be distracted so easily. God, your "statutes and decrees" do not seem so readily clear-cut at times. The best we can do is to be as those leaders of old who found a quiet place or sanctuary, or the dead of night, in order to clear the space of noise and people. From these quiet places and times, we emerge with an answer—though not always a distinct one—because it is your nature to answer those who call upon you. And loving God, it is your character to forgive us our misdeeds, though we still face the consequences of our actions. For directions and answers and consequences we give thanks to you, O God.

### MORNING

As you have directed in the past, make your way clear
before us today, O Guiding Pillar.
*(Prayers of Intercession)*

### EVENING

Exalted and wondrous God, you have spoken by and to your people.
We worship you in the place of your choosing.
*(Prayers of Intercession)*

---

**"THERE IS NO QUESTION TOO GREAT FOR GOD; THERE IS NO ANSWER TOO INSIGNIFICANT."**
*(Pray the Prayer of Our Savior.)*

---

### MORNING

Forgiving God who listens when
we pray, I bless you for answering in
expected and unexpected ways.
In Jesus' name. Amen.

### EVENING

In the calm of night, O God, speak
clearly to my heart. In Jesus' name.
Amen.

# November 9

*(Read Isaiah 45:1–7)*

### MORNING

Undisputed God of all creation, remind me that you choose the most unlikely people to carry out your will. May I not turn away from anyone, thinking you could never speak to me or change my life through such a person.

### EVENING

Undisputed God of all creation, I am reminded that you choose the most unlikely people to carry out your will. May I be among those who honor you with my life.

God, we believe that you are for peace and not war. Yet today we read of war. Cyrus was chosen to become the ruler of Syria and did not know it. What a thought: that you may use someone I consider a foreigner and an enemy to show that you are sovereign over all. As we realize this, how do we address the world where we live, when we are told to choose sides constantly? How do we do the work of justice? Teach us, O God.

### MORNING

God, we acknowledge that through ordinary and obscure people
you show yourself to be mighty.
*(Prayers of Intercession)*

### EVENING

God, may we acknowledge that you have strengthened us.
For the sake of your people, we respond to your call.
*(Prayers of Intercession)*

---

"FROM THE RISING OF THE SUN UNTIL THE PLACE WHERE IT SETS,
PEOPLE WILL KNOW THERE IS NONE BESIDES GOD."
*(Pray the Prayer of Our Savior.)*

---

### MORNING

It is easy to dismiss people as insignificant or unimportant. Yet, God, I do not want to be guilty of missing your hand in my life or in the lives of those around me. In Jesus' name. Amen.

### EVENING

If I missed your presence in an unlikely source today, O God, forgive me. Increase my understanding that you are not bound by my human ideas of who should or should not be chosen. In Jesus' name. Amen.

# November 10

*(Read Psalm 96:1–13)*

### MORNING
Majestic God, we worship you in great humility.

### EVENING
Majestic God, we honor your great and glorious strength.

All creation is singing praise to you, Maker of all the heavens and earth. Help us not to destroy your witness among the created order by our own selfish abuse of nature. You alone are to be reverenced and honored. For in spite of injustices, troubles, and turmoil, the world is firmly established by your love, and you, O God, will judge every action of humanity with equality and justice. You are a righteous judge in an unseemly world. In a world of falsehoods, your truth will prevail in righteousness. May these realities be my song both day and night.

### MORNING
Giver of songs, as wind whispers of your splendor among treetops,
so I offer my songs up to you.
*(Prayers of Intercession)*

### EVENING
Giver of songs, I turn from all my idolatries
and worship you in all your splendor and glory.
*(Prayers of Intercession)*

---

### "DECLARE GOD'S GLORY AMONG THE NATIONS,
### GOD'S MARVELOUS WORKS AMONG ALL THE PEOPLES."
*(Pray the Prayer of Our Savior.)*

---

### MORNING
Our world is so full of ugliness, horror, and pain. It is difficult to see your glory in the midst of it all, O God.
Today help me to sing of your grace and righteousness even in the presence of unrighteousness. In Jesus' name. Amen.

### EVENING
Our world has so much possibility. Nature sings of it. May my heart sing along. In Jesus' name. Amen.

# November 11

(Read 1 Thessalonians 1:1–10)

### MORNING

Living and true God, help me to be a model of one
who believes in your active presence in our world.

### EVENING

Living and true God, help me to model with full conviction
your sustaining grace.

In the pressures of living are we known, Living Presence. Authentic witness to Jesus the Christ must be made with more than words; it also must be made in power and in the Holy Spirit and with full conviction. Deliver us from lip service and half-hearted devotion. May our work be in faith. May it be a labor of love. May we have a tenacious hope in Jesus the Christ. Increase our joy in service, so that the love of Christ is evident to all who are greeted by us. We wait expectantly for your divine interruption in our lives. In the meantime, help us imitate our Savior in every way.

### MORNING

Divine Joy and Hope of Heaven,
give us grace and peace to enter the world with full conviction.
*(Prayers of Intercession)*

### EVENING

Divine Joy and Hope of Heaven,
give us peace and grace to share your gospel with full conviction.
*(Prayers of Intercession)*

---

**"WE ALWAYS GIVE THANKS TO GOD FOR ALL OF YOU AND MENTION YOU IN OUR PRAYERS."**
*(Pray the Prayer of Our Savior.)*

---

### MORNING

I want to be an imitator of you, gracious God. I want to imitate your love and care and power for and in the world. May I welcome those whom you welcome to serve you, living and true God. In Jesus' name. Amen.

### EVENING

I wait for your interruption into my life, O God. I want to experience your resurrection power each day and labor in love toward your destiny. In Jesus' name. Amen.

# November 12

*(Read Jeremiah 33:14–16)*

### MORNING
Covenant-keeping God, spring up within me today,
that I may welcome your coming.

### EVENING
Covenant-keeping God, thank you for guiding me through the day and
leading me in paths of righteousness. Now grant me a night of recovery and rest.

In a culture that feeds on individualism and is forever promoting measures to actualize the self, we need a visitation from the One who can fill our deepest needs—the God of Abraham, Isaac, and Jacob; the God of Jesus, the Christ. Our efforts at self-redemption are ever so dangerous, leaving humankind bankrupt and shipwrecked. We have lost our sense of righteousness by covenanting with the gods of self-aggrandizement. Covenant-keeping God, break through these disordered lives of ours with your redeeming presence. Cause your righteous branch to spring up within us, for we cannot save ourselves.

### MORNING
God of newness, today help me to be present to all that is righteous,
all that is just, and all that is of you.
*(Prayers of Intercession)*

### EVENING
Merciful God, you have companioned me today.
You have broken forth in many ways to lighten my burden. Thank you.
*(Prayers of Intercession)*

### WITH DEEPLY FELT LONGINGS I PRAY.
*(Pray the Prayer of Our Savior.)*

### MORNING
O dawning God, lead me in causes of righteousness and justice, that the new may spring forth in those who are weary and worn down. Through Jesus, the Christ. Amen.

### EVENING
I rejoice, O God. You are my salvation and you will care for me through the night and guide me in all tomorrows. Through Jesus, the Christ. Amen.

# November 13

*(Read Psalm 25:1–5)*

**MORNING**

Caring and Loving One, as the day breaks open to me,
so does your grace. I lift up my soul to you, O God of my salvation.

**EVENING**

Caring and Loving One, through the rush and hurry of the day,
you have led me safely through treacherous pathways. Thank you.

Ever consistent God, you are faithful, always steady, and trustworthy. God, you are Protector, keeping us safe from enemies that would reign over us. God, you are Caretaker, mindful of the human condition and its fragility. In our pain and grief, you come to us with an embracing love. There is no suffering that you do not know or share. Your presence heals us and grants us peace. Let us lift up our souls to you and find wholeness.

**MORNING**

Grant me the patience to remain in you through this day, O God.
Help me to know your ways and walk your paths.
*(Prayers of Intercession)*

**EVENING**

O God of my salvation, you have nourished me today with your
faithfulness. I have remembered your tender care and now await
the gift of rest.
*(Prayers of Intercession)*

**TRUSTING IN GOD I PRAY.**

*(Pray the Prayer of Our Savior.)*

| **MORNING** | **EVENING** |
|---|---|
| O Eternal One, lead me in your truth. Teach me how to wait. Guard me against evil ways. Through Jesus, the Christ. Amen. | You have blessed me through the day. As shadows lengthen and the night comes, comfort and replenish my soul. Through Jesus, the Christ. Amen. |

# November 14

*(Read Psalm 25:6–10)*

**MORNING**

Loving God, I am redeemed by your mercy, nourished by your grace.
Grant me your unfailing love, that I may be found in your will.

**EVENING**

Loving God, in this day just past, you have remembered me.
Your mercy has renewed my life and enabled me to walk confidently
in your way. Thank you, kind and living God.

We reside in a world where men and women, boys and girls are so very angry! Sharp, cutting, and destructive words flow freely from our mouths, bringing pain and division to people and institutions. In these days, your values are brutally disregarded, O God. Compassion and kindness often seem more distant than near. Hatred seems strong; love seems weak. Forgive us, O God, when we forget that your tender care and unfailing love are sufficient. Help us to remember that love and goodness, sacrificially rendered, defeat all the enemies of life and love.

**MORNING**

I face today with hope because I know God loves me
and bears me no ill will for my past transgressions.
*(Prayers of Intercession)*

**EVENING**

As the sun falls beneath the western sky, I rejoice that
my God is good and upright and leads me along right paths.
*(Prayers of Intercession)*

**WHILE GOD'S MERCY IS ALWAYS AVAILABLE,
IT IS ONLY ACCESSIBLE THROUGH A HUMBLE HEART.**
*(Pray the Prayer of Our Savior.)*

| MORNING | EVENING |
|---|---|
| God of new beginnings, as this day opens before me, may I be present to all your graces. Through Jesus, the Christ. Amen. | God of rest, lift from me the burdens of this past day and shelter me with your gentle love. Through Jesus, the Christ. Amen. |

# November 15

*(Read 1 Thessalonians 3:9–13)*

MORNING

Loving One, as the sun rises in the eastern sky, help me to rise
in adoration and thanksgiving to you and to Jesus.

EVENING

Loving One, in the midst of evening cares, come forward with
your healing rest. Hold me in your grace and restore my soul to
meet the joys and hopes that tomorrow will bring.

Refreshing God, when you came in Jesus, the Christ, it was cause for
great thanksgiving, love, and joy. When you come, our hearts are
strengthened, we know wholeness, and our very identities are defined.
When you come, love increases, and affection and respect for others
abound. When you come, the restoration of the divine brings refreshment to the soul and cleanses the social order. Come, Jesus. Come and
grant us wholeness and peace.

MORNING

O Jesus Christ, open my eyes to your presence.
Help me bring love and joy to all the experiences that the day presents.
*(Prayers of Intercession)*

EVENING

O God of rest, with my energy diminished by the labors of the day,
I pray that you will be present with me as I sleep and as I wake.
*(Prayers of Intercession)*

"AND MAY GOD MAKE YOU INCREASE AND ABOUND IN LOVE

FOR ONE ANOTHER AND FOR ALL."
*(Pray the Prayer of Our Savior.)*

| MORNING | EVENING |
|---|---|
| Dawn upon me, O glory of God, that | Restore me in the evening hours, that |
| I may arise today and bask in your | I may seek you in the morning and |
| light and proclaim your love faithfully. | serve you throughout the day ahead. |
| Through Jesus, the Christ. Amen. | Through Jesus, the Christ. Amen. |

# November 16

*(Read Luke 21:25–28)*

**MORNING**

Mighty God, open my eyes to the sights and sounds
that today holds, so that I may witness your appearing
and be held in your power.

**EVENING**

Mighty God, thank you for the day just concluded
and for all the graces you have granted within it.

As Jerusalem was under siege, so are we. Ecological tremors and changes
are so very real and haunting. Wars rage between nations. Violence esca-
lates and claims the souls of humankind. Personal anxiety and worry carve
deep furrows in our psyches. Fearful and fainting, we move from one day
to another with little confidence and hope. O God, help us to rise up and
see you coming to redeem us through the tremors and tribulations.

**MORNING**

Approaching God, may your face and glory bring peace to the
roars and waves of this raging and violent world.
*(Prayers of Intercession)*

**EVENING**

Today you came into my confused and fear-filled life and gave me
hope. Thank you, O God of my salvation.
*(Prayers of Intercession)*

---

GOD ALWAYS BREAKS THROUGH LIFE'S ROAR, RESCUES GOD'S PEOPLE
FROM THEIR DISTRESSES, AND SAVES THEM FROM ALL UPHEAVAL.
*(Pray the Prayer of Our Savior.)*

---

| **MORNING** | **EVENING** |
|---|---|
| God, help me to stand up, raise my head, and see you in the day that is before me. May I not faint with fear but rise in hope, for your redemption is drawing near. Through Jesus, the Christ. Amen. | Thank you for coming to me, O God, helping me to claim your power and glory as today unfolded. Now give me rest and renew me for tomorrow. Through Jesus, the Christ. Amen. |

# November 17

*(Read Luke 21:29–33)*

### MORNING

O Advent God, help me to pay attention to your nearing presence.
Give me wisdom to understand your teaching,
that I may not miss you when you come.

### EVENING

O Advent God, you have held me in your love
throughout the hours of this day. Thank you. Now hold me
as the evening deepens into night.

With each sprouting leaf, hope is declared. As the buds of spring presage the abundance of summer leaves, autumn collects them, and winter provides space for their rest and regeneration. Such are the rhythms and contours of life. And through each stage, God, you draw nearer to the generations. Your realm keeps inching ever closer to our time and space. May our eyes be wide and our hearts open to see and receive your love.

### MORNING

God of new beginnings, help me to look for "leaf sprouts"
as I live in and through this day.
*(Prayers of Intercession)*

### EVENING

God, you have been an enduring presence in my life today.
As I enter the night, remain with me.
*(Prayers of Intercession)*

---

**THE WORD OF GOD NEVER FADES. IT ENDURES FROM GENERATION TO GENERATION.**
*(Pray the Prayer of Our Savior.)*

---

### MORNING

Today, help me to see you in the events of my life, O God. Give me ears for hearing and a mind for understanding your unfolding truth. Through Jesus, the Christ. Amen.

### EVENING

Today, I glimpsed a part of what you are about, O God. Grant me rest now and help me to discern your will in even deeper ways tomorrow. Through Jesus, the Christ. Amen.

# November 18

*(Read Luke 21:34–36)*

### MORNING
Incarnate God, may gratitude reign in my heart today
as I enjoy your many gifts and graces.

### EVENING
Incarnate God, you are my strength. All through the day you have visited me
and kept me from being seduced by the plastic gods of this age. Thank you.

We are so very beset by the concerns of the present age, so busy with much
that is trivial and secondary. No wonder we are drunken and weighted
down! Trapped and beleaguered in the snares of this world, we see our
power dissipate and we are filled with anxiety. We long for the Presence,
the Eternal Other, the Child of God. So let us pray fervently and continually that you, majestic God, will come and live with and within us.

### MORNING
Almighty God, I fear that you will come to me today and find me
asleep or engaged in work that is devoid of Christ's love. Open me
to your will, that I may celebrate your coming.
*(Prayers of Intercession)*

### EVENING
As this holy day ends, may I retire in peace, knowing that my redeemer comes.
*(Prayers of Intercession)*

---

COME, LIVING GOD, RUSH SPEEDILY TO MY ANXIOUS AND HEAVY-LADEN HEART.
I WAIT FOR YOU.
*(Pray the Prayer of Our Savior.)*

---

### MORNING
How joyous is the day when
I am the beneficiary of God's love!
May I live confidently in God's love
today and always. Through Jesus,
the Christ. Amen.

### EVENING
Hour by hour, you have sustained me
through this day, O God. Your love has
enabled me to stand strong and live
with confidence. Now watch over me in
my sleep, that tomorrow I may rise to
do your will. Through Jesus,
the Christ. Amen.

# November 19

*(Read Psalm 123)*
*Sing "God of Grace and God of Glory" or another familiar hymn.*

**MORNING**
Dearest Jesus, as I open my eyes to behold a new day,
may they fall on you and only you.

**EVENING**
Dearest Jesus, as dusk settles in, may your mercy surround me.
Enable me to extend your mercy to others.

Ever-abiding God, when I search for you, I find that you have always been with me. In the midst of my searching, I learn what is most important, enabling me to let go of all the scorn and contempt that I have endured from others. Help me always to remember that in the midst of those who would scorn and speak evil of me, you will never leave my side. For your supporting presence, my focus will always remain on your mercy and love for me.

**MORNING**
Most merciful God, you have shown me your mercy and love.
Help me to pass that love and mercy on to others.
*(Prayers of Intercession)*

**EVENING**
Today, I walked aware of your goodness and mercy. Grant me the courage
and wisdom to be always aware of the need to reach out to others.
*(Prayers of Intercession)*

---

REMAINING IN YOUR PRESENCE, MY SEARCHING ENDS.
IN YOUR MERCY AND LOVE, I FIND PEACE.
*(Pray the Prayer of Our Savior.)*

---

**MORNING**
How great is your faithfulness,
most merciful God. Morning after
morning, new mercies I see.
In Jesus' name. Amen.

**EVENING**
As I close my eyes, I rest filled with
your love, mercy, and a grateful heart.
In Jesus' name. Amen.

# November 20

*(Read Psalm 90:1–8)*

**MORNING**

Eternal and everlasting God, your voice wakes and
summons me to rise and begin this new day. I give thanks to
the One who calls me by name.

**EVENING**

Eternal and everlasting God, Rock of Ages,
cleft for me, let me hide myself in thee.

Never-changing God of the ages, throughout all generations you have
been a safe dwelling place. You existed before the beginning of time and
will continue to exist beyond what I could ever think or imagine. Knowing
that you are omnipresent—everywhere at once—I can hide myself in you,
in the bosom of your safety. I never will escape trials and tribulations, but
I can accept them with joy, knowing that I am in your great love.

**MORNING**

With wisdom and power, our Redeemer reigns.
What an awesome God we serve! Sing hallelujah to our Parent,
Teacher, and Sovereign God.
*(Prayers of Intercession)*

**EVENING**

Where God leads me I will follow, knowing that God gives me
grace and glory and goes with me every step of the way.
*(Prayers of Intercession)*

---

**FROM EVERLASTING TO EVERLASTING, YOU ARE GOD, THE ALPHA AND OMEGA.**
*(Pray the Prayer of Our Savior.)*

---

**MORNING**

Omnipotent and forgiving God,
who reproves me with righteous anger
when I need it, wash away my sins.
In Jesus' name. Amen.

**EVENING**

Protector, I close my eyes in sweet
rest, knowing that as long as I cling
to you in love, you will keep and
surround me in your protection.
In Jesus' name. Amen.

# November 21

*(Read Psalm 90:9–12)*

**MORNING**
Ancient One of days, satisfy me in the morning
with your steadfast love, so that I may rejoice and be glad all of my days.

**EVENING**
Ancient One of days, teach me to be aware of my limited number
of days, in order that I might use them wisely.

God, teach me to make the most of my days here on earth, so that I may not waste an hour or minute of the day. Christ, from your teachings you have shown us the importance of placing nothing before our relationship with you and others. Help me to make the most of my relationships, realizing that when I leave this temporary home and enter into my heavenly home, you are all that I will take with me.

**MORNING**
As the rising of the sun extinguishes the darkness of the night,
allow me to live this day to its fullest as if it were the last.
*(Prayers of Intercession)*

**EVENING**
Praise and glory to you, most Holy One,
for another day in your service.
*(Prayers of Intercession)*

**MAKE US GLAD AS MANY DAYS AS YOU HAVE AFFLICTED US.**
*(Pray the Prayer of Our Savior.)*

**MORNING**
I rise this day begging for forgiveness of my sins, that the few days of my life may be spent seeking your wisdom. In Jesus' name. Amen.

**EVENING**
As this day draws to a close, may your Spirit descend upon me, that I might feel your presence now and forever. I await the Holy Spirit! In Jesus' name. Amen.

# November 22

*(Read Matthew 25:14–30)*

### MORNING
Creator of all that is, I arise this day asking for your help. Help me to invest
my services for the betterment of your dominion here on earth.

### EVENING
Creator of all that is, I pray that the fruits of my labor
have been beneficial. This increase I gladly give to you.

Giver of life, I raise my voice and lift my hands in praise to you, for
your presence in my life means more to me than life itself. I pray that
the gifts and talents you have so richly blessed me with will be used for
the uplifting of your realm here on earth. Use me, God, for I am your
willing and faithful servant.

### MORNING
Granter of talents and gifts, help me to realize the magnitude of the many
talents and gifts you have bestowed upon me. Help me to use them, share them,
and sharpen them, for I know that my doing so will be pleasing in your sight.
*(Prayers of Intercession)*

### EVENING
Gracious and compassionate God, this day I pray that the fruits of my labor
are acceptable in your eyes. Grant that I may hear, "Well done, good, trustworthy,
and faithful servant. Enter into the joy of my arms."
*(Prayers of Intercession)*

### WE ARE ACCOUNTABLE!
*(Pray the Prayer of Our Savior.)*

### MORNING
I work hard, loving Parent, to apply
my meager talents in the fashion that
you set before me. Bless my efforts,
that you may enjoy the work I have
done. In Jesus' name. Amen.

### EVENING
As I prepare to rest my physical body, I
bring to you, my Parent, the interest from
my talents. The spoken and unspoken
word, the touch of kindness, the smile of
your presence in my life as it lightened
one heart, comforted one soul, and
brought relief to one wayfarer are my love
offerings to you. In Jesus' name. Amen.

# November 23

*(Read 1 Thessalonians 5:1–11)*

### MORNING

Almighty and everlasting God, thanks be to you, who save me! As I awaken,
I rise from my gloom with the assurance that if I remain faithful to you,
gracious God, I will see the glory of the coming Christ.

### EVENING

Almighty and everlasting God, I pray that all who are separated from you
because of the sins of this world will turn to you and walk in obedience.

God, you paid a great price to redeem me, and I give you my life and
my loyalty. Because Christ Jesus died for my sins, I will choose daily to
love and serve you. I wait fearlessly, patiently, and with peace and confidence for your second coming, because I know that you have delivered
me from my sins and I now walk in obedience. Hallelujah, for the reward of obedience is waiting for me!

### MORNING

Send your light, merciful God, that I might find my way.
Lead and guide me along my journey.
*(Prayers of Intercession)*

### EVENING

Redeeming God, help me to keep my eyes on the path
of righteousness. I want to follow you each step of the way.
Order my steps in your Word; I want to walk worthy!
*(Prayers of Intercession)*

---

**"ENCOURAGE ONE ANOTHER AND BUILD UP ONE ANOTHER, AS YOU ARE INDEED DOING."**
*(Pray the Prayer of Our Savior.)*

---

### MORNING

Understanding and forgiving God, I
thank you for your redemptive love and
place all my hope in you. Help me as I
strive to walk in your way, encouraging
my brothers and sisters along my journey.
In Jesus' name. Amen.

### EVENING

Abide with me, fast falls the eventide,
the darkness deepens. God, with me
abide. In Jesus' name. Amen.

# November 24

*(Read Judges 4:1–7)*

**MORNING**

God of a new day, yesterday's mistakes are behind me. Grant that I might listen
to the Holy Spirit's instructions and with renewed strength stand!

**EVENING**

God of a new night, allow your given victories of this day to
strengthen my efforts to walk in the way of righteousness.

When the turmoil and turbulence of this life cause me to drift away
from you, bring judgment into my life to direct its course back to you.
With faith, I know that you will hear my cries and guide me. You will
deliver me from the enemy of my soul and cause me to be victorious.
Your love and faithfulness endure forever.

**MORNING**

Gracious God, give me the wisdom to hear your instruction.
Direct my life in accordance with your desire.
*(Prayers of Intercession)*

**EVENING**

My soul rejoices in praises for your unending direction and guidance.
*(Prayers of Intercession)*

---

I SEEK DIVINE JUDGMENT. IF I BUT LISTEN, YOU WILL SET MY FEET
ON THE PATH OF RIGHTEOUSNESS. I WILL LISTEN AND OBEY.
*(Pray the Prayer of Our Savior.)*

---

**MORNING**

I will not find you in the voices of
contemporary society. I, however, will
find you in the most unexpected
places. From the lips of strangers, I
will hear your still, small voice. And I
will obey your command. In Jesus'
name. Amen.

**EVENING**

Did I listen? Did I hear myself? Did I
obey? Did I close my ears to the deaf-
ening sounds of this world? Did I shut
them out and hear your words? Did I
stand for Christ? As I prepare to slumber this night, I pray that I heard and
obeyed. In Jesus' name. Amen.

# November 25

*(Read Zephaniah 1:7, 12–18)*

### MORNING

Compassionate and forgiving God, I have sinned and
do not deserve your grace. I pray for your forgiveness, that I
might be a willing and able servant.

### EVENING

Compassionate and forgiving God, I prostrate myself before you.
Forgive me for conforming to the materialistic path of society.
Teach me your ways.

Sun-rising God, your day is coming. I will be commanded to stand
accountable for my sins before you, a God who is omnipotent, all-
knowing, compassionate, and merciful. Sinner that I am, I seek this day
and every day the forgiving grace of Jesus Christ, knowing that Jesus is
a forgiving and loving parent. Cleanse me of all unrighteousness and
anoint me from head to toe with your Holy Spirit, in order that I might
be a willing and able servant.

### MORNING

Search me, God, that I may rid myself of the hidden sins
that I do not want to see.
*(Prayers of Intercession)*

### EVENING

Bring your lamp, your light, the light of the world,
and save me from my sins.
*(Prayers of Intercession)*

---

**THE LIGHT OF THE WORLD IS JESUS.**
*(Pray the Prayer of Our Savior.)*

---

| MORNING | EVENING |
|---|---|
| Out of the chaos of the world, wandering on its willful way, let the light of your grace fall on me. In Jesus' name. Amen. | I have no fear. My life is founded on the rock of Jesus Christ. When the day of God comes, I will be victorious. In Jesus' name. Amen. |

# November 26

*(Read Joshua 24:1–3, 14–25)*

### MORNING
God of the universe, take me in your hands; help me to yield
to your shaping and molding. Empower me to be faithful to what
you have called me to be and to do today.

### EVENING
God of the universe, you ordered this day for all creation according
to your plan. Today you held my hand over rough places and
calmed the tumults of my heart. Grant rest to my body and peace
to my soul, for in your love alone are absolute acceptance and joy.

Sovereign God, thank you for people of faith like Joshua. By his story, you help me see more keenly whose I am. Turn Joshua's words into a sword to slay the idols in my life. Remind me of your love and the certainty of your judgment. Teach me to be grateful, and in my gratitude empower me to serve you. Help me to extend a life of service beyond myself by living out my faith, so that my household and my friends will recognize you as their God and themselves as your servants. Grant me the courage of Joshua, and remind me of your sacrificial love through Jesus Christ.

### MORNING
God, in this world of many choices, help me to choose you above
all else, with all my heart, with all my soul, and with all my mind.
*(Prayers of Intercession)*

### EVENING
God, write in my heart an everlasting covenant with you.
Grant that my life seeks, above all, to fulfill it.
*(Prayers of Intercession)*

---

**"BUT AS FOR ME AND MY HOUSEHOLD, WE WILL SERVE GOD."**
*(Pray the Prayer of Our Savior.)*

---

### MORNING
Loving God, enable me to live
Joshua's story today. In your precious
name, I pray. Amen.

### EVENING
Loving God, I rest in your love
and unconditional acceptance. In your
precious name, I pray. Amen.

## November 27

*(Read Psalm 78:1–7)*

### MORNING

Divine Teacher, your wisdom and power are boundless,
and your mercy is beyond measure. Wash me anew of my sins
and refresh my soul with the lessons of all generations.

### EVENING

Divine Teacher, thank you for your lessons. I learn slowly,
and the tests are not easy. But the faithful you always pass.
God of mercy, hallelujah!

Gracious God, thank you for your commandments and teachings in my lifetime and over all generations. You wrote them in my conscience, in the laws of your creation, and in the lives of your faithful witnesses. The wonders of your deeds fill the Scriptures. My sins and the sins of humankind are many, and only the saving blood of Jesus can satisfy your justice and holiness. Help me to learn my lessons well and to share your love with people I meet through the power of your Holy Spirit.

### MORNING

Divine Teacher, make me teachable and empower me
to be a model to the people I love.
*(Prayers of Intercession)*

### EVENING

God, give me a holy memory to remember your glorious deeds.
*(Prayers of Intercession)*

---

**"WE WILL TELL TO THE COMING GENERATION THE GLORIOUS DEEDS OF GOD."**
*(Pray the Prayer of Our Savior.)*

---

### MORNING

Loving God, enable me to live out your teachings. Help me to brighten a young person's day. In your precious name, I pray. Amen.

### EVENING

Loving God, continue to create in my consciousness love for your ways and obedience to your laws. In your precious name, I pray. Amen.

# November 28

*(Read Amos 5:18–24)*

### MORNING

Loving God, I tremble in the face of your disapproval and judgment.
But morning always brings the hope of a new day. By the power of your
renewing Spirit, help me to have a fresh start today.

### EVENING

Loving God, I offer my life as a continuing act of worship to you.
May it be pleasing in your sight.

Holy God, you call your people to a life of wholeness and integrity. You require that the words of our prayers match the deeds of our lives. You ask your people to offer their lives as a living sacrifice and worship to you. You call us to a life of serving and caring, not acquiring and using. Help me to serve you by caring for the weak and the poor and by working for justice in a society that favors the rich and the powerful. Forgive my sins of inaction and timidity and the injustices of my generation.

### MORNING

Holy God, bless your people with personal righteousness
and social justice.
*(Prayers of Intercession)*

### EVENING

Holy God, may the words of your people, the meditations
of their hearts, and the deeds of their hands be pleasing in your sight.
*(Prayers of Intercession)*

---

"LET JUSTICE ROLL DOWN LIKE WATERS AND RIGHTEOUSNESS
LIKE AN EVER-FLOWING STREAM."
*(Pray the Prayer of Our Savior.)*

---

### MORNING

Holy God, make me an instrument
of your justice and righteousness.
In your precious name, I pray. Amen.

### EVENING

Holy God, refresh me in the shower
of your justice, and nourish me in the
spring of your righteousness. In your
precious name, I pray. Amen.

# November 29

*(Read Proverbs 6:17–20)*

### MORNING
Holy and Gracious God, your holiness reveals the reality
of my sinfulness. Forgive my sins, and help me celebrate this day
as a forgiven and beloved child of a gracious God.

### EVENING
Holy and Gracious God, forgive my sins again. Is it ever
possible not to sin? Ah, I can only rest in your assurance that
nothing can separate me from your love.

Holy God, you know me so well. You know that I have feet of clay. My experiences with other people have taught me to be defensive and mistrustful, and I have learned to put myself first above others. Thank you, Gracious God, for not giving up on me. You forgive my sins and cast them away as far as the east is from the west. Your love for me is as great as the heavens are far from the earth. Bless me with friends and mentors who would be willing to point out my errors and show me your way. Grant me an obedient and forgiving heart.

### MORNING
Holy God, I pray that I may be as ready to forgive myself
and others as you are to forgive me.
*(Prayers of Intercession)*

### EVENING
Create in me, O God, a real and abiding consciousness
that I am holy just because I am your child.
*(Prayers of Intercession)*

---

**"THE RIGHTEOUS WILL LIVE BY FAITH."**
*(Pray the Prayer of Our Savior.)*

---

### MORNING
Holy God, help me to be righteous
and keep me from being judgmental
of others. In your precious name,
I pray. Amen.

### EVENING
Gracious God, your righteousness
is with those who love you and obey
your commandments. In your
precious name, I pray. Amen.

# November 30

*(Read Psalm 70)*

**MORNING**

Thank you, God, for being my Protector. Your power is absolute,
and your reliability is sure. Whom shall I fear?

**EVENING**

Thank you, God, for the sun has set and my enemies lurk
in the shadows. But your light will reveal their injustice and
protect me from their evil plot.

Almighty God, when I make a stand for what is right, help me to be steadfast. Remind me that the loss of my earthly possessions, my job, my friends, or my social status does not compare to the gain of your heavenly realm. Protect me from the enemies of justice and righteousness by thwarting their plans. Bring to my side sisters and brothers of wisdom and courage. Bring down failure to my enemies and deliver me success, so that your name will be glorified and your people encouraged.

**MORNING**

Great God, I pray for courage and faith for all in the world
who suffer persecution for the sake of justice and righteousness.
*(Prayers of Intercession)*

**EVENING**

Triumphant God, the war is won, and you are the victor.
May I rest in the assurance of your final victory.
*(Prayers of Intercession)*

---

**"LET ALL WHO SEEK YOU REJOICE AND BE GLAD IN YOU."**
*(Pray the Prayer of Our Savior.)*

---

| **MORNING** | **EVENING** |
|---|---|
| Almighty God, deliver us from evil. | Almighty God, you are my Shield |
| In your precious name, I pray. Amen. | and my Deliverer. In you do I trust. |
| | In your precious name, I pray. Amen. |

# December 1

*(Read 1 Thessalonians 4:13–18)*

**MORNING**
Glorious and Loving God, thank you for the assurance
of life everlasting with you in the company of your people in glory.

**EVENING**
Glorious and Loving God, remind me of the faith stories
from the life of my departed loved ones.

Glorious God, thank you that death is not the finality of life. But, God, I dread death even though it seems to be the threshold to eternal life. The loss of a loved one in death feels so final and the loss so great to bear. Thank you, God, for your assurance in the Bible that the saints who died are with you and that we will have a reunion in heaven at your appointed time. There is no greater comfort than this. Thank you, Jesus, for your sacrifice on the cross, which opened the doors of heaven for your people. In response to your sacrificial love, help me to live a life that will bring a little bit of heaven on earth through the power of your Holy Spirit.

**MORNING**
Loving God, I pray for your comfort
for grieving people in the world.
*(Prayers of Intercession)*

**EVENING**
Loving God, grant that your people may sleep in heavenly peace.
*(Prayers of Intercession)*

---

**"DO NOT GRIEVE FOR THOSE WHO HAVE DIED AS OTHERS DO WHO HAVE NO HOPE."**
*(Pray the Prayer of Our Savior.)*

---

| **MORNING** | **EVENING** |
| --- | --- |
| Loving God, help us to be thankful and to celebrate the life of our loved ones. In your precious name, I pray. Amen. | Loving God, thank you for the cloud of witnesses. Teach us the lessons of their faith. In your precious name, I pray. Amen. |

# December 2

*(Read Matthew 25:1–13)*

**MORNING**

Jesus, help me to make ready for your coming.
May each breaking dawn serve as a reminder of your glorious return.

**EVENING**

Jesus, as I switch on the lights each evening, teach me anew
the lessons of the parable of the ten bridesmaids.

Jesus, thank you for coming into the world and into my life. You first came as a helpless baby, unknown and unwanted by the world. But you will come again as a triumphant ruler, and every knee will bow before you, and every tongue will sing praises of your glory. Jesus, allow me to take part in the welcoming chorus. As you have written your laws in my heart, let my life be an anthem of faith and obedience. As you have washed my sins away by your sacrifice on the cross, let me be part of the cleanup crew to get things ready for your arrival. Jesus, I am not worthy, but just say the word and my spirit will be made whole.

**MORNING**

Jesus, I do not know when you will come; help me to be ready always.
*(Prayers of Intercession)*

**EVENING**

Jesus, as I lie down to sleep, grant me peace and joy,
knowing that I may wake up in heaven.
*(Prayers of Intercession)*

---

**"KEEP AWAKE, THEREFORE, FOR YOU KNOW NEITHER THE DAY NOR THE HOUR."**
*(Pray the Prayer of Our Savior.)*

---

| **MORNING** | **EVENING** |
| --- | --- |
| Jesus, thank you for the anticipation of your coming. In your precious name, I pray. Amen. | Jesus, bless my soul and let your Word be a lamp to my feet. In your precious name, I pray. Amen. |

# December 3

*(Read Isaiah 7:1–2)*

### MORNING

Sweet God of eternal life, am I prepared today to stand
on your Word despite the odds? Do I have the courage today
to lean on you for my needs, sweet Jesus?

### EVENING

Sweet God of eternal life, thank you for allowing me to lean on you today.
Guide me safely through this night. Let me continue to lean on you.

Everything around me reminds me of the tinsel Christmas. The Christmas trees, the decorations, the imitation Santas, and the brightly colored wrapped gifts neatly tied and tucked under the twinkling, singing green pine. In all of these distractions, help me to have courage to stand in your name in the face of adversity. Let me find comfort in your presence and see your face in your people. Blessed sweet Jesus, let me stand without fear on the promises of your coming!

### MORNING

Spirit of the living God, breathe courage into my life today.
Give courage to . . .
*(Prayers of Intercession)*

### EVENING

O God of grace, I thank you for this day. Like the house of David,
have I leaned on you today for courage? Bless the courage of . . .
*(Prayers of Intercession)*

---

**LEANING ON GOD'S COURAGE, I CAN STAND WITH CHRIST IN ANY SEASON!**
*(Sing "What a Fellowship" or another familiar hymn.)*

---

### MORNING

As I begin this day with new courage, O God, give me courage to celebrate the coming of Jesus Christ. Allow me the privilege to encourage others to seek you in the power of the Holy Spirit. In the precious name of the Christ. Amen.

### EVENING

Thank you, God, for the small measures of success today. Let these lessons remind me of your presence. Bless me with a restful night, and rock me in your arms of courage to enter a new day of peace. In the precious name of the Christ. Amen.

# December 4

*(Read Isaiah 7:5–9)*

### MORNING

Holy Spirit and Ever-living Creator, can my heart
be rekindled to trust God's promise?

### EVENING

Holy Spirit and ever-living Creator, what promise did I fulfill this day in faith?
Have I accepted the rewards of your promises through faith?

In the busyness of the season, it is easy for me to forget that I am a faithful person. There seems to be more month left than money, and there's never enough time to do anything. This is an impossible time of year. But I must remember to stand on my faith and remember that this holy season is also a season of gift giving. God, thank you for the gift of Jesus Christ, our Savior. In Christ I have hope, and in hope I live in faith. In faith I expect the miracle of your blessings!

### MORNING

Holy God, let me exercise my faith. May you give new faith to . . .
*(Prayers of Intercession)*

### EVENING

Gracious God of day and night, thank you for increasing my faith
and celebrating your presence today. Bless the faith of . . .
*(Prayers of Intercession)*

---

**"IF YOU DO NOT STAND FIRM ON YOUR FAITH YOU SHALL NOT STAND AT ALL!"**
*(Sing "The Solid Rock" or another familiar hymn.)*

---

| MORNING | EVENING |
|---|---|
| Sweet Creator, as I meet the permeating light of this new day, increase my faith in you. Like the waters of the stream, let my words increase the pool of faithful others I greet this day, I pray. In the precious name of the Christ. Amen. | Whispering Holy Spirit, as I lie down to rest this night, remind me if I was faithful in some way. Release me from the thought of failure, and bless me with a peaceful rest. In the precious name of the Christ. Amen. |

# December 5

*(Read Psalm 80:1–3)*

**MORNING**

Creator God of the quiet morning, touch my heart to see your
help. Can I see your mighty hand assisting me in my daily work?

**EVENING**

Creator God of the quiet evening, thank you for restoring me to you this day.
Have I seen your hand at work in my life? Or was I too busy with my own life?

God of joy and peace, when I begin the day, I feel close to you. Yet in the
midst of controversy, you seem silent. Am I impatient and angry today
and so fail to see your work on my behalf? How often do I operate in fear,
hatred, or intolerance? Intervene, sweet God, on my behalf. God, open
my eyes to see you in the middle of the day, healing my brokenness.

**MORNING**

O blessed God whose light illuminates all things and makes them
known, help me to see your mighty acts in my life.
Illuminate your healing power in . . .
*(Prayers of Intercession)*

**EVENING**

God of the vespers light, have I seen your hand at work today?
At this moment as the sun disappears into the shadows, I know
you have restored me. Thank you for being with . . .
*(Prayers of Intercession)*

**"RESTORE US, O GOD. LET YOUR FACE SHINE!"**
*(After sixty seconds, repeat.)*

| **MORNING** | **EVENING** |
|---|---|
| Today, I claim the restoration of my relationship with God. Can God's Spirit illuminate through me to restore others as I am restored? Allow me to give glory to your name this day. In the precious name of the Christ. Amen. | As the evening shadows greet the fading lights, I accept God's love and forgiveness. Can these gifts of restoration begin a new journey of peace and love of others in my life? In Christ I claim this peace and love this night. In the precious name of the Christ. Amen. |

# December 6

*(Read Psalm 80:4–7)*

**MORNING**

Holy Spirit, Source of all goodness, let me begin this day with a spirit of peace.
Is the battle I fight within myself? Can I draw near to you and be at rest?

**EVENING**

Holy Spirit, as the battle ends today, thank you for hearing
my prayers. Shall I find inner peace from my turmoil knowing you
are now listening to my prayers?

God, often the confusion in life is a direct result of my inability to hear
and seek you. I know, however, the very moment you turn away from
me because I actively seek your attention. Can I empty my bed of tears
in your pool of mercy and accept grace? Can I empty my life and turn
it to Christ for guidance, doing your will?

**MORNING**

Searching to drink from your spiritual cup of new life, sweet
Savior, let me share in your blessing with . . .
*(Prayers of Intercession)*

**EVENING**

As the Creator of all life, God, you have spared my life for another day.
Give me, a weary warrior of my inner battle, rest and peace this night.
Let your grace fall upon us, especially . . .
*(Prayers of Intercession)*

**GOD HEARS MY PRAYERS AND ANSWERS THEM!**
*(Sing "Have Thine Own Way, Lord" or another familiar hymn.)*

**MORNING**

O God, I begin this day in your care.
Can I choose not to battle with you
and accept your will? Can you help
me to accept your will and show me
how? In the precious name of the
Christ. Amen.

**EVENING**

Soul of Christ, I come to you for rest.
Hold me in the palm of your hand, and
renew my strength for another day.
Thank you, God, for ending my battle
and allowing me to do your will. In the
precious name of the Christ. Amen.

# December 7

*(Read Psalm 80:17–19)*

### MORNING
Thank you, God, for this day. On this day, how can I forget who I am
and whose I am? Can I praise you today and know your presence?

### EVENING
Thank you, God, for this night. How blessed I have been today as your hand
led my life. Have I praised and thanked you for your blessings?

As I do last-minute shopping, I often forget the lives of people living in
war-torn countries, hungry children, and homeless families. O God,
have I forgotten your strength and how you give us life? In this holy season of gift giving, can I praise you for allowing us to live and have our
being? Awaken my soul today to praise you, O God, regardless of the
events of this day.

### MORNING
Dearest Jesus, you lived and died for us to call on your name
in love. Let me celebrate your gift of life with . . .
*(Prayers of Intercession)*

### EVENING
Holy giving Spirit of God, Spirit of life, thank you for loving me
and holding me in your hand. Your signs are clear. Bless . . .
*(Prayers of Intercession)*

### PRAISE GOD! GOD HAS GIVEN US LIFE!
*(Sing "Great Is Thy Faithfulness" or another familiar hymn.)*

### MORNING
Holy God of the morning dew,
lift me up to grow in life to praise you
for your grace and love. May I always
draw near to you with praise and love.
In the precious name of the Christ.
Amen.

### EVENING
God of sunsets and life, be in my
heart and on my lips this night.
Let me praise you in my waking and
sleeping moments. And allow me to
rest in your peace and grace, so I may
be refreshed. In the precious name
of the Christ. Amen.

# December 8

*(Read Matthew 1:1–17)*

**MORNING**

Dear God of my ancestors, God of my enslaved brothers and sisters,
let me meet the morning knowing who I am and whose I am this day.
Will I see the grace of your love?

**EVENING**

Dear God of my ancestors, as the day ends, thank you for the privilege
of knowing who I am. In you, have I seen the love of my brothers and sisters?
Or have I seen the rush for temporal satisfaction in toys?

In my veins runs the blood of kings and queens, thieves and robbers, and the faithful and unfaithful. The ancestral ties, retold through Scripture, remind me of who I am and whose I am. God, as your child, co-heir with Christ, can I accept your forgiveness and forgive myself for my sins? Can I claim my ancestral ties and celebrate your gift of new life?

**MORNING**

Holy ageless Spirit, you move through time and are known
to my ancestors; be known to me and heal . . .
*(Prayers of Intercession)*

**EVENING**

Holy God of grace and glory, thank you for the privilege
of working out my self-forgiveness. Forgive and heal . . .
*(Prayers of Intercession)*

---

**THE GOD OF OUR ANCESTORS FORGIVES AND ALLOWS ME TO FORGIVE MYSELF.**
*(Sing "Blessed Assurance" or another familiar hymn.)*

---

**MORNING**

Let this day be a new beginning, a new life, in Christ, seeking to forgive myself and accept the blessings of God in love. In the precious name of the Christ. Amen.

**EVENING**

As the evening draws near, I thank you, God, for forgiveness and ancestors. Let me always rest in the cradle of your love, assured of my history of forgiveness. Renew my love in you as I rock in your tender care. In the precious name of the Christ. Amen.

# December 9

*(Read Romans 1:1–7)*

### MORNING
Care-giving God, in the break of this day, have I seen the young woman with child seeking a place to rest? Will I be obedient to your call to offer love and receive discipleship and grace?

### EVENING
Care-giving God, the good news of Christ is not easy. Distractions from prayer and obedience are ramped up in the Christmas season. Have I stayed focused on my discipleship? Did I rest in your grace in peace?

What am I willing to do today to be obedient to your Word and yield to the work of the Holy Spirit? The season of giving is clouded with mixed messages of spending money to show love. Yet didn't you illustrate supreme love through the birth of an infant, born to a teenage mother? How much more can I do to illustrate discipleship today?

### MORNING
God of grace, remove the anxiety from my life.
Let me rest in you and be obedient. Remember . . .
*(Prayers of Intercession)*

### EVENING
Merciful God, you have blessed my life as a disciple. Let me continue to live with Christ as my focus, leading my faith. Remember . . .
*(Prayers of Intercession)*

---

**OBEDIENCE OF FAITH ILLUSTRATES JESUS CHRIST IN LOVE!**
*(Sing "Give Me a Clean Heart" or another familiar hymn.)*

---

### MORNING
In the newness of life I begin a day of obedience to God's love with the faith of a mustard seed. Let this faith increase, my words encourage, my hand build up the love of Christ. In the precious name of the Christ. Amen.

### EVENING
As I lay my head upon the pillow of faith and rest myself upon the bed of grace, I thank God for guiding me. In obedience to your love, blessed Christ, I submit this day to your care. In the precious name of the Christ. Amen.

# December 10

*(Read Luke 3:7–14)*

### MORNING
Divine Wisdom, thank you for a new day with new opportunities,
new experiences, new demands, new choices. Help me to let go of yesterday
and embrace this new day with courage, enthusiasm, and commitment.

### EVENING
Divine Wisdom, the day is now past. Bless my faithfulness,
forgive my failures. Let me rest in the blessed assurance that I am
yours and you are mine.

Almighty God, examine my life and my fruit today. Let my repentance be more than guilty or remorseful feelings. Let my repentance lead to sharing with the destitute, honesty in business, and contentment with my wages. Let me not be content that my name is on a church roll. Let me be content knowing that my actions are pleasing to you.

### MORNING
At the beginning of this new day, guard my lips, lest my words
offend you; guide my feet, lest I go in the wrong direction; clear
my path, lest I stumble along the way; purify my thoughts, lest I
imagine vain things; sanctify my motives, lest I deceive myself.
*(Prayers of Intercession)*

### EVENING
Now I lay me down to sleep, entrusting myself to you all night long.
*(Prayers of Intercession)*

---

**LEAD ME NOT INTO TEMPTATION, BUT DELIVER ME FROM EVIL.**
*(Pray the Prayer of Our Savior.)*

---

### MORNING
Let the words of my mouth and the
meditation of my heart be acceptable
in your sight all day long. In the name
of the Christ child. Amen.

### EVENING
Guard me in the silence of this
evening. Watch over me through
the night. Keep me in the center of
your love. In the name of the
Christ child. Amen.

# December 11

*(Read Zephaniah 3:14–20)*

### MORNING

Triumphant God, I claim the promise of your presence at the beginning
of this new day. Help me hold on to that promise all day long.

### EVENING

Triumphant God, as you have been with me all day, you will not
leave me during the night. I close my eyes for sleep now, knowing
that I rest in your watch care.

Triumphant God, you have revealed yourself to your children as a victorious warrior. When I feel discouraged, I need that image. When I feel defeated, I need that image. When I feel distraught, I need that image. When I feel inadequate, I need that image. Help me to see you today as a victorious warrior in my life; unafraid, resolute, courageous, and brave. When I am weak and timid and unsure, let my thoughts return to that image. Then I will be steadfast and strong.

### MORNING

Christ Jesus, lover of my soul, let me enjoy your divine embrace
all day long and, in the assurance of your love, let me embrace others.
*(Prayers of Intercession)*

### EVENING

Wonderful Counselor, as you did for the psalmist, counsel me also
during my sleep. Let me awaken in the morning rested and wiser.
*(Prayers of Intercession)*

### WITH CONFIDENCE I PRAY.

*(Pray the Prayer of Our Savior.)*

### MORNING

O God of new beginnings, I delight
in the rebirth of day. Give me courage
to live this day in its fullness. In the
name of the Christ child. Amen.

### EVENING

Help me, Heavenly Guide, to sort,
sift, and process all the events of the
day. Keep me in the center of
your love. In the name of
the Christ child. Amen.

# December 12

*(Read Zephaniah 3:16–17)*

**MORNING**

Powerful God, strengthen my hands with hope today.
Let me face each new demand unafraid and with confidence.

**EVENING**

Powerful God, the deeds of today are past. The deeds of tomorrow are seeds
yet to be planted. Give me quiet rest so that I may arise in the morning with new
strength to plant in hope of a full harvest.

Almighty God, I have known the paralysis of fear and hopelessness in
times of pain and confusion and distress. But I hear your words that
say, "Do not let your hands fall limp." Rescue me from "limp hands"
and the emotional paralysis that robs me of vitality. Let me know today
that you "are in my midst." And if I forget, give me helpful reminders.

**MORNING**

Help me to lay aside the garment of sleep and take up
the garment of wakefulness. Help me to embrace this new day
with energy and enthusiasm.
*(Prayers of Intercession)*

**EVENING**

Cleanse me, O God, and I will be clean.
Still me, and I will have rest.
*(Prayers of Intercession)*

**IN BOLDNESS I PRAY.**

*(Pray the Prayer of Our Savior.)*

**MORNING**

Good morning, God. I trust in the
goodness of the morning because you
are good. Lead me in your goodness
all through the day. In the name
of the Christ child. Amen.

**EVENING**

Let my bed be a meeting place
for my soul and your Spirit. In this
place of holiness, give me pleasant
sleep, insightful dreams, sweet peace,
and renewing rest. In the name
of the Christ child. Amen.

# December 13

*(Read Philippians 4:4–7)*

**MORNING**

O God of Glory, let this be a day of rejoicing, not because
everything that will happen today is good, but because I know
there is good, regardless of what happens.

**EVENING**

O God of Glory, as this precious day comes to a close,
accept my thanks and praise for another day of life. Give me
the gift of quiet rest and a calm heart.

God of joy, if Paul could rejoice in prison, then help me to rejoice in the
privileges of freedom that I enjoy today. When I am feeling discouraged;
help me to rejoice. When I am feeling sorrow; help me to rejoice. When
I am feeling depressed; help me to rejoice. When I am feeling over-
worked and undervalued and taken for granted, let me remember prison
words of praise, "Rejoice in God always, and again I will say, rejoice!"

**MORNING**

The night has passed, the day has come. Blessed be the name of God.
*(Prayers of Intercession)*

**EVENING**

Almighty God, let your strong arms surround me,
your eternal love enfold me, your watchful eye guard me all night long.
*(Prayers of Intercession)*

**REJOICING, I PRAY.**
*(Pray the Prayer of Our Savior.)*

**MORNING**

As I open my eyes to a new day,
open my heart to receive your Word
of guidance, instruction, inspiration,
and conviction. In the name
of the Christ child. Amen.

**EVENING**

As the shadows of the night surround
and envelop me, I am reminded that
night is not gloomy to you, and I am
glad. Be with me through the night—
an ever-seeing eye. In the name of the
Christ child. Amen.

# December 14

*(Read Philippians 4:5)*

### MORNING
Dear Heavenly Parent, I greet this new day as an opportunity to continue my life journey. Today when I face conflict, give me patience. When I face confusion, give me clarity. When I face restlessness, give me peace.

### EVENING
Dear Heavenly Parent, I rest tonight knowing that I am your child. Use my dreams to instruct and correct me.

Immanent God, your Word reminds me that you are near. But sometimes you seem so far away. Remind me of your nearness all during the day: during my conversations, during my decision making, during my commute, and during my time with the family. Be nearer to me than my own breath, and at the end of the day, I will give you thanks.

### MORNING
Divine Wisdom, you have counseled me to number my days so that I might gain wisdom. Let me treat this new day as a day that counts.
*(Prayers of Intercession)*

### EVENING
Replace my restlessness with your rest, my anxiety with your peace, my activity with your stillness, so that I can sleep all night long.
*(Prayers of Intercession)*

---

**IN THE COMPANY OF YOUR PRESENCE, I PRAY.**
*(Pray the Prayer of Our Savior.)*

---

### MORNING
In the stillness of the dawn, I am aware of my weakness. Help me to claim your strength so that I can face this day with courage. In the name of the Christ child. Amen.

### EVENING
The day is over. A page in my life book is finished. I rest tonight anticipating continuing the journey tomorrow. In the name of the Christ child. Amen.

# December 15

*(Read Isaiah 12:2–6)*

### MORNING

Omniscient God, in this moment of worship, put a song
in my heart and on my mind so that I can sing to you all day long.
Let this be a day in which I can give an answer to others for the
hope that lies deep within me.

### EVENING

Omniscient God, I close my eyes to sleep, knowing that you never
slumber or sleep. With that calm assurance, I rest now in peace.

Source of eternal life, I come to this time of worship, that I might draw
water from the springs of salvation. Like fresh artesian wells, let your
life overflow in me today. Quench the thirsty, parched, dry places in my
soul with your refreshing presence. Like a tree planted by springs of
water, let my life be a blessing and a witness to others around me.

### MORNING

Creator of the Light, as the light of day dawns,
let me live in the light as you are in the light.
*(Prayers of Intercession)*

### EVENING

In the stillness of this night, help me to be still.
Still my thoughts, fears, and worries that I might rest.
*(Prayers of Intercession)*

---

**WITH EVER-FLOWING STREAMS OF LOVE, I PRAY.**
*(Pray the Prayer of Our Savior.)*

---

### MORNING

God of the new day, help me
to accept all the new beginnings of
my life with the same hope as I accept
this new day. In the name of
the Christ child. Amen.

### EVENING

Place your loving arms around me
during this night and protect me from
all harm. In the name of
the Christ child. Amen.

---

# December 16

*(Read Philippians 4:4–7)*

### MORNING

Creator God, on this Sabbath day, give me such a sense of your presence
that my worship will continue long after the services of my church are past.

### EVENING

Creator God, just as I prepare for sleep, help me to lay aside
the worries and cares of the day, that I might be "anxious for nothing."

Centering God, I hear the words of your servant that call me to be anxious for nothing. But I am anxious—anxious for my health; anxious for my career; anxious for my family; anxious for my future. I want to let go of my anxiety and receive your incomprehensible peace. But I don't know how. Lead me today into new ways of thinking so that my anxieties may be overwhelmed by your peace.

### MORNING

At the break of this new day, I give you thanks for all that is good.
I also give you thanks for difficulties.
*(Prayers of Intercession)*

### EVENING

All that did not get done this day, I commit to you this night. Let me awaken
with new resolve to complete the tasks that await me in the morning.
*(Prayers of Intercession)*

---

### WITH ASSURANCE, I PRAY.
*(Pray the Prayer of Our Savior.)*

---

### MORNING

As the branch abides in the vine,
let me abide in you this day. Let your
light, life, and love flow through me
to all that I meet. In the name of
the Christ child. Amen.

### EVENING

As I bow to sleep, bless those that I
cannot bless, touch those that I cannot
touch, help those that I cannot help,
be near those that I cannot be near,
comfort those that I cannot comfort.
With confidence that you hear my
prayer, let me rest in peace. In the
name of the Christ child. Amen.

# December 17

*(Read Psalm 148)*

MORNING

O God, the Mother who gives birth to the dawning sun,
I praise you. Filled with anticipation, I ask you for guidance in preparing
my mind, soul, and body for the birth of the Christ.

EVENING

O God, the Father whose hands protect me through the night's deep slumber,
I give thanks for the vivid and hidden blessings I have encountered this day.

My hands begin, O God, motionless in a moment of praise for you, joining with the hands of simple carpenters and shepherds who became the agents of your vision. My mind begins, O Creator, open and hungry in a soft moment of your revelation. My soul begins, O Sustainer, glistening in the light of truth which is your promise. I come, O God, ready to receive the hope that will inspire me beyond the birth of that promise to its fulfillment in seeking justice and offering compassion with all the gifts I have to offer.

MORNING

God of Love, may my mind, body, and soul be opened and filled
with a love that seeks you and lends your mercy to all.
*(Prayers of Intercession)*

EVENING

God of justice, grant rest to all the tired souls of the world, teach each of us
your gentle mercy, and teach us to heal one another through word and deed.
*(Prayers of Intercession)*

PRAISE YAHWEH FROM THE HEAVENS; PRAISE YAHWEH IN THE HEIGHTS!
*(Embrace your family and friends.)*

| MORNING | EVENING |
|---|---|
| As my body awakens, may I come to know the light that brings hope to the dim world of the forsaken. Teach me strength, and teach me justice. In Christ's name. Amen. | Though my tired eyes find rest, my soul still longs for your presence and my hand still longs to touch your face. Teach me peace, and teach me patience. In Christ's name. Amen. |

# December 18

*(Read Isaiah 61:10–11)*

### MORNING
Mysterious and glorious God, I greatly rejoice in you. I greet you
in the warmth of the sun and the freshness of the winter air.

### EVENING
Mysterious and glorious God, I greatly rejoice in you as I conclude this day.
I long to know the whys and hows of this society and world.

Glorious God, even as I joyfully praise your name, my eyes fill with tears, for I know that the path to Bethlehem eventually leads to Golgotha. I look to the discord in the Middle East, the chaos that haunts Israel, the iniquity in my own society, the often unseen violence in my own neighborhood, and the hurt I have inflicted on others, and I wonder where you are. When will you cause righteousness and praise to spring up before all the nations? This hurting world craves you, O God. Will you not come to us? I praise your works, O God; they do not go unseen, but so often I feel that you do. Yet I ask for light to see your righteousness, and I ask for the strength to preserve it.

### MORNING
I speak of the citizens of a hurting world, so that they might know your love.
*(Prayers of Intercession)*

### EVENING
May you watch over the sleeping earth, O God,
whose seas and skies are filled with the joys and fears of your many peoples.
*(Prayers of Intercession)*

---

### So Yahweh will cause righteousness and praise
### to spring up before all the nations.
*(Embrace those who suffer oppression both at home and abroad.)*

---

### MORNING
O God, I hunger for you, and this
world aches for your gentle touch.
In Christ's name. Amen.

### EVENING
May your face be both the soft
light and the soothing darkness that
usher in my dreams.
In Christ's name. Amen.

# December 19

*(Read Luke 2:34–35 and Isaiah 62:1–3)*

**MORNING**
God of wonders who awakens,
I come filled with the breath of a December morning.

**EVENING**
God of wonders who puts to rest, as you wrapped your Word
into the garments of flesh to become the most human of humans,
wrap me in a garment of your Word.

The weight of incarnation is so heavy, O God. We wait for you—a God who is human. A God who suffers and dies on the cross and yet a thousand times more. A God who comes into this world. A God who is cruelly berated, beaten, raped, and abandoned. A God who will be lynched, who will suffer from AIDS, whose body will be eaten away by cancer. You come, O God, and you bring us a portion of something totally unlike what we know. But when you come, you become like us. Your presence is so human and yet so divine—so gloriously sad, so wrenchingly beautiful—that it will pierce our very souls. We awaken to your presence, O God. We await your becoming.

**MORNING**
God with us, be with us still.
*(Prayers of Intercession)*

**EVENING**
Your name is my evening prayer, O God, as I remember the names
of the many others who long for freedom, comfort, and peace.
*(Prayers of Intercession)*

**A SWORD WILL PIERCE YOUR OWN SIDE, TOO.**
*(Embrace mothers whose children are in pain.)*

**MORNING**
O God, this day of your creation
gives birth to more of the beautiful
moments of my life.
In Christ's name. Amen.

**EVENING**
O God, I have been visited by you so
many times today. You have brought
all the laughter and tears of life to my
door. In Christ's name. Amen.

# December 20

*(Read Isaiah 63:7–9)*

**MORNING**

God of Loving Kindness and Tender Mercies,
it is with gratitude that I awaken with glad joy!

**EVENING**

God of Loving Kindness and Tender Mercies,
it is with a grateful spirit that I submit to you my offerings of this day.

Coming Savior, how awestruck I am that you would dare to come again! In just five more days we will celebrate your birth. It's mind blowing! It's mind boggling! And it's the inspiration for my praise. How thankful I am. You came once, saw personally just how awful we are, and even after you ascended back to glory, you returned! Surely, you are our salvation, now and forevermore. Forgive my sin. Let my life reflect your coming into my heart.

**MORNING**

God who comes, I lift those who need a fresh experience
of your coming.
*(Prayers of Intercession)*

**EVENING**

Savior of the world, it is indeed a blessed assurance
that your coming was not in vain.
*(Prayers of Intercession)*

---

**OUR GOD CAME, IS PRESENT, AND WILL COME AGAIN!**

---

**MORNING**

In appreciation of your coming
to me, allow me to be fully present to
those I encounter today. In the
matchless name of the Christ.
Amen.

**EVENING**

In acknowledgement of your being
with me all this day, I offer myself to
your keeping power in the watches
of the night. In the matchless name
the Christ. Amen.

# December 21

*(Read Isaiah 63:9–11)*

**MORNING**
Remembering God, thank you for the Sonlight
that continues to shine this day.

**EVENING**
Remembering God, your love and your pity
carried me all day long.

Angel of Presence, you have allowed yourself to be afflicted with our human afflictions. It was not required that you move into our community, put on our flesh, walk in our shoes, and conquer all of our foes. You decided not only to come to earth, but to die and be buried in the earth so that you might win for us eternal salvation and everlasting life. You chose to be born to die! What a mighty, awesome God you are! Forgive my sin and help me to be prepared, this day, to give evidence, by my life, that I am indeed grateful for your first coming. Help me to be a living testimony, causing others to desire to be made ready to receive you when you come again. For it is certain that you will soon come again!

**MORNING**
Healing Presence, be with those who come to mind as I pray.
Allow your healing presence to enfold them even now.
*(Prayers of Intercession)*

**EVENING**
Carrying God, all day long you have borne me
in your capable arms. Rock me now in the cradle of your love,
especially now as I pray for these.
*(Prayers of Intercession)*

---

**GOD CREATED. GOD CARRIES. GOD REALLY DOES CARE!**

---

**MORNING**
Shine on me! In the matchless name
of the Christ. Amen.

**EVENING**
Remember me! In the matchless name
of the Christ. Amen.

---

355

# December 22

*(Read Psalm 148:1–6)*

**MORNING**

Worthy God, your created order sustains my everlasting praise!

**EVENING**

Worthy God, the moon and the stars continue to call forth my praise!

Creating God, help me to slow down and to appreciate all that you have ordered in this world. As the hustle and bustle seeks to consume me, allow me the space of these few minutes to remember how you took time to create a beautiful, magnificent and reproducing world as a birthday gift for ungrateful humans. It was our desire to be you that allowed sin to enter the world and for you to decide to take on our flesh to reunite us through Jesus. You spoke and the world came into being. Yet, you took the time to play in the dirt as you formed us and gave us dominion over your gift to us. As you prepare to come again, forgive my sin and let my deeds today reflect my sincere appreciation for the gift of Jesus Christ.

**MORNING**

I am the gift you send out into the world this day!
I pray for these . . .
*(Prayers of Intercession)*

**EVENING**

I have encountered many people this day
who need your special attention now . . .
*(Prayers of Intercession)*

**THE GREATEST GIFT IN THE WHOLE WIDE WORLD IS JESUS!**

**MORNING**

Spirit of the Living God,
fall afresh on me. In the matchless
name of the Christ. Amen.

**EVENING**

Spirit of Refreshment,
rock me now, in the cradle of your
divine love. In the matchless name
of the Christ. Amen.

# December 23

*(Read Psalm 148:7–14)*

### MORNING

Majestic Sovereign, as the whole earth prepares to join in praise
to you this day, I lift my voice in the unending concert.

### EVENING

Majestic Sovereign, hail, snow and clouds might
reign outside, but the breath of your love has hovered over me
all day long. I offer grateful praise.

Exalted One, kings, queens, state legislators, men, women, and children are preparing for your coming. Some will never mention your name. Some will never attend a worship service to give you praise. Some will use this season as a time for parties, exploiting others and providing the rich with "things." In their place, your glory is exalted among the elements you have created. The mighty winds sing praise. The mountains and hills testify to your worthiness. Fruitful trees, creeping vines, and flying things give honor to the grandeur of your name. For you alone are worthy. Your name is exalted in my mouth. Forgive my sin and renew a right spirit in me, I pray.

### MORNING

There are many who have no song of praise on their lips;
I lift them to you.
*(Prayers of Intercession)*

### EVENING

I have encountered many today who are singing the wrong tunes;
for these I pray.
*(Prayers of Intercession)*

---

**PRAISE THE NAME OF GOD, WHOSE NAME ALONE IS EXALTED!**

---

| MORNING | EVENING |
|---|---|
| Let my life be praise unto your worthy name. In the matchless name of the Christ. Amen. | My soul rests content in the God of creation. In the matchless name of the Christ. Amen. |

# December 24

*(Read Hebrews 2:10–18)*

**MORNING**

Death-defying Savior, my eyes, my mind,
and my spirit awake in gratitude for this new gift of life.

**EVENING**

Death-defying Savior, your solicitous help has nurtured
and encouraged us on this busy day.

Helper of the Helpless, we approach you like the pregnant Mary and anxious Joseph sought refuge in the inn. How great, how wonderful, how awesome it is that you always make room for us! God, like the poor shepherds tending the needs of lowly sheep, we await the bright stars that will lead us this day to the Hope of the Ages! And like the heavenly choir that leaned over the banisters of glory to sing songs of praise for the birth of a newborn king, let my life be the song, as you are the melody. Forgive my sin. Fill me with your Holy Spirit. Give me a new song of praise this day.

**MORNING**

As you have been gracious in aiding me and mine,
I pray for these . . .
*(Prayers of Intercession)*

**EVENING**

You have allowed me the privilege of being an aid to others,
I lift their names to you . . .
*(Prayers of Intercession)*

**JESUS CAME TO SUFFER, BE TEMPTED, AND DIE JUST TO BE OUR CAPABLE HELPER!**

| **MORNING** | **EVENING** |
|---|---|
| I'm leaning on the everlasting arms! | I have been carried all day long. |
| In the matchless name of the Christ. | I rest in thee now. In the matchless |
| Amen. | name of the Christ. Amen. |

# December 25

*(Read Matthew 2:13–18)*

**MORNING**
Morning Glory, I awake with
joyous expectations and praise.

**EVENING**
Evening Glory, the day has been filled
with joy-filled delights.

Well, the Baby has been born! We thank you that the long wait of Advent has ended. We love you for coming again. In spite of our horrible world conditions and even our bad state of affairs in your church, you dared to come again. Thank you for continued instructions, guidance, and directions on how to avoid death. Forgive my sin and bless me to be just the perfect gift to someone this day. I pray in the name of the God who comes!

**MORNING**
Babe Born in Bethlehem, many are the forces of death
seeking to destroy these for whom I now pray.
*(Prayers of Intercession)*

**EVENING**
Sovereign of Love, for these who may not have experienced
your glory today, I pray.
*(Prayers of Intercession)*

**JESUS WAS BORN TO DIE!**

**MORNING**
Very God of Very God,
live in me this day. In the matchless
name of the Christ. Amen.

**EVENING**
Mary's Baby, let the
night lullabyes comfort my spirit now.
In the matchless name of the Christ.
Amen.

# December 26

*(Read Matthew 2:16–23)*

**MORNING**

Comforter of the Disconsolate, let my life speak peace in the world today.

**EVENING**

Comforter of the Disconsolate, thank you for staying around,
even as the tinsel begins to fade.

As I approach your throne of grace, God of infants, aged, and all in between, it is with full certainty that the spirit of Herod lives today. There are simply too many mothers—Rachels—in too many places around the world, lamenting for lost children. Christmas is not always a happy time. There is the reminder of those small gifts called children who were snatched away by death way before their divine potential could be developed. Plastic smiles have been stuck upon faces, yet the real pain lays upon broken hearts. I pray for every Rachel. I add my lamentations, my tears, and my great mourning with theirs. Send the power of comfort this day, I pray. Forgive my sin and let me be an agent of healing as I encounter an undercover Rachel!

**MORNING**

Great God who is mother, father, sister, and brother,
we need your comfort as we pray for all mothers.
*(Prayers of Intercession)*

**EVENING**

Nurturing God, we have witnessed your concern for Rachel
this day and call her name before you now.
*(Prayers of Intercession)*

---

**GOD CARES AND KNOWS ABOUT THOSE HANDS THAT ROCK CRADLES
AS WELL AS THOSE HEARTS THAT ARE BROKEN!**

---

**MORNING**

Spirit of Compassion, let me be a
healing balm today. In the matchless
name of the Christ. Amen.

**EVENING**

Spirit of Compassion, thank you
for allowing me to offer you the work
of my hands. In the matchless name
of the Christ. Amen.

# December 27

*(Read Isaiah 9:2–7)*

**M O R N I N G**
Brightness of the Noon Day Sun, we approach
these awakening hours with hope in our hearts. Thanks for the gift
of your only begotten son.

**E V E N I N G**
Twinkling of the Midnight Moon, we come to these hours of rest
with gratitude for your keeping power all day long.

Giver of every good and perfect gift, as the trees come down, the wrapping papers are thrown away, the day-after sales are slowing, and the good will of the previous week is fading fast, I come to you with joy. Thank you for the gifts of family, friends, and community. Thank you for angels, hourly workers, little children, and those who share their gifts. Thank you for the quiet hours, the sweet melodies of carols, and the memories that bring both tears and smiles. Thank you for the abundance of food that you provided and for those with whom I have broken bread over these holy days. Forgive me of the sin that would keep me from you. Allow the light of your presence to make my heart a prepared home for you to remain all the year. For unto us a child has been born. Unto us your son has been given. Thanks be unto a generous God.

**M O R N I N G**
For those who have little to remember with joy, I pray.
*(Prayers of Intercession)*

**E V E N I N G**
For those who have made too few good memories, I plead.
*(Prayers of Intercession)*

### JESUS IS A WONDERFUL COUNSELOR!

**M O R N I N G**
For the living of this day, I offer
myself as a gift. In the matchless name
of the Christ. Amen.

**E V E N I N G**
For the rest of this night, I offer what
I have given in your name. In the
matchless name of the Christ. Amen.

# December 28

*(Read Isaiah 9:2–7)*

**MORNING**

God of every nation, I lift my eyes and my voice
in a chorus of praise.

**EVENING**

God of every nation, I close my weary eyes with thanks
for your never slumbering or sleeping.

Peace Giver, how soon we forget your reign of loving shalom. How soon we return to our ugly ways. How soon we go back to war, rumors of war, and hostility toward one another. For a couple of days there are sweet sounds of harmony. For a couple of days there are the cords of community. For a couple of days it seems as if we have almost understood your message sent in Jesus Christ. Then, the afterglow fades. The music of peace dies. The smiles disappear. The sounds of war grow louder. God, forgive the sin in me. I want there to be peace on earth. And I do want it to begin with me. Work through me this day, is my prayer.

**MORNING**

For those who have had little peace, I pray.
*(Prayers of Intercession)*

**EVENING**

For those who don't know the meaning of inner peace, I plead.
*(Prayers of Intercession)*

**JESUS IS THE PRINCE OF PEACE!**

| **MORNING** | **EVENING** |
| --- | --- |
| I offer myself as a bearer | I bring all the scattered pieces |
| of your shalom this day. Use me. | I collected this day. Restore me. |
| In the matchless name of the Christ. | In the matchless name of the Christ. |
| Amen. | Amen. |

# December 29

*(Read Psalm 96)*

**MORNING**

Music Maker God, I awake with a psalm of praise on my lips.

**EVENING**

Music Maker God, I offer my closing anthem of thanksgiving to you.

Coming One, thanks for the gift of yet another day. Thanks for a song of gratitude in my heart. Thanks for the opportunity to join in the great and varied hallelujahs that will be offered in praise of your creation today. The winds sing. The snow and rain offer their own distinct tunes. The flying birds and creeping wild animals are in one accord. Help me to be a bringer of joyous sounds to all those I meet today. Let the discord in my life be silenced as I think of all the wonder you have set before me to discover this day. Honor, majesty, strength, and beauty are yours. Yet, you have given me eyes to behold the glory of your creation. Let me add my voice in exalted hymns of delight. Forgive me of the sin that tells me to sing the blues! Play a new song upon the strings of my heart.

**MORNING**

For those who sing the blues, I pray.

*(Prayers of Intercession)*

**EVENING**

For those who feel they have no song, I plead.

*(Prayers of Intercession)*

**LET THE WHOLE EARTH BRING FORTH NEW SONGS OF PRAISE!**

**MORNING**

As morning gilds the sky, my heart's awakening cry is "Let Jesus Christ be praised!" In the matchless name of the Christ. Amen.

**EVENING**

As the moon mounts its pulpit and shines forth its glorious note, I rest my weary soul in the anchor that holds. In the matchless name of the Christ. Amen.

# December 30

*(Read Titus 2:11–14)*

**MORNING**

Great God and Glorious Savior of Grace, thank you
for another fresh opportunity to get it right!

**EVENING**

Great God and Glorious Savior of Grace, with gratitude
I approach the ending of another day.

Daily Provider, this is another year drawing to a close. My heart offers thanks for the living of these days. For many who began the journey of this year have been called home for eternal rest. Many who are in pain and distress are longing to be with you before the ending of this year. The days seem to rush past. The weeks are over too soon. There is so much I had planned to do. There are so many I had planned to visit, send a card to, make a phone call to. Yet, the days of this year are closing on us. You have been so faithful, so loving, and so kind. I ask forgiveness for the sin that lives in me. For you were gracious enough to send Jesus as a role model of a self-controlled, upright, and godly life. As I take stock of my days, I find myself so short of his mark. Help me to take stock of this year and to make better use of my life.

**MORNING**

For those who need the knowledge of Jesus Christ, I pray.
*(Prayers of Intercession)*

**EVENING**

For those who have tried to make a permanent
and positive impact on the world, I pray.
*(Prayers of Intercession)*

**JESUS IS OUR BLESSED HOPE!**

| MORNING | EVENING |
|---|---|
| Manifest yourself through my life this day. In the matchless name of the Christ. Amen. | May God be glorified in my living of this day. In the matchless name of the Christ. Amen. |

# December 31

*(Read Luke 2:15–20)*

**MORNING**
Great Shepherd of the Sheep, I offer my treasures to you this day.

**EVENING**
Great Shepherd of the Sheep, another year of my life
is offered as my testimony to you.

Record Keeping God, the pages of another year are drawing to a close. The ledgers will be balanced. I will be found wanting, lacking, and short! For the things you gave me as an assignment—I did not do them all. I made excuses. I was scared. I didn't know how to accomplish all the great tasks. Then, the things you told me not to do, I did. I didn't sin boldly, but I didn't love others as you had commanded. I didn't really give sacrificially, but I offered you less than I give a good waitress or waiter! Some of my gifts, I hid. For I was too tired to add one more project to my list of things to do. Yet, the year is closing, and, I have to offer you an accounting. Forgive me of my sin. I have no other excuse. Restore me, I pray, in the name of Jesus Christ.

**MORNING**
Gift of All, this is the last day of the year
and I am prayerful for your world.
*(Prayers of Intercession)*

**EVENING**
Yesterday, today, and tomorrow, you are God,
and many need you now!
*(Prayers of Intercession)*

I'M DETERMINED TO WALK LIKE JESUS, YES, I AM!

**MORNING**
Today is the end of another
year-long gift of life. Thank you!
In the matchless name
of the Christ. Amen.

**EVENING**
This night folds one year into
another, and a fresh beginning is
mine. In the matchless name
of the Christ. Amen.

# Other books from The Pilgrim Press

## KRAZY KINFOLK
### Exploring Dysfunctional Families of the Bible

BARBARA J. ESSEX

0-8298-1654-2/paper/$16.00

Essex continues her popular series with the discussion of families
in the Bible. Each study unit reviews the stories of selected biblical
"dysfunctional" families such as 1) Abraham, Sarah, and Hagar;
2) Jacob, Leah, and Rachel; 3) Moses, Miriam, and Aaron.

## BAD BOYS OF THE NEW TESTAMENT
### Exploring Men of Questionable Virtue

BARBARA J. ESSEX

0-8298-1672-0/paper/$16.00

This seven-week small group study focuses on stories of selected
biblical "bad boys" in the New Testament. Stories such as the elder
brother of the prodigal son parable, the Pharisees, Judas Iscariot,
Pontius Pilate, and Ananias. A short commentary follows each
scripture. Reflection questions conclude each unit, offering participants
the opportunity to start a discussion about what can be learned from
these characters and their stories.

## BAD BOYS OF THE BIBLE
*Exploring Men of Questionable Virtue*

BARBARA J. ESSEX

0-8298-1466-3/paper/$14.00

Cain, Abraham, Adam, Samson, Lot, Jacob, and Jepthah are well-known men of the Bible who were strong and faithful, yet also weak and challenged. In this best-selling text, Essex takes readers on a journey to explore male giants of faith.

## BAD GIRLS OF THE BIBLE
*Exploring Women of Questionable Virtue*

BARBARA J. ESSEX

0-8298-1339-X/paper/$14.00

Designed as a fourteen-week study, this resource explores biblical accounts of traditionally misunderstood or despised women as they are presented in the Bible. Reflection questions are included as well as suggestions for preaching and teaching.

## FROM LITERAL TO LITERARY
*The Essential Reference Book for Biblical Metaphors, second edition*

JAMES ROWE ADAMS

978-0-8298-1788-1/paper/$25.00

The newly updated second edition of this professional reference tool examines more than 165 biblical metaphors—fifteen of which are new—and includes an index to Hebrew and Greek words, along with many other features.

**To order these or any other books from The Pilgrim Press call or write to:**

THE PILGRIM PRESS
700 PROSPECT AVENUE EAST
CLEVELAND, OHIO 44115-1100

Phone orders: 1-800-537-3394  ■  Fax orders: 216-736-2206

*Please include shipping charges of $6.00 for the first book and $1.00 for each additional book.*

*Or order from our web sites at www.pilgrimpress.com and www.ucpress.com.*

Prices subject to change without notice.